The Design of the Eurosystem's
Monetary Policy Instruments

Contributions to Economics

www.springer.com/series/1262

Ulrike Neyer

The Design of the Eurosystem's Monetary Policy Instruments

With 27 Figures

Physica-Verlag

A Springer Company

PD Dr. Ulrike Neyer
Martin-Luther-University Halle-Wittenberg
Department of Economics
06099 Halle/Saale
Germany
neyer@wiwi.uni-halle.de

Library of Congress Control Number: 2007934412

ISSN 1431-1933

ISBN 978-3-7908-1977-9 Physica-Verlag Heidelberg New York

Physica-Verlag is a part of Springer Science+Business Media

springer.com

© Physica-Verlag Heidelberg 2007

Production: LE-TEX Jelonek, Schmidt & Vöckler GbR, Leipzig
Cover-design: WMX Design GmbH, Heidelberg

SPIN 12091072   134/3180YL - 5 4 3 2 1 0   Printed on acid-free paper

Preface

A number of people provided valuable comments on various parts of this book which I presented as my "Habilitationsschrift" to the Martin-Luther-University Halle-Wittenberg in December 2005. However, in particular I would like to thank Rüdiger Pohl and Frank Ebel for their advice, encouragement, criticisms, and their patience during the various productive discussions we had. I also appreciate the helpful comments and suggestions of Ulrich Bindseil, Axel Brüggemann, Diemo Dietrich, Frank Heyde, Dieter Nautz, and Jürgen Wicmers. Furthermore, I would like to thank Rüdiger Pohl, Martin Klein, and Uwe Vollmer for refereeing this thesis.

Halle/Saale, May 2007 *Ulrike Neyer*

Contents

1

Introduction

On 1 January 1999 a new currency, the euro, was launched and a new institution, the Eurosystem,[1] took over responsibility for the single monetary policy in the euro area, which is one of the largest developed economic areas in the world.[2] However, the euro area is not only large but it is also a heterogeneous economic area since it comprises individual countries with different economic and financial structures. With regards to the size and the heterogeneity of the euro area, the creation of a single currency and a single monetary policy has faced extraordinary challenges, among them the design of suitable instruments and procedures, i.e. of a suitable operational framework, for the conduct of monetary policy.

---

[1] The term "Eurosystem" has been chosen to describe the institution being responsible for monetary policy in the euro area, namely the ECB and the national central banks in the *euro area* (European Central Bank, 2001g, p. 9). The European System of Central Banks (ESCB) comprises the European Central Bank (ECB) and the national central banks of *all Member States of the European Union*. For the sake of simplicity, the terms "ECB" and "Eurosystem" are used interchangeably throughout this work.

[2] Measured in terms of population, the euro area has been the largest developed economy in the world: In 2002, the euro area had a total population of 308 million. As a comparison, the population of the U.S. and Japan were 289 million and 127 million respectively. Measured in terms of its share of world GDP, the euro area has been the second largest economy with a weight of 15.7% followed by Japan (7.1%). The largest economy was the U.S. with a share of 21.1%. (Data: ECB and OECD. Share of world GDP is expressed in terms of purchasing power parity).

In January 1997, the European Monetary Institute[3] published its first conceptual design of a set of monetary policy instruments for the Eurosystem (European Monetary Institution, 1997). This work served as the base for the development of the monetary policy instruments and procedures with which the Eurosystem started its work in January 1999.[4] Main elements of this operational framework were and still are: *open market operations*, these are mainly credit operations which are executed in the form of fixed rate or variable rate tender procedures, two *standing facilities*, and a *minimum reserve system*.[5]

The Eurosystem's operational framework has experienced already a number of changes since its introduction in 1999. Most of them were relatively small and did not gain much public attention.[6] However, there have also been two major alterations to the framework. Alterations, for which the ECB even launched a public consultation in advance. The first major modification, which came into effect in 2004, concerned the main refinancing operations (MROs), which are the most important open market operations of the ECB, and the minimum reserve system. The second major modification concerned the Eurosystem's collateral framework.[7] This shows that the Eurosystem's operational framework is not a non-modifiable institution, but that it can and has been changed to adjust to an altered environment or to correct apparent flaws in its design. The ECB itself states that "The Governing Council of the ECB may, at any time, change the instruments, conditions, criteria and procedures for the execution of Eurosystem monetary policy operations." (European Central Bank, 2005b, p. 12)

---

[3] The European Monetary Institute (EMI) was a temporary institution established in 1994. The EMI prepared the creation of the euro and the single monetary policy in the euro area. It went to liquidation when the ECB was established in June 1998 (European Central Bank, 2004c, p. 110).

[4] For a detailed documentation of this starting operational framework see European Central Bank (1998).

[5] These elements will be described in detail in Chap. 2.

[6] One example for such a change is the update of specific eligibility criteria of assets which may serve as collateral for credit operations with the Eurosystem. Revised versions of the "General documentation on ESCB monetary policy instruments and procedures" (European Central Bank, 1998) in which the changes to the framework are documented were published in November 2000, April 2002, February 2004, and February 2005. They are available on the ECB's website (www.ecb.int).

[7] In Chap. 2, these two major modifications to the Eurosystem's operational framework will be described in detail.

Aim of this Work

The aim of this work is to evaluate the Eurosystem's operational framework against a number of requirements and to suggest possible measures to improve this framework. The requirements we consider in our analysis are the following:[8]

- The framework shall ensure that monetary policy decisions are fed through as precisely and quickly as possible to short term money market rates (principle of operational efficiency).
- Credit institutions shall be treated equally irrespectively of their size and where they are located in the euro area (principle of equal treatment).
- In the past, several MROs were characterized by under- or over-bidding behaviour, i.e. total bids significantly exceeded or remained under the amount of liquidity the Eurosystem aimed to allot. This unbalanced bidding behaviour shall be avoided.
- The minimum reserve system in the euro area enables the credit institutions to make use of averaging provisions of required reserves over a reserve maintenance period. However, to enhance the buffer function of the minimum reserve system, strategic shifting of reserves should be avoided, i.e. in the absence of liquidity shocks reserves should be provided evenly over a maintenance period.

Theoretical Analysis and Main Results

In order to evaluate the Eurosystem's operational framework against these requirements, we develop a model framework which captures the main characteristics and institutional features of the euro area. Within this model framework, we analyze the liquidity management of credit institutions and the consequences of their liquidity management for the behaviour of the interbank market rate. An important feature of our model framework is the *heterogeneity of the banking sector*. Banks have different opportunity costs of holding collateral. Therefore, they face different costs when borrowing liquidity from the central bank. Further main elements of our theoretical framework are: *credit operations with the central bank* which have to be based on collateral and a *minimum reserve system* which allows for averaging provisions of required reserves and in which reserves are remunerated. Within this framework, we first develop a simple one-period base model to make the reader familiar

---

[8] We will comment on these requirements in more detail in the Chaps. 2 and 3.

with the basic structure of the framework. Then, we present three two-period models which differ in the maturity of the central bank credits and the way in which reserves are remunerated, and discuss within each model the following questions: Does the aggregate demand for central bank credits deviate from the central bank's benchmark amount? Are reserves provided unevenly over the reserve maintenance period? Are banks affected differently by a monetary policy impulse? What is the behaviour of the interbank market rate?

The first result of our theoretical analysis shows that when there is heterogeneity in the banking sector, intermediation occurs. Banks with relatively low opportunity costs of holding collateral borrow more liquidity from the central bank than they need for themselves and lend the excess liquidity, via the interbank money market, to banks with relatively high opportunity costs. This intermediation results in a positive spread between the interbank market rate and the rate on the central bank credit operations. Concerning the central bank's operational framework, the main results of our theoretical analysis are the following. Overlapping maturities of two subsequent credit operations and the remuneration of required reserves at the average of the rates on the central bank credit operations over a maintenance period will lead to uneven provisions of required reserves over the reserve maintenance period and to a deviation of the aggregate demand for central bank credits from the central bank's benchmark amount if the central bank changes the interest rate on its credit operations within the reserve maintenance period. Furthermore, banks will be affected differently by this monetary policy impulse. If the maturities of two subsequent credit operations do not overlap and if reserves are not remunerated at that average rate but at the current rate on central bank credits, reserves will be provided evenly over a reserve maintenance period, aggregate demand for central bank credits will correspond to the central bank's benchmark amount, and banks will not be affected differently by the monetary policy impulse.

The intuition behind these results is the following. The starting point is that banks are required to hold minimum reserves. They can fulfil these reserve requirements by making use of averaging provisions over two periods. However, in order to enhance the buffer function of the minimum reserve system the central bank prefers smooth provisions of required reserves over this reserve maintenance period in the absence of liquidity shocks. The aggregate demand for central bank credits which allows for these smooth provisions corresponds to the central bank's benchmark amount. Overlapping maturities of central bank credits and the remuneration of reserves at the average rate described above imply that interest costs and interest yields of holding reserves will fall apart within a reserve maintenance period if the central bank changes its interest rate within that maintenance period. If the central bank cuts (raises) its interest rate, holding reserves will be cheaper in the second (first) period resulting in credit institutions strategically shifting their reserve holdings which implies that aggregate demand for central bank credits deviates from the central bank's benchmark amount. For shifting reserves, banks must borrow the relevant liquidity from the central bank. Since the marginal costs of borrowing this liquidity differs from bank to bank, the amount of reserves they can profitably shift does as well. Consequently, the benefits from this reserve shifting differ between banks which implies that they are affected differently by a monetary policy impulse since it is the change in the rate on central bank credits which triggers the reserve shifting. If the maturities of the central bank credits do not overlap and if reserves are remunerated at the current rate on the central bank's credit operations, holding required reserves will be neutral with regard to interest payments to and interest yields from the central bank so that the banks will not have an incentive to shift their reserves, the aggregate demand for central bank credits will not deviate from the central bank's benchmark amount, and banks will not be affected differently even if the central bank changes its interest rate within the reserve maintenance period.

Transferring these results to the euro area leads us to the following implications. The redesign of the Eurosystem's operational framework in 2004 must be evaluated positively since the under- and overbidding problem and related problems, will generally be solved as long as the ECB does not change interest rates within the reserve maintenance period. However, to enhance the operational efficiency of the Eurosystem's operational framework, we propose to change the way in which reserves are remunerated. Holdings of required reserves should be remunerated at the end of each week at the current central bank credit rate instead of at the average rate described above. As a consequence, the present commitment of the governing council deciding on interest rate changes only at the beginning of a reserve maintenance period would no longer be necessary. Decisions on interest rate changes could then be made whenever the assessment of relevant information requires this - without breaking a commitment, i.e. monetary policy could be conducted more flexibly.

Related Literature

The bulk of the literature on credit institutions' liquidity management
and the behaviour of the interbank money market rate refers to credit
institutions in the U.S. and the federal funds rate. Developing a model
in which individual banks compare the liquidity benefit of excess reserves with the federal funds rate, Ho and Saunders (1985) derive different federal funds demand functions and provide several explanations
for specific features of the federal funds market. Clouse and Dow (2002)
model the reserve management of a representative bank as a dynamic
programming problem capturing main institutional features of the federal funds market to discuss the effects of various changes in the operating environment and monetary policy instruments. A large part of the
literature which deals with the federal funds market analyses why the
federal funds rate fails to follow a martingale within the reserve maintenance period, i.e. why banks obviously do not regard reserves held on
different days of the maintenance period as perfect substitutes (Hamilton, 1996; Clouse and Dow, 1999; Furfine, 2000; Bartolini, Bertola, and
Prati, 2001, 2002).

However, the results of these works for the U.S. cannot be easily
transferred to the banks' liquidity management and the behaviour of
short term interest rates in other countries because country specific
institutional features and the style of central bank intervention play an
important role as shown by Bartolini, Bertola, and Prati (2003) and
Bartolini and Prati (2006).

Consequently, the literature dealing with the liquidity management
of the credit institutions and the behaviour of the interbank market
rates in the euro area considers specific institutional features of the
euro area. A main difference to the U.S. is that the ECB does not
provide the bulk of the liquidity to the banking sector via outright purchases of securities but via *credit operations* which are executed in form
of tender procedures. Nautz (1998) develops one of the first models of
banks' liquidity management which explicitly considers that banks can
borrow liquidity directly from the central bank in form of securities re-
purchase agreements (repos). He designs a two-period model in which
the crucial point is that refinancing conditions (rate and volume) at
the central bank in the second period are uncertain. He shows that
if this uncertainty increases, banks will increase their demand for reserves in the first period. Therefore, he concludes, the central bank
can influence the interbank market rate just by being more or less
vague or more or less determined about future monetary policy. A bulk
of the more recent literature dealing with the liquidity management

of euro area banks analyzes the causes and consequences of the observed over- and underbidding behaviour in the Eurosystem's MROs. Examples are the works by Ayuso and Repullo (2001, 2003), Ewerhart (2002), Breitung, Linzert, and Nautz (2003), Nautz and Oechssler (2003), and Bindseil (2005). We will come back to these works in the course of this work. Studies explicitly analyzing the influence of specific institutional aspects regarding the behaviour of the interbank market rate in the euro area can be found, for example, in Pérez-Quirós and Rodríguez-Mendizábal (2006) and Välimäki (2001). Pérez-Quirós and Rodríguez-Mendizábal construct a model in which the interest rates of the Eurosystem's two standing facilities play a crucial role in determining the behaviour of the interbank market rate. Välimäki presents an interbank market model to analyze the performance of alternative fixed rate tender procedures.

Contribution to the Literature

The contribution of this work to the literature is the provision of a model framework which allows the analysis of the credit institutions' liquidity management and the consequences of this liquidity management for the behaviour of the interbank market rate. This model framework focusses on the main characteristics and institutional features of the euro area which to date, as far as we know, have not been subject to a scrutinized analysis. Central to these characteristics and institutional features are a heterogeneous banking sector, central bank credit operations which have to be based on collateral, the maturity of these credit operations and the remuneration of reserves. This approach allows us, inter alia, to identify the causes and the problems of the observed under- and overbidding in the Eurosystem's tender procedures, to evaluate the changes to the operational framework the Eurosystem undertook in 2004, and to discuss further possible measures to improve the Eurosystem's operational framework.

Outline

Chapter 2 gives a brief overview of the Eurosystem's monetary policy instruments, with a special focus on those instruments and their features which are important for our theoretical analysis. Chapter 3 documents evidence of stylized facts the subsequent theoretical analyses are called to explain. Chapter 4 introduces the basic structure of the theoretical models presented in this work by developing the one-period base model. The Chaps. 5, 6, and 7 expand this base model by a second period and the introduction of a minimum reserve system. The models presented in these three chapters differ in their assumptions concerning the maturity of the central bank credits and the way in which reserves are remunerated. In Chap. 8, the implications of the theoretical analysis for the Eurosystem's operational framework are drawn. We discuss which of the presented models most closely captures the characteristics necessary for meeting the requirements of the Eurosystem's operational framework, we evaluate the 2004-changes to the Eurosystem's operational framework, and we suggest further measures to improve the framework. Finally, Chap. 9 briefly summarizes the main findings of this work.

2

Monetary Policy Instruments of the Eurosystem

2.1 Introduction

To achieve its primary goal of maintaining price stability in the euro area, the Eurosystem aims at steering short-term money market rates. The EONIA[1], the reference rate in the interbank market for overnight loans, is the Eurosystem's operating target. For steering the short-term interest rates, the Eurosystem has at its disposal a set of monetary policy instruments. These instruments are part of the Eurosystem's operational framework which comprises all of the instruments and procedures used to implement the single monetary policy in the euro area (European Central Bank, 2004c, p. 71). While designing this operational framework, a set of principles has had to be considered. We will briefly present these principles in the next section.

In the euro area, the liquidity needs of the banking sector mainly arise from minimum reserve requirements and the so-called autonomous factors, such as banknotes in circulation and government deposits with the Eurosystem. These liquidity needs can only be covered by the Eurosystem since it is the sole issuer of banknotes and the sole provider of bank reserves. The monetary policy instruments at the disposal of the Eurosystem for providing this liquidity can be roughly divided into open market operations and standing facilities. The former can be conducted as main refinancing operations (MROs), longer-term refinancing operations, fine-tuning operations and structural operations. The MROs play a key role in providing liquidity to the banking sector in the euro area. From January 1999 to November 2005 on average about 75%

---

[1] The EONIA (European Overnight Index Average) is a market index computed as the weighted average of unsecured overnight transactions undertaken by a panel of banks. For more information on this reference rate see www.euribor.org.

of the banking sector's liquidity needs were met through the MROs. In the same period, the longer-term refinancing operations satisfied about 24% of the credit institutions' liquidity needs and less than 1% were met by the fine-tuning operations, structural operations and the lending facility.[2] These short stylized facts can also be seen in table 2.1 which represents a simplified consolidated balance sheet of the Eurosystem.[3]

Table 2.1: Simplified balance sheet of the Eurosystem (numbers are based on the consolidated financial statement of the Eurosystem given in the ECB Monthly Bulletin October 2005, p. S 6).

Eurosystem

Assets	(30 September 2005, EUR billions)		Liabilities
Autonomous Liquidity Factors		**Autonomous Liquidity Factors**	
Net Foreign Assets	315.31	Banknotes in Circulation	533.21
Other Autonom. Factors (net)	44.49	Government Deposits	65.43
Monetary Policy Instruments		**Current Accounts**	
Main Refinancing Operations	293.50	**(Covering Min. Reserves)**	145.10
Longer-term Refinan. Operations	90.00		
Marginal Lending Facility	0.51	**Monetary Policy Instruments**	
		Deposit Facility	0.07
	743.81		743.81

In section 2.2 we introduce the principles behind the design of the Eurosystem's monetary policy instruments. We then describe the instruments in more detail by focussing on the minimum reserve system and the main refinancing operations because these are the instruments we refer to in our theoretical analysis. We will introduce the other Eurosystem's monetary policy instruments only briefly and refer the reader for more details to European Central Bank (2005b) where these instruments are described at length.

---

[2] The time series data on which these numbers are based are available on the ECB's website (www.ecb.int).

[3] For a detailed description of the liquidity demand and the liquidity supply in the euro area see European Central Bank (2002b).

2.2 Guiding Principles Behind the Design of the Eurosystem's Monetary Policy Instruments

General principles behind the design of the Eurosystem's monetary policy instruments are laid down in Article 105 in the Treaty establishing the European Community: The European System of Central Banks "shall act in accordance with the principle of an open market economy with free competition, favouring an efficient allocation of resources...". In addition, the ECB has formulated the following principles (European Central Bank, 2004c, p. 71-72): The most important principle is that the operational framework shall ensure that monetary policy decisions are fed through as precisely and quickly as possible to short term money market rates (principle of operational efficiency). Furthermore, the principle of equal treatment shall be considered when designing the operational framework, i.e. credit institutions shall be treated equally irrespective of their size and where they are located in the euro area. Further principles are the principle of decentralization, i.e. monetary policy operations shall be carried out by the national central banks, and the principles of simplicity, transparency, continuity, safety and cost efficiency. The latter means that operational costs shall be as low as possible for both, the Eurosystem and the credit institutions. In this work, we will focus on the principles of operational efficiency and of equal treatment.

2.3 Minimum Reserve System

In the euro area, credit institutions are required to hold a fixed amount of compulsory deposits on the accounts with the Eurosystem. The rationale for imposing reserve requirements given by the ECB is twofold (see European Central Bank, 2005b, p. 55): First, since the minimum reserve system in the euro area enables the credit institutions to make use of *averaging* provisions, the reserve requirements contribute to the stabilization of money market interest rates since short-term transitory liquidity shocks can be buffered by these reserve holdings. Second, the minimum reserve system creates or enlarges a structural liquidity shortage in the euro area banking system.[4]

---

[4] In the twentieth century, various justifications have been put forward in industrialized countries for the implementation of reserve requirements. Besides the two arguments given above, Bindseil (2004, chapter 6) has found five justifications, for example, that reserve requirements were supposed to help to ensure the liquidity

The amount of compulsory reserves to be held by any given credit institution is determined in relation to specific elements of its balance sheet. At present, the minimum reserves amount to 2% of certain short-term liability items. In order to fulfil reserve requirements, averaging provisions are allowed over a one-month reserve maintenance period. Until March 2004, any reserve maintenance period started on the 24th calendar day of each month and ended on the 23rd calendar day of the following month, i.e. it was independent of the dates of the Governing Council meetings where interest rate changes were decided. Since March 2004, maintenance periods start on the settlement day of the first MRO following the Governing Council meetings where interest rate changes are usually decided, and end on the day preceding the corresponding settlement day in the following month. The reason for changing the timing of the maintenance period was to avoid speculation on interest rate changes within a maintenance period, something which led to under- or overbidding behaviour in cases of expected interest rate changes.[5]

A further important feature of the minimum reserve system in the euro area is that holdings of required reserves are remunerated. According to the ECB, this remuneration shall ensure that the minimum reserve system does not impose a competitive drawback for the banking sector in the euro area and that it does not hinder the efficient allocation of resources (European Central Bank, 2004c, p. 78). Within a reserve maintenance period, normally four MROs are conducted. Required reserve holdings are remunerated at the end of the reserve maintenance period at the average of the rates on these MROs.[6]

---

of the banking sector and that they were supposed to contribute to generating central bank income. However, as pointed out by Bindseil, today minimum reserve systems in general are specified in such a way that they only support the two justifications also given by the ECB.

[5] We will define under- and overbidding in section 2.4.1 and describe and comment on the observed under- and overbidding behaviour in the euro area in section 3.2.

[6] For a detailed description of the current *minimum reserve system* we refer the reader to European Central Bank (2005b, chapter 7), for a description of the reserve system before the changes were effective to European Central Bank (2002d). For details concerning the reason why the Eurosystem has changed its minimum reserve system see European Central Bank (2003a).

2.4 Open Market Operations

2.4.1 Main Refinancing Operations

As shown above, the MROs constitute the key operations of the Eurosystem to provide liquidity to the banking sector in the euro area. They are credit transactions, i.e., contrary to the Federal Reserve System, for example, which provides the liquidity to the banking sector mainly via outright purchases of securities, the Eurosystem provides the bulk of liquidity via loans to the banking sector.[7] The MROs are executed weekly either as a fixed rate or a variable rate tender. From the launch of the euro in January 1999 until June 2000, tenders were conducted exclusively as fixed rate tenders. Since then, only variable rate tenders with a minimum bid rate have been used. With effect from March 2004, the maturity of the MROs has been reduced from two weeks to one week in order to avoid overlapping maturities which induced under- or overbidding behaviour in the MROs in case of expected interest rate changes.[8]

Under- and Overbidding Behaviour: Definition

The ECB refers the term underbidding to MROs in which aggregate bids fall below the Eurosystem's benchmark allotment and the term overbidding to those MROs in which aggregate bids exceed this benchmark (European Central Bank, 2002b, p. 46). For calculating the benchmark allotment of a MRO, the ECB assesses the liquidity needs of the banking sector for the maturity of the MRO. For this assessment, the liquidity needs arising from autonomous factors and minimum reserve requirements are taken into account so that reserve requirements are fulfilled, on aggregate, smoothly over the maintenance period (European Central Bank, 2002b, p. 47).[9] The definition of the benchmark allotment reveals that although a single bank may fulfil its

---

[7] For a detailed comparison of the Eurosystem's and the Federal Reserve System's operational frameworks see, for example, Ruckriegel and Seitz (2002). Bartolini and Prati (2003), also comparing the two central banks, focus on the different approaches to the execution of the monetary policy.

[8] For a detailed description of the current design of the *MROs* we refer the reader to European Central Bank (2005b), for a description of the MROs before the changes were effective to European Central Bank (2002d). For details concerning the reason why the Eurosystem has changed the design of the MROs see European Central Bank (2003a).

[9] For more information on the benchmark allotment concept see European Central Bank (2004a, p. 16-18).

reserve requirements unevenly over the maintenance period, the Eurosystem aims on aggregate a smooth fulfilment. The reason given is that smooth provisions of required reserves enhance the buffer function of the minimum reserve system against short-term transitory liquidity shocks (European Central Bank, 2002b, p. 47). We will describe and comment on the observed under- and overbidding behaviour in the euro area in section 3.2.

Collateral Framework

Article 18.1 of the Statute of the European System of Central Banks requires all Eurosystem credit operations, i.e. also the MROs, to be based on adequate collateral in order to protect the Eurosystem against financial risk (European Central Bank, 2001a). In the models presented in this work, opportunity costs of holding collateral play a pivotal role. Therefore, we take a closer look at the Eurosystem's collateral framework.

Assets which can be used as collateral for the underlying credit operations with the Eurosystem must fulfil a multitude of specific criteria. Examples are that eligible assets must meet high credit standards and that they must be denominated in euro.[10] The ECB has defined a list of eligible assets which fulfil these criteria. This list is published and updated daily on the ECB's website (www.ecb.int).

Especially at the beginning of Stage III of the Economic and Monetary Union in January 1999, differences in financial structures across Member States had to be considered when defining the list of eligible assets. These differences have led to a distinction between two categories of eligible assets, referred to as tier one and tier two. Tier one consists of assets which fulfil uniform euro-area wide eligibility criteria, tier two consists of assets being particularly important for a given national financial market and banking system. Tier two assets fulfil criteria established by the national central banks (note that these specific criteria are subject to approval by the ECB).

One leading principle that has guided the development of the Eurosystem's collateral framework is the equal treatment of credit institutions (European Central Bank, 2001a). However, so far it has been difficult to ensure a level playing field for all credit institutions (European Central Bank, 2003f), although the credit institutions can use all

---

[10] The entire list of criteria eligible assets have to fulfil is given in European Central Bank (2005b, chapter 6).

eligible assets, i.e. also the tier two assets, on a cross-border basis.[11] The problem is that the costs of collateral vary across countries and therefore across financial institutions within the euro area (Hämäläinen, 2000; Bruno, Ordine, and Scalia, 2005). The ECB argues that a lack of transparency due to the heterogeneity of the assets in the tier two lists of different member countries may contribute to this problem (European Central Bank, 2003f). Therefore, the ECB has decided to replace the two-tier framework by a single list.[12] However, this revision of the collateral framework will require a gradual implementation over a number of years. One reason for the long time horizon is the necessary legislative adaption in some countries (European Central Bank, 2003f).

But even if in some time the single list will be established and even if in some time differences in financial structures will be so small that they will not be relevant anymore, banks will nevertheless face different opportunity costs of holding collateral. Thus, the problem of the violation of the principle of equal treatment, will be reduced over the course of time but not solved. This is due to the heterogeneity of the banking sector in the euro area. Banks differ in size and - as shown by Bruno, Ordine, and Scalia (2005) - in the euro area size plays an important role for opportunity costs of holding collateral.[13] Furthermore, banks focus on different business segments. As a consequence of this specialization their asset structures are distinct from another which implies that they have different opportunity costs of holding collateral.

2.4.2 Longer-Term Refinancing Operations, Fine-Tuning and Structural Operations

A further source of refinancing for the credit institutions in the euro area are the *longer-term refinancing operations*. They are conducted once a month and have a maturity of three months. From the ECB's point of view the provision of this longer-term liquidity to the banking

---

[11] All eligible assets, also the tier two assets, are potentially available for use by any credit institution regardless of its location in the euro area.

[12] In June 2003, the ECB launched a public consultation on this measurement (European Central Bank, 2003f). Almost all responses received during this consultation supported the proposed reform (European Central Bank, 2004b). For details concerning the steps towards establishing the single list see European Central Bank (2005b, chapter 6).

[13] One may argue that these size effects are a consequence of the non-transparency which will be reduced if the single list is established since bigger (multinational) banks can cope better with this non-transparency. However, even if the single list will be established at a future date, bigger banks may still obtain and evaluate information on eligible assets at lower costs.

sector is useful because it prevents the rolling over of all the liquidity provided to the banking sector each week. These operations are executed in the form of pure variable rate tenders with pre-announced allotment volumes. They do not play an active role in the ECB's liquidity management. In its public consultation on measures to improve the efficiency of its operational framework, the ECB did not only proposed to change the timing of the reserve maintenance period and the maturity of the MROs but also to suspend the longer-term refinancing operations (European Central Bank, 2002c). However, an overwhelming majority of the respondents were against the suspension of these operations since they would play an important role in the credit institutions liquidity management (European Central Bank, 2003g).

The *fine-tuning operations* are a further instrument of the Eurosystem to provide but also to absorb liquidity. These operations are not standardized and when using this instrument the Eurosystem aims at smoothing the effects on interest rates of unexpected liquidity fluctuations in the money market. Until the last quarter of 2004, these operations have mainly been related to unexpected events such as the terrorist attacks on 11 September 2001. However, since the last quarter of 2004, the Eurosystem has conducted a fine tuning operation nearly every month on the last day of the reserve maintenance period.[14] With these operations it has aimed at restoring neutral liquidity conditions, i.e. at preventing the EONIA to deviate from the ECB's target rate.

The liquidity imbalances at the end of the reserve maintenance period have resulted from substantial forecast errors concerning autonomous factors, especially concerning government deposits with the Eurosystem. These forecast errors have been mainly due to the changes to the Eurosystem's operational framework which came into effect in 2004 (the changes to the timing of the reserve maintenance period and to the maturity of the MROs). As a result of these changes, the allotment of the last MRO in a maintenance period always takes place eight days before the maintenance period ends. Before the changes to the operational framework the last allotment took place on average four days before the end of the maintenance period (note that under the old framework the timing of the last allotment varied from month to month). This means that under the new framework, the ECB has to forecast liquidity needs over an eight-day horizon, while under the previous framework on average only a five-day horizon had to be forecasted. This difference is decisive: The standard deviation of the autonomous factor forecast error over eight days is about 7 billion euro,

---

[14] See ECB-statistics available on the ECB's website, www.ecb.int.

while it is only about 3 billion euro over five days (European Central Bank, 2005c). We will come back to this aspect of liquidity imbalances at the end of the maintenance period in Chap. 8 when discussing the implications of our theoretical models for the Eurosystem's operational framework.

Structural Operations are a further possibility to adjust the structural liquidity position of the Eurosystem vis-à-vis the banking system. Yet, by the end of November 2005, the Eurosystem had not conducted any such operations aimed at influencing the structural liquidity position of the banking sector.[15]

2.5 Standing Facilities

The Eurosystem offers two standing facilities to the credit institutions in the euro area. The marginal lending facility provides and the marginal deposit facility absorbs liquidity with an overnight maturity on the initiative of the credit institutions. Access to both facilities is unlimited, however, the lending facility can only be used against collateral. Access to the facilities is generally possible throughout the day until 6.30 p.m., i.e. until thirty minutes after the closing of the payment system. The interest rate on the marginal lending facility normally provides a ceiling, the rate on the deposit facility a floor for the rate in the interbank market for overnight loans. Consequently, the standing facilities contribute to the stabilization of short-term interest rates. Up to now, the interest rates on the standing facilities have formed a symmetric corridor around the MRO-rate, and have been changed since April 1999 in parallel with the MRO-rates, i.e. they have had no independent role in signalling the stance of monetary policy (Bindseil, 2004, p. 137).[16]

---

[15] The European Central Bank (2004c, p. 84) states that by the end of June 2003 it had not conducted any such operations aimed at influencing the structural liquidity position of the banking sector. From January 1999 to November 2005, ECB-statistics (available on the ECB's website, www.ecb.int) disclose two one-week operations under this item. One in May 2001, the other in November 2001. However, in both cases, these operations were conducted to offset the liquidity deficit which had accumulated as a result of underbidding in these maintenance periods (see European Central Bank, 2001b, p. 24 and European Central Bank, 2002a, p. 17), i.e. they were not conducted in order to influence the structural liquidity position of the banking sector in the euro area.

[16] A detailed description and discussion of this symmetric corridor approach implemented by the Eurosystem can be found in Bindseil (2004, chapter 3). For further information on standing facilities in general we refer the reader to Bindseil (2004,

2.6 Summary

To achieve its primary goal of maintaining price stability in the euro area, the Eurosystem aims at steering short-term interest rates. For steering these interest rates, the Eurosystem has a set of monetary policy instruments at its disposal. The following list summarizes main features of these instruments, features which are also captured by the theoretical models we will present in this work.

- The liquidity needs of the banking sector in the euro area mainly arises from autonomous factors and reserve requirements imposed by the Eurosystem.
- For fulfilling required reserves averaging provisions are allowed over a maintenance period.
- Required reserves are remunerated at the average, over the maintenance period, of the rates on the MROs conducted in that maintenance period.
- The bulk of the banking sector's liquidity needs in the euro area is satisfied via the MROs.
- The MROs are credit transactions which have to be based on collateral.
- The banks in the euro area differ in their opportunity costs of holding these collateral.
- Until March 2004, the maturities of two subsequent MROs overlapped as these operations were conducted weekly but had a two-week maturity. Since March 2004, the maturity of the MROs is one week, i.e. there is no overlapping in the maturities anymore.

Besides the description of the Eurosystem's monetary policy instruments, this section has presented briefly the principles behind the design of the Eurosystem's operational framework. The principles we will focus on in this work are the principles of operational efficiency and of equal treatment of credit institutions.

---

chapter 4) and on specific aspects concerning the standing facilities in the euro area to European Central Bank (2005b, chapter 4).

Stylized Facts and First Explanations

3.1 The Overnight Rate

The Eurosystem aims at steering the interbank money market rates in
the euro area, the EONIA is its operational target. Figure 3.1 shows
that the EONIA has tracked closely the MRO-rate, i.e. the ECB policy rate, so that from this point of view the Eurosystem's operational
framework has performed well.

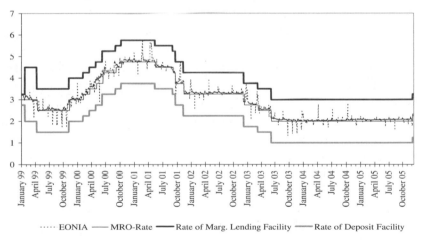

····· EONIA ——— MRO-Rate ——Rate of Marg. Lending Facility ——Rate of Deposit Facility

Fig. 3.1: EONIA and Key ECB Interest Rates. (Daily data from 4 January 1999 to
13 December 2005. Numbers are in percentages. The MRO-rate is the rate applied
to the fixed rate tenders and the minimum bid rate of the variable rate tenders.
Data sources: ECB and Deutsche Bundesbank.)

Furthermore, the figure reveals that the interest rate on the marginal
lending facility provides a ceiling and the interest rate on the marginal

deposit facility a floor for the overnight interbank market rate. However, the figure also demonstrates that the EONIA has hardly been close to these boundaries, but it has usually been close to the MRO-rate, except for infrequent spikes which coincide with some special episodes and effects during the period being considered. These are:

- Underbidding episodes in February, April and October 2001, December 2002 and March 2003. More underbidding episodes occurred in April 1999, November 2001 and June 2003, but they did not lead to tight conditions in the interbank market and, thus, had no significant effect on the EONIA. We will come back to this underbidding behaviour in the next section.
- Anomalous allotment on 18 September 2001, i.e. in the week following the terrorist attack on the US.
- End of year and cash changeover effects.
- Periods between the governing council's announcement of an interest rate change and its implementation.
- End of reserve maintenance periods effects. The allowance of averaging provisions of required reserves over a reserve maintenance period typically results in strong activities in the interbank market on the last days of the maintenance period and, therefore, results in strong fluctuations in the EONIA during these days.

It is immediately apparent that since December 2004 the volatility of the EONIA has decreased. One reason for this is that since then the ECB has regularly conducted fine-tuning operations due to strong liquidity imbalances at the end of several reserve maintenance periods. According to the ECB, under the new operational framework, i.e. since March 2004, these liquidity imbalances have been stronger than those under the old framework (see also p. 16), so we can conclude that the average amplitudes of the EONIA would also have been higher without the fine-tuning operations (European Central Bank, 2005c).

Figure 3.1 already indicates that the EONIA does not fluctuate evenly around the MRO-rate but, in general, there is a positive spread between the interbank market rate and the MRO-rate which is explicitly illustrated by Fig. 3.2.

However, when comparing the EONIA with the MRO-rate, i.e. with the rate applied to the fixed rate tenders and the minimum bid rate of the variable rate tenders, there are two potential biases that might affect the spread. Firstly, differences in credit risk may bias the spread upwards since the MROs are collateralized, whereas the EONIA refers to unsecured interbank market transactions. Secondly , the MRO-rate

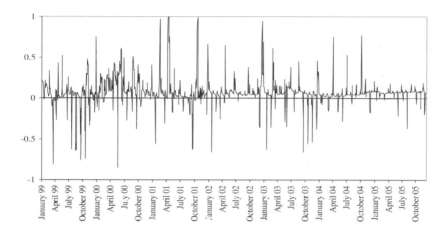

Fig. 3.2: Spread between the EONIA and the MRO-Rate. (Daily data from 4 January 1999 to 13 December 2005. Numbers are in percentage points. The MRO-rate is the rate applied to the fixed rate tenders and the minimum bid rate of the variable rate tenders. Data sources: ECB and Deutsche Bundesbank.)

refers to credit transactions with a two-week/one-week maturity[1] while the EONIA refers to overnight transactions which implies that the MRO-rate has a positive term premium when compared to the EO-NIA. This should bias the spread downwards.[2]

The first bias should be small since the panel banks contributing to the EONIA are generally banks of first class credit standing. With regard to the second bias, we have also compared the one-week EURI-BOR[3] with the ECB-rate. In addition, we have used for the ECB-rate the weighted average rate instead of the minimum bid rate because the weighted average rate of the variable rate tenders is a more appropriate rate for comparing the costs of an interbank market credit with those

---

[1] With effect from March 2004, the MRO-maturities have been reduced from two weeks to one week. See section 2.4.1 for details.

[2] Concerning a discussion of these two potential biases see also Ayuso and Repullo (2003).

[3] The EURIBOR (Euro Interbank Offered Rate) is a market index computed as the weighted average of transactions undertaken by a panel of banks. The same panel banks contributing to the EONIA also quote for the EURIBOR. The EURIBOR is the reference rate for maturities of one, two and three weeks and for twelve maturities from one to twelve months. For more information on these reference rates see www.euribor.org.

of a central bank credit.[4] Moreover, comparing the costs of these two types of credits is the focus of our theoretical analysis. It should be noted that the weighted average rate is higher than the minimum bid rate, i.e. for proving that a positive spread is more unfavourable. Nevertheless, this spread between the one-week EURIBOR and the fixed rate/the weighted average rate of the ECB-tenders is also generally positive as Fig. 3.3 illustrates.

Neyer and Wiemers (2004) test the null hypotheses of a non-positive spread against the alternative of a positive spread between a number of euro area interbank market rates and ECB-rates.[5] For all cases they can reject the null-hypothesis of a non-positive spread on a confidence level of 1%.

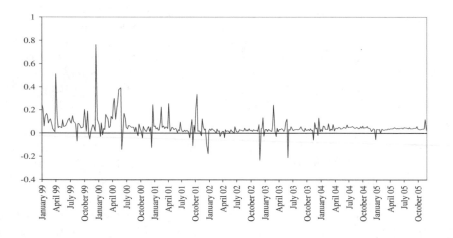

Fig. 3.3: Spread between the One-Week EURIBOR and the MRO-Rate. (Settlement days of the MROs from 7 January 1999 to 30 November 2005. Numbers are in percentage points. The MRO-rate is the rate applied to the fixed rate tenders and the weighted average rate of the variable rate tenders. Data sources: ECB and Deutsche Bundesbank.)

A positive spread between the interbank market rate and the central bank rate has been also confirmed by Ayuso and Repullo (2003), Ejer-

---

[4] The marginal rate in the variable rate tenders normally lies slightly above the minimum bid rate, i.e. actually no bank pays the minimum bid rate.

[5] They test the null hypotheses of a non-positive spread against the alternative of a positive spread between the EONIA and the fixed rate/minimum bid rate, between the one-week EURIBOR and the fixed rate/weigthed average rate, and between the two-week EURIBOR and the weighted average rate.

skov, Moss, and Stracca (2003), and Nyborg, Bindseil, and Strebulaev (2002), for example.

According to the theoretical analysis of this work, the positive spread can be explained by a heterogeneous banking sector which has been already briefly described in the introduction. In Ayuso and Repullo (2003), the positive spread supports their hypothesis of an asymmetric objective function of the Eurosystem in the sense that the Eurosystem, which wants to steer the interbank rate towards a target rate, is more concerned about letting the interbank rate fall below the target. This would be consistent with the desire of a young central bank to gain credibility for its anti-inflationary monetary policy. Ayuso and Repullo focus on the behaviour of the central bank and its relationship with the credit institutions. Our paper complements their work by focussing on the behaviour of the credit institutions and their interrelationship. We will come back to this issue when discussing the implications of our theoretical analysis for the Eurosystem's operational framework in Chap. 8.

3.2 Bidding Behaviour in the Main Refinancing Operations

3.2.1 Observed Bidding Behaviour

The first striking aspect is that only a small fraction of euro area banks actually takes part in the Eurosystem's MROs. Considering that more than 2000 credit institutions fulfil the criteria for participating in the MROs,[6] the number of actively bidding institutions is relatively small as Fig. 3.4 illustrates. The theoretical analysis of this work will offer a heterogeneous banking sector as one explanation for this phenomenon. Banks' costs differ with regards to borrowing liquidity directly from the central bank which results in a kind of intermediation by banks with relatively low marginal costs (we have already briefly described this idea in the introduction to this work).

A further striking feature of the observed bidding behaviour is that several MROs were characterized by severe under- or overbidding behaviour. The term underbidding describes a situation in which the total number of bids fall below the Eurosystem's benchmark allotment, the

---

[6] At the end of 2000 (June 2003), the criteria for participating in the MROs were fulfilled by 2542 (2242) credit institutions (European Central Bank (2001g, p. 63); European Central Bank (2004c, p.75)).

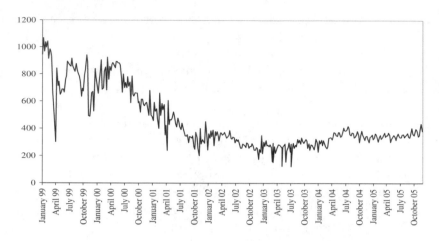

Fig. 3.4: Number of Participants in the MROs. (Data source: ECB.)

term overbidding describes a situation in which the total number of bids exceed this benchmark (see p. 13 for details).

Auctions characterized by overbidding behaviour were conducted in the last quarter of 1999 and in the first half of 2000. Assuming that the actually allotted amounts in that period were at least close to the Eurosystem's benchmark allotment, the extremely low allotment quotas (see Fig. 3.5, allotment quota = amount allotted divided by total amount of bids) indicate significant overbidding behaviour. Furthermore, it should be noted that despite the extremely low allotment quotas, that period was not characterized by a liquidity shortage: The EONIA did not increase significantly above the MRO-rate (see Fig. 3.1), and there was only a moderate recourse to the marginal lending facility (see figure 3.6).

Underbidding in the MROs has occurred so far nine times: in April 1999, February 2001, April 2001, October 2001, November 2001, December 2002 (two times), March 2003, and in June 2003. Despite an allotment quota of one, i.e. despite the fact that all bids were satisfied, the liquidity was not enough to allow for the smooth provisions of the required reserves over the concerned reserve maintenance period. In February 2001, April 2001, October 2001, and in December 2002, the ECB was not willing to allot in the subsequent MROs the amount of liquidity which would have been necessary to restore neutral liquidity conditions. Consequently, there has been a significant increase in the EONIA (see Fig. 3.1) and a relatively high recourse to the marginal lending facility (see Fig. 3.6). In April 1999, November 2001, March

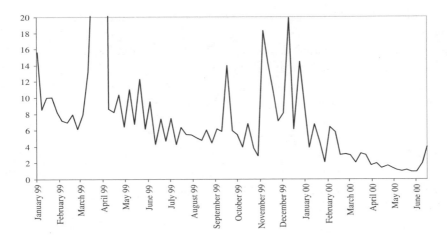

Fig. 3.5: Portion of Allotted Bids under the Fixed Rate Tender. (Numbers are in percentages. In the MRO conducted at the beginning of April 1999, the allotment quota was equal to 100%. Data source: ECB.)

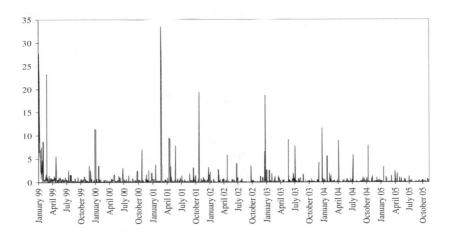

Fig. 3.6: Recourse to the Marginal Lending Facility. (Daily data from 1 January 1999 until 8 November 2005. Numbers are in EUR billions. Data source: ECB.)

2003, and in June 2003, the ECB restored neutral liquidity conditions, i.e. the banks had not to take recourse to the marginal lending facility and, with the exception of March 2003, the EONIA did not increase significantly.[7]

---

[7] In March 2003, the Eurosystem conducted an additional MRO with a maturity of one week to restore neutral liquidity conditions without generating a considerable difference between the sizes of the two outstanding MROs (European Central

Interestingly, the Eurosystem seems to have changed its attitude towards the banks' underbidding behaviour. In 2001 and 2002, the ECB generally did not want to offset totally the liquidity deficits due to the underbidding behaviour in order to make clear that underbidding is a non-profit-making strategy for the banks (European Central Bank, 2001d, p. 16 and European Central Bank, 2003d, p. 13). However, concerning the underbidding cases in March and June 2003, the Eurosystem restored neutral liquidity conditions. In March 2003, it conducted an additional MRO with a maturity of one week, and in June 2003, it increased accordingly the allotment quota in the subsequent MRO (European Central Bank, 2003c, p. 12 and European Central Bank, 2003b, p. 13).

3.2.2 Interest Rate Change Expectations as a Possible Trigger for the Under- and Overbidding Behaviour

Referring to the expectations theory and the liquidity premium theory of the term structure of interest rates, we use the spread between the one-month EURIBOR and the MRO-rate as a proxy for interest rate expectations in the euro area. Large positive values indicate that the MRO-rate is expected to increase and negative values indicate expectations of a decreasing MRO-rate. Thus, Fig. 3.7 indicates the importance of interest rate change expectations for the unbalanced bidding behaviour:

- All underbidding cases (April 1999, February 2001, April 2001, October 2001, November 2001, December 2002, March 2003 and June 2003) fall in periods characterized by expectations of interest rates decreasing.[8]

Bank, 2003c, p. 12). The significant increase in the EONIA took place before the additional operation was conducted. For details concerning the monetary policy operations and liquidity conditions in the reserve maintenance periods in which the underbidding behaviour occurred see: April 1999: European Central Bank (1999); February 2001: European Central Bank (2001c); April 2001: European Central Bank (2001d); October 2001: European Central Bank (2001e); November 2001: European Central Bank (2001f); December 2002: European Central Bank (2003d); March 2003: European Central Bank (2003c); June 2003: European Central Bank (2003b).

[8] In February 2001, the spread was not negative but it was close to zero which is, in the light of the liquidity premium theory of the term structure of interest rates, also an indicator for expectations of interest rates decreasing.

- The extreme overbidding behaviour in the last quarter of 1999 and
  in the first half of 2000 occurred in a situation characterized by
  expectations of interest rates increasing.[9]

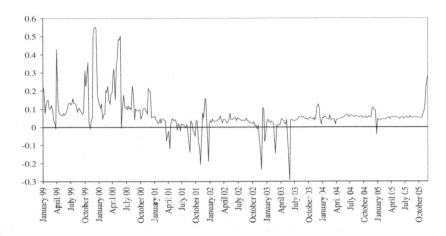

Fig. 3.7: Spread between the One-Month EURIBOR and the MRO-Rate. (Days of
settlement of the MROs from 7 January 1999 to 30 November 2005. Numbers are
in percentage points. The MRO-rate is the rate applied to the fixed rate tenders
and the weighted average rate of the variable rate tenders. Data sources: ECB and
Deutsche Bundesbank.)

The theoretical analysis of this work confirms the importance of interest rate change expectations for the observed under- and overbidding
behaviour. In the literature, the importance of expectations of interest
rate changes for the observed *underbidding* behaviour in the MROs is
not a controversial issue of discussion unlike their importance regarding the observed *overbidding* behaviour. The European Central Bank
(2000, 2003a) as well as Bindseil (2005) state that expectations of interest rate changes were the sole triggers of the overbidding problem.

Ayuso and Repullo (2001, 2003) argue that an asymmetric objective
function of the ECB (see p. 23 for details) led to liquidity allotment
decisions which resulted in tight liquidity conditions. These tight liquidity conditions again implied such a large positive spread between
the interbank market rate and the MRO-rate that banks overbid in
order to profit by arbitrage from this interest rate differential.

---

[9] For empirical analyses confirming the importance of interest rate expectations for
the overbidding behaviour see Breitung and Nautz (2001) and Ehrhart (2001).

Nautz and Oechssler (2003) argue that expectations of interest rate changes cannot explain why the overbidding increased over time, or on other words why the allotment quota "vanished" over time, i.e. expectations of interest rate changes cannot explain the large extent of the overbidding at the end of the fixed rate tender period in May/June 2000. For explaining the "vanishing quota puzzle", Nautz and Oechssler model a stylized game between banks. Each bank can cover its liquidity needs either by participating in a central bank's auction and demanding liquidity at a fixed rate, and/or by borrowing liquidity in the interbank market. In the interbank market, a bank can also lend liquidity. If a bank bids its true demand and receives this amount, the bank will realize its cost minimum. There are two crucial assumptions in the Nautz-Oechssler model: First, banks are boundedly rational players. They have adaptive expectations. Second, banks are rationed, i.e. the allotment quota is strictly smaller than one. Under these assumptions, Nautz and Oechssler obtain the intuitively convincing result that the bidding process explodes. We will illustrate their idea with the following numerical example: In all periods, the banks' true aggregate demand is 100 liquidity units. In period t, they bid this amount but receive only 90 units, i.e the allotment quota is equal to 0.9. Keeping in mind this allotment quota, the banks will bid for 111 units in period $t + 1$. In that period, the central bank allots again only 90 units, i.e. the allotment quota falls to 0.8. This implies that in period $t + 2$, total bids are equal to 125 units and so on, i.e. overbidding increases and the allotment quota vanishes. Note that this process implies that the central bank is not willing to satisfy the banks' true liquidity demand (see Nautz and Oechssler, 2003, p. 214). By assumption $A_t < D_t$, where A_t is the total allotment and D_t total *true* demand (not total bids). We will come back to the Nautz-Oechssler explanation for the observed overbidding behaviour when the implications of our theoretical analysis for the Eurosystem's operational framework in Chap. 8 are discussed. Experimental evidence in favour of the Nautz-Oechssler model can be found in Ehrhart (2001).

Nautz and Oechssler (2006) evaluate the empirical relevance of the three different hypotheses (interest rate change expectations hypothesis, tight liquidity hypothesis and rationing hypothesis). Their main result is that none of these hypotheses alone can explain the observed overbidding behaviour. We will come back to these hypotheses when the implications of our theoretical models for the Eurosystem's operational framework in section 8 are discussed.

3.2.3 Problems of the Under- and Overbidding Behaviour

In the literature, to date there is no in-depth discussion about the problems related to the observed unbalanced bidding behaviour. Bindseil (2005) emphasizes the inefficient allocation of reserves as a consequence of the overbidding behaviour and Nautz and Oechssler (2003), also when referring to the overbidding behaviour, mention in addition that the low allotment quotas obscure the ECB's policy signals and that banks take unnecessary risks. Ewerhart (2002) argues that underbidding behaviour may unbalance the dynamic system of bidding volumes, tender conditions, and money market rates. The theoretical analysis of this work identifies two possible problems related to under- and overbidding behaviour: First, a reduction in the buffer function of the minimum reserve system. The intuition is that underbidding/overbidding is combined with extremely uneven provisions of required reserve which implies that there are periods in which aggregate minimum reserve holdings are relatively low (see section 3.3). Second, the unbalanced bidding behaviour involves a violation of the Eurosystem's principle of equal treatment which has been already outlined in the introduction to this work.

3.2.4 Reactions of the Eurosystem to the Under- and Overbidding Behaviour

The reaction of the ECB to this bidding behaviour has been threefold. First, in June 2000, the governing council decided to switch from fixed rate tenders to variable rate tenders as a response to the severe overbidding (European Central Bank, 2000). Second, in November 2001, the governing council decided to discuss interest rate changes at the first of its bi-monthly meetings only because discussing this issue at both meetings would lead every two weeks to speculations about interest rate changes (Duisenberg, 2001). Third, in January 2003, the governing council decided to change its operational framework (European Central Bank, 2003e). It decided to reduce the maturity of the MROs from two weeks to one week and to change the timing of the reserve maintenance period (see sections 2.3 and 2.4.1 for details).

The first two reactions were not convincing solutions to the under- and overbidding problem. The switch from fixed rate tenders to variable rate tenders with a minimum bid rate only solved the overbidding problem. As shown by Breitung, Linzert, and Nautz (2003), the underbidding problem would have also been solved if the ECB had decided to use pure variable rate tenders, i.e. variable rate tenders without a minimum bid rate. However, when abandoning the minimum bid rate and the fixed rate tenders, the ECB may not be able to signal the monetary policy stance as clearly as it wants to, or, to put it differently, instruments will be given up which may be the most appropriate ones in specific situations. The decision to make interest rate decisions only at the governing council's first monthly meeting did not solve the problem either. Under the old operational framework, i.e. until March 2004, only the frequency of the unbalanced bidding behaviour was reduced while at the same time the flexibility of monetary policy has been curtailed. According to the theoretical analysis of this work, the third reaction of the ECB (the changes to its operational framework) moves into the right direction, since interest rate change expectations should no longer influence the banks' bidding behaviour and, therefore, should not be the trigger for further unbalanced bidding behaviour. However, the problem of the ECB's self-commitment remains.

3.3 Fulfilling of Required Reserves

In the euro area, a bank can make use of averaging provisions to fulfil its reserve requirements. But on the aggregate level, the ECB prefers smooth provisions of reserve requirements since it enhances the buffer function of reserve holdings against liquidity shocks (European Central Bank, 2002b). However, there are maintenance periods characterised by extremely uneven provisions of aggregated required reserves, as Fig. 3.8 illustrates. For instance in the maintenance period January/February 2001 required reserves were 120 billion Euro and provisions varied from 92 billion Euro to 182 billion Euro.

Taking a closer look at the periods characterized by extremely uneven provisions reveals that interest rate expectations seem to have a significant influence on banks' allocation of reserve holdings over a maintenance period. For example at the beginning of November 2001 market participants anticipated that the ECB would decide at its meeting on 8 November 2001 to reduce the MRO-rate with effect from the MRO which was settled on 14 November (see Fig. 3.7). Figure 3.9 illustrates that in the week prior to this MRO, reserve holdings were relatively low and after this date relatively high.

Similar patterns can be observed in April 1999, February 2001, April 2001, October 2001, December 2002, and June 2003, i.e. in periods also characterized by expectations of interest rates decreasing. During

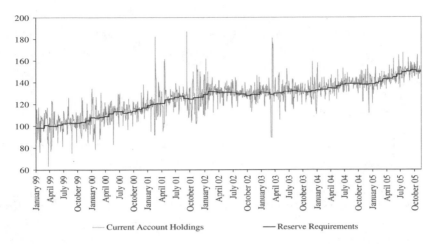

Fig. 3.8: Current Accounts and Required Reserves. (Daily data from 1 January 1999 to 28 November 2005. Numbers are in EUR billions. Data source: ECB.)

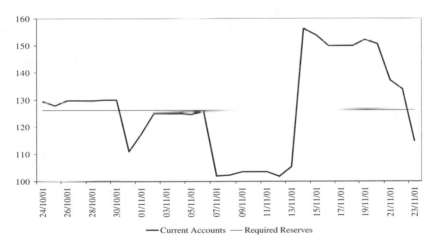

Fig. 3.9: Current Accounts and Required Reserves in the Reserve Maintenance Period October/November 2001. (Daily data. Numbers are in EUR billions. Data source: ECB.)

the identified periods of expectations of interest rates increasing an analogous fulfilling of required reserves could not be observed.

The explanation our theoretical analysis offers for the reserve shifting is due to the specific design of the Eurosystem's operational framework. Namely, overlapping maturities of central bank credits and the remuneration of required reserves at an average rate, banks can reduce their liquidity costs by this reserve shifting as it was briefly described in the introduction. That no frontloading of required reserve could be observed before the ECB raised interest rates is simply due to the fact that the ECB did not allot the necessary liquidity which would have allowed the frontloading of reserves.

3.4 Summary

This section has documented evidence of the following stylized facts the analyses in the next chapters are called to explain.

- The interbank market rate in the euro area tracks closely the Eurosystem's MRO-rate but the interbank market rate does not fluctuate evenly around the MRO-rate. However, in general there is a positive spread between these two rates.
- Several MROs were characterized by underbidding (overbidding) behaviour in the periods characterized by expectations of interest rates decreasing (increasing).
- Expectations of interest rates decreasing led to relatively low reserve holdings in the week prior to the MRO for which the interest rate cut was expected and they led to relatively high holdings in the subsequent week.

4

Base Model: Banks' Liquidity Management and Interbank Market Equilibrium

4.1 Introduction

The aim of this chapter is twofold. First, we will introduce in a rather simple framework the basic structure of the theoretical models presented in this work. Second, we will present a key result of this work by providing the rationale behind the existence of the interbank money market.

The basic structure of the theoretical models is as follows: In a first step, a single bank is considered which can cover its liquidity needs either by borrowing from the central bank or in the interbank market, where it can also place excess liquidity. Both forms of procuring liquidity are costly. Besides interest costs, the bank faces opportunity costs of holding collateral when borrowing from the central bank and transactions costs when borrowing or placing liquidity in the interbank market. The bank minimizes its total liquidity costs by choosing its optimal borrowing from the central bank and its optimal transactions in the interbank market. In a second step, the whole banking sector is considered. The crucial point is that this banking sector is heterogenous. The banks differ in their costs of obtaining funds from the central bank because they differ in their marginal opportunity costs of holding collateral. This heterogeneity is the rationale for the existence of the interbank market. Banks with relatively low costs borrow more liquidity from the central bank than they need in order to cover their own liquidity needs to lend the excess liquidity via the interbank market to those banks with relatively high costs of obtaining funds from the central bank.

4.2 Optimal Liquidity Management of a Single Bank

4.2.1 Liquidity Costs

We consider an isolated, price-taking bank. Its liquidity needs arise from autonomous factors, for example banknotes in circulation, and from reserve requirements imposed by the central bank. In this base model, these liquidity needs are summarized by the exogenous variable A. To cover its liquidity needs A, the bank can borrow liquidity from the central bank or in the interbank market where it can also place excess liquidity.

The loan borrowed from the central bank is denoted by K, with $K \geq 0$. The central bank specifies the interest rate l (repo rate) and, as a start, we assume that the bank receives the amount of liquidity from the central bank it wishes to borrow from at this rate. Later, in the sections 6.3.3 and 7.3.4, we suggest that the bank will be rationed if aggregate liquidity demand at the central bank exceeds a specific benchmark.[1] An important aspect is that this credit transaction has to be based on adequate collateral. We assume that rate of return considerations induce a strict hierarchy of the bank's assets,[2] and the assets which can serve as collateral have a relatively low rate of return due to the specific criteria they have to fulfil. Consequently, there are increasing marginal opportunity costs of holding collateral: The more liquidity the bank borrows from the central bank, the more collateral it must hold at the dispense of other assets. This is combined with increasing marginal costs due to the assumed hierarchical order of the bank's assets. These opportunity costs of holding collateral are given by

$$Q(K) = qK + f(K), \tag{4.1}$$

where $f(K) \geq 0$, $f(0) = 0$, $f' \geq 0$, $f'' > 0$, $f'(A) < \infty$, and $q \geq 0$.[3] In our model, the parameter q plays a crucial role: When we will look at the banking sector as a whole (section 4.3), we assume that the banks

---

[1] We will comment on this benchmark in more detail on p. 48

[2] This approach can be compared with the approach of Blum and Hellwig (1995). Blum and Hellwig consider a bank with deposits and equity. The bank can put these funds into loans to firms, government bonds or reserves of high powered money. Blum and Hellwig assume that rate of return considerations induce a strict preference for loans over bonds and for bonds over reserves.

[3] The assumption $f'(A) < \infty$ implies that the bank does not face infinite marginal costs when it covers its total liquidity needs A at the central bank.

differ in their levels of marginal opportunity costs of holding collateral, i.e. in q. It is a bank-specific cost parameter.

In the interbank market, the bank can demand liquidity or place excess liquidity. The bank's position in the interbank market is given by

$$B = A - K \lesseqgtr 0. \tag{4.2}$$

Trading in the interbank market, the bank faces transaction costs given by

$$Z(B) = zh(B), \tag{4.3}$$

where $h(B) \geq 0$, $h(0) = 0$, $h'(B > 0) > 0$, $h'(B < 0) < 0$, $h'(0) = 0$, $h''(B) > 0$, $h'(A) < \infty$, and the parameter $z > 0$. Furthermore, we assume the cost function to be symmetric, i.e. $h(B) = h(-B)$. Equation (4.3) represents a common approach of modelling transaction costs in the interbank market (see, for example, Campbell, 1987; Bartolini, Bertola, and Prati, 2001). The convex form of this cost function reflects increasing marginal costs of searching for banks with matching liquidity needs and those resulting from the need to split large transactions into many small ones to work around credit lines. It should be noted that in this one-period model, the convexity of both cost functions $Q(\cdot)$ and $Z(\cdot)$, and, therefore, of the functions f and h is not a necessary condition for our results. We will comment on this in more detail on p. 36.

Denoting the interbank market rate by e, the bank's total liquidity costs are

$$C(K) = Kl + B(K)e + Q(K) + Z(B(K)). \tag{4.4}$$

The first term on the right hand side describes interest payments to the central bank, the second describes either interest costs or revenues from transactions in the interbank market, and the last two terms represent opportunity costs of holding collateral and transaction costs.

4.2.2 Optimization

The bank minimizes its total liquidity costs by choosing the optimal level of K, subject to $K \geq 0$. The Lagrangian is

$$L(K, \lambda) = Kl + B(K)e + Q(K) + Z(B(K)) - \lambda K \tag{4.5}$$

and the first order conditions are

$$l + q + f'(K) - e - zh'(B(K)) - \lambda = 0, \tag{4.6}$$

$$\lambda K = 0, \quad \lambda \geq 0, \quad K \geq 0. \tag{4.7}$$

The first order condition given by equation (4.6) reveals that if the bank covers its liquidity needs at the central bank and in the interbank market, marginal costs of central bank funds $(l + q + f')$ will be equated to marginal costs of funds borrowed in the interbank market $(e + zh')$. If the bank places liquidity in the interbank market, the sum of the marginal costs of central bank funds and marginal transaction costs in the interbank market $(l + q + f' - zh')$ will be equated to marginal revenues in the interbank market e. (Note, that in case the bank places liquidity in the interbank market $h' < 0$.) It should be noted that in this base model, the convexity of both cost functions $Q(\cdot)$ and $Z(\cdot)$ is not necessary for obtaining a unique cost minimum: The second order condition given by

$$f''(K) + zh''(B(K)) > 0 \tag{4.8}$$

reveals that one of the functions can be linear or even concave. Crucial is that the bank must face *in total* increasing marginal costs.

Equation (4.6) implicitly gives the optimal central bank borrowing $K^{opt}(e, l, q, A, z)$. Using the implicit function theorem we find that for $K > 0$ optimal central bank borrowing is decreasing in q:

$$\frac{\partial(K^{opt}|K > 0)}{\partial q} = -\frac{1}{f'' + zh''} < 0. \tag{4.9}$$

The reason is obvious: An increase in q implies c.p. higher marginal costs of borrowing liquidity from the monetary authority so that the bank reduces its central bank borrowing and covers a higher part of its own liquidity needs in the interbank market or reduces its investment in the interbank market (see the comments to the first order condition on p. 36).

The condition $K \geq 0$ introduces a non-differentiable point in the partial derivative $\partial K^{opt}/\partial q$. We find this point by setting K equal to zero and solving equation (4.6) for q. Denoting this upper threshold for q by $\bar{q}$ we obtain

$$\bar{q} = e - l - f'(0) + zh'(A). \tag{4.10}$$

If $q \geq \bar{q}$, the bank's opportunity costs of holding collateral will be that high so the bank will prefer to cover its total liquidity needs in the interbank market, i.e. $K^{opt} = 0$ and $B = A$.

Evaluating equation (4.6) at $K = A$ and solving for q, we also find a lower threshold for q given by

$$\underline{q} = e - l - f'(A) + zh'(0) = e - l - f'(A). \qquad (4.11)$$

If $q < \underline{q}$, the bank's opportunity costs of holding collateral will be that low so it will be advantageous to borrow from the central bank to place liquidity in the interbank market. In this case, the bank borrows more reserves from the central bank than it actually needs to cover its own requirements, i.e. $K^{opt} > A$ and $B < 0$.

Thus, the bank's optimal central bank borrowing and its resulting optimal transactions in the interbank market are described by the following functions:

$$K^{opt}(e, l, q, A) = \begin{cases} (K^{opt}|A \leq K)(e, l, q, A) & \text{if} \quad q \leq \underline{q} \\ (K^{opt}|0 < K < A)(e, l, q, A) & \text{if} \quad \underline{q} < q < \bar{q} \\ 0 & \text{if} \quad \bar{q} \leq q, \end{cases} \qquad (4.12)$$

and

$$B^{opt}(e, l, q, A) = \begin{cases} (B^{opt}|B \leq 0)(e, l, q, A) & \text{if} \quad q \leq \underline{q} \\ (B^{opt}|0 < B < A)(e, l, q, A) & \text{if} \quad \underline{q} < q < \bar{q} \\ A & \text{if} \quad \bar{q} \leq q. \end{cases} \qquad (4.13)$$

If $q < \underline{q}$, the bank will borrow more reserves from the central bank than it needs to cover its own liquidity needs and will place the excess liquidity in the interbank market. If $q = \underline{q}$, the bank will borrow exactly the amount of central bank credit from the central bank it needs to cover its own requirements. If $\underline{q} < q < \bar{q}$, the bank will cover its liquidity needs at the central bank and in the interbank market; and finally, if $q \geq \bar{q}$, the bank will cover its liquidity needs exclusively in the interbank market. Figure 4.1 illustrates this result. It should be noted that the slope of the curve between 0 and $\bar{q}$ has been chosen arbitrarily. Its exact shape depends on the form of the cost functions $Q(\cdot)$ and $Z(\cdot)$.

4.3 Interbank Market Equilibrium

4.3.1 Heterogeneous Banking Sector

Looking at the banking sector as a whole, we consider a continuum of measure one of isolated, price-taking banks. The crucial point is that the banks differ in their level of marginal opportunity costs of holding

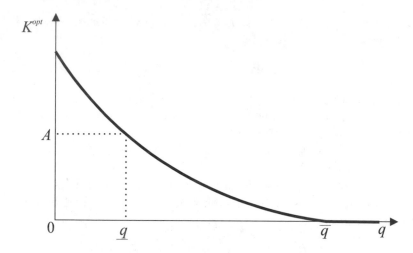

Fig. 4.1: Base Model: Optimal Borrowing from the Central Bank

collateral q, i.e. q is a bank-specific cost parameter. This heterogeneity of the banking sector leads to the development of an interbank market. Banks with relatively low opportunity costs of holding collateral ($q < \underline{q}$) borrow more liquidity from the monetary authority than they need to cover their own liquidity needs in order to place the excess liquidity in the interbank market, while banks with relatively high opportunity costs of holding collateral ($q > \underline{q}$) cover their liquidity needs partially or totally in the interbank market. Consequently, the banks with the relatively low opportunity costs act as intermediaries.

In our (deterministic) model, banks do not enter the interbank market in order to balance individual daily liquidity imbalances. This interbank market function could be considered by modelling A as a bank-specific random variable or by adding bank-specific liquidity shocks. However, this would make our analysis more complex without changing our main results so that we neglect this interbank market function. In our analysis, the interbank market exists because of a heterogenous banking sector, banks differ in costs of obtaining funds from the central bank because their opportunity costs of holding collateral are different.

Concerning the heterogeneity of the banking sector, we will briefly comment on two aspects: price discrimination and the survival of banks with relatively high costs. Concerning the first, it should be noted that we have assumed a competitive interbank market. Neither the banks which supply nor those which demand liquidity in that market have any market power. Therefore, in the interbank market there is only one price e. Price discrimination by charging the banks with higher costs of obtaining funds at the central bank (which, therefore, have a higher reservation interbank market interest rate), a higher rate e is not possible, or to put it differently, consumer surplus cannot be captured. Concerning the second aspect, where the described heterogeneity of the banking sector does not imply that banks with relatively high costs are squeezed out of the financial markets by the banks with relatively low costs, it should be noted however that we consider only *one* financial market, the interbank market, and we assume that the banks with relatively high costs will have cost advantages when acting in other financial markets, i.e. we assume that banks specialize in different business segments.

4.3.2 Equilibrium Interbank Market Rate

For determining the equilibrium interbank market rate c^*, we assume that q is distributed in the interval $[0, q^{max}]$ across banks according to the density function $g(q) = G'(q)$ with $G(0) = 0$. Since at e^*, liquidity supply equals liquidity demand, e^* is implicitly given by[4]

$$
\int_0^{\bar{q}} (B^{opt}|q < \bar{q})g(q)dq + \int_{\underline{q}}^{q} (B^{opt}|q < \bar{q})g(q)dq
$$
$$
+ \int_{\bar{q}}^{q^{max}} (B^{opt}|q \geq \bar{q})g(q)dq = 0. \tag{4.14}
$$

The first term in equation (4.14) represents the liquidity supply in the interbank market, while the second term and the third term represent the liquidity demand. The liquidity demand captured by the second term consists of banks covering a part of their liquidity needs in the interbank market, the last term consists of banks satisfying their total liquidity by borrowing reserves in that market.[5]

4.3.3 Determinants of the Equilibrium Interbank Market Rate

According to equation (4.14), the equilibrium interbank market rate is determined by the repo rate, the transaction costs in the interbank

---

[4] To keep the base model as general as possible, we do not specify the distribution of q across the banks and determine the equilibrium interbank market rate e^* only implicitly.

[5] In equation (4.14) the first two integrals can be written as one integral since the integrand is the same. However, we have chosen to split the integral to separate supply and demand.

market, the total liquidity needs of the banking sector, the opportunity costs of holding collateral and the distribution of the latter across banks. When applying the implicit function theorem, we obtain:[6]

$$\frac{\partial e^*}{\partial l} = 1, \tag{4.15}$$

$$\frac{\partial e^*}{\partial z} = \frac{-\int_0^{\bar{q}} \frac{h'}{f''+zh''} g(q)dq}{\int_0^{\bar{q}} \frac{g(q)}{f''+zh''} dq} \gtreqless 0, \tag{4.16}$$

$$\frac{\partial e^*}{\partial A} = \frac{1 - \int_0^{\bar{q}} \frac{zh''}{f''+zh''} g(q)dq}{\int_0^{\bar{q}} \frac{g(q)}{f''+zh''} dq} > 0. \tag{4.17}$$

Equation (4.15) reveals that there is a positive relationship between the interbank market rate e^* and the *repo rate l*. An increase in l results in increasing marginal costs of borrowing from the central bank implying that banks on the demand as well as on the supply side in the interbank market reduce their borrowing from the central bank. Consequently, supply in the interbank market decreases and demand increases inducing the interbank market rate to rise.

Equation (4.16) reveals that the effect of a change in the *transaction cost parameter z* is ambiguous. Let us assume that there is an increase in z. Then, marginal costs of placing and borrowing in the interbank market increase so that supply as well as demand will fall. It depends on the shape of the cost functions $Q(\cdot)$ and $Z(\cdot)$, in more detail on the functions f and h, and on the density function $g(q)$ which effect outweighs the other and, thus, whether there is a decrease or increase in e^*.

Equation (4.17) shows that there is also a positive relationship between the interbank market rate e^* and *total liquidity needs A*. This result is driven by the functions f and h. If both functions are convex, as assumed, the banks which supply liquidity in the interbank market will cover their additional liquidity needs by reducing their supply in that market *and* by borrowing more funds from the central bank, while

---

[6] In equation (4.16) the sign is ambiguous because for $0 \leq q < \underline{q}$, $h' < 0$ and for $\underline{q} < q < \bar{q}$, $h' > 0$. In equation (4.17) the sign is positive: The functions h and f are assumed to be strictly convex, i.e. $0 < zh''/(f'' + zh'') < 1$. This implies that $\int_0^{\bar{q}} (zh''/(f'' + zh'')) g(q)dq < 1$. (Note that $\int_0^{q^{max}} g(q) = 1$ and that $\bar{q} < q^{max}$.)

the banks on the demand side will cover their additional needs by borrowing more funds in the interbank market *and* from the central bank.[7] Consequently, in the interbank market, the supply decreases and the demand increases implying a rising interbank market rate e^*. However, it should be noted that the convexity of both functions, f and h, is not a necessary condition for the result $\partial e^*/\partial A > 0$. This result will also hold if only one cost function is convex and the other is linear, and it may also hold if one is convex and the other is concave. Crucial is that the second order condition for a cost minimum $f'' + zh'' > 0$ is fulfilled (see also p. 36).

4.3.4 Spread Between the Interbank Market Rate and the Repo Rate

We have argued that the heterogeneous banking sector implies that banks with relatively low costs of obtaining funds from the central bank act as intermediaries between the central bank and those banks with relatively high costs. It is obvious that this results in a positive spread between the equilibrium interbank market rate and the repo rate ($s = e^* - l > 0$), otherwise no bank would be willing to borrow from the central bank in order to place the liquidity in the interbank market. This spread is determined by the transaction costs in the interbank market, the total liquidity needs of the banking sector, the opportunity costs of holding collateral and the distribution of the latter across banks, and $\partial s/\partial z = \partial e^*/\partial z$ and $\partial s/\partial A = \partial e^*/\partial A$ (see equations (4.16) and (4.17)).

4.3.5 Illustration

In order to illustrate our results graphically, we postulate the cost functions to be quadratic:

$$Q(K) = qK + \frac{p}{2}K^2 \tag{4.18}$$

and

$$Z(B(K)) = \frac{z}{2}B(K)^2 \tag{4.19}$$

with the parameters $p, z > 0$. Furthermore, we assume a uniform distribution of q, with $g(q) = 1$. Figure 4.2 shows the interbank market equilibrium considering these assumptions.

---

[7] Formally, one obtains this result by using equation (4.6) and employing the implicit function theorem which reveals that $\partial(K^{opt}|K > 0)/\partial A < 1$.

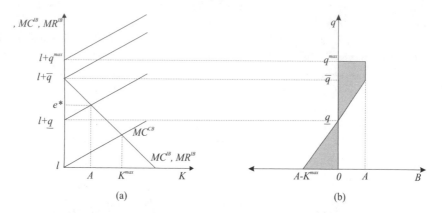

Fig. 4.2: Base Model: Interbank Market Equilibrium

In panel (a), the upwards sloping curves represent marginal costs of borrowing from the central bank given by

$$MC^{CB} = l + q + pK. \tag{4.20}$$

Since there is a continuum of banks differing in q, which is distributed in the interval $[0, q^{max}]$, there is a continuum of marginal cost curves between $(l + 0 = l)$ and $(l + q^{max})$. The downwards sloping curve represents marginal costs of borrowing in the interbank market. For banks placing liquidity in that market this curve depicts net marginal revenues (interest yield on interbank loans minus transaction costs). These marginal costs and revenues are given by

$$MC^{IB} = MR^{IB} = e + z(A - K). \tag{4.21}$$

Looking at panel (a) and comparing the marginal costs of borrowing from the central bank with the marginal costs of borrowing in the interbank market/marginal revenues from placing liquidity in the interbank market leads to the following results: For banks with $q > \bar{q}$ the marginal costs of borrowing from the central bank are always higher than those of borrowing in the interbank market. Consequently, $(K^{opt}|q \geq \bar{q}) = 0$ (we break ties in favour of borrowing in the interbank market). Banks with $\bar{q} > q > \underline{q}$ partially cover their liquidity requirements at the central bank and in the interbank market, i.e. $0 < (K^{opt}|\bar{q} > q > \underline{q}) < A$. The bank-specific amount $(K^{opt}|\bar{q} > q > \underline{q})$ is found at the point where the bank-specific marginal cost curve $(MC^{CB}|\bar{q} > q > \underline{q})$ and the marginal cost curve MC^{IB} intersect. Credit institutions with $q < \underline{q}$ borrow more reserves than they need to cover their own liquidity needs to place the excess liquidity in the interbank market, i.e. $(K^{opt}|q < \underline{q}) > A$. The bank-specific amount $(K^{opt}|q < \underline{q})$ is determined by the intersection of the bank-specific marginal cost curve $(MC^{CB}|q < \underline{q})$ and the marginal revenue curve MR^{IB}. K^{max} denotes the central bank loan of the bank with the lowest level of marginal opportunity costs of holding collateral, i.e. with $q = 0$.

Panel (b) in Fig. 4.2 represents aggregate demand and supply in the interbank market. The shaded area to the left of the vertical q-axis represents aggregate supply, the respective area to the right aggregate demand. In equilibrium, both areas have to be of the same size. The equilibrium interbank rate e^* is determined by the intersection of the specific marginal cost curve $(MC^{CB}|q = \underline{q})$ and the marginal cost/revenue curve $(MC^{IB} = MR^{IB})$, i.e. where $K^{opt} = A$ (see equation (4.21) and replace K by A).

Figure 4.3 illustrates the consequences of an increase in the central bank rate l, liquidity needs A, and transaction costs z on liquidity demand and supply in the interbank market. The index 0 (1) marks variables before (after) the increase in l, A and z.

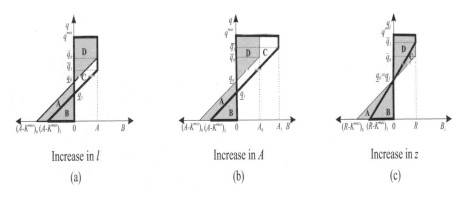

Fig. 4.3: Base Model: Comparative Static Analysis

An increase in l implies that in Fig. 4.2 the continuum of the marginal cost curves MC_i^{CB} shifts parallel upwards. The consequent decrease in K^{max}, $\underline{q}$ and $\bar{q}$ implies that in Fig. 4.3, panel (a) aggregate supply shrinks from the area (A+B) to the triangle B. Aggregate demand, on the other hand, increases from the area D to the area (C+D). Consequently, there will be a rise in e to restore market equilibrium. Graphically, this rise in e shifts the marginal cost/revenue curve $(MC^{IB} = MR^{IB})$ upwards, implying that K^{max}, $\underline{q}$ and q will increase again, until the areas to both sides of the vertical q-axis are the same size again.

In Fig. 4.2, an increase in A leads to a parallel upward shift of the marginal cost/revenue curve ($MC^{IB} = MR^{IB}$). Furthermore, on the horizontal axis, A moves to the right. The shift of the marginal cost/revenue curve implies that K^{max} will increase, but since this increase must be smaller than the rise in A ($\partial K^{opt}/\partial A < 1$) the distance $\overline{AK^{max}}$ becomes smaller which implies that $\underline{q}$ decreases. The upper threshold $\bar{q}$, on the other hand, increases. Therefore, as Fig. 4.3, panel (b) illustrates, aggregate supply shrinks from the area (A+B) to B, whereas aggregate demand increases from the area D to (D+C). Hence, the interbank market rate e will rise to restore the market equilibrium.

In Fig. 4.2, an increase in z implies the marginal cost/revenue curve ($MC^{IB} = MR^{IB}$) to turn clockwise in that point where it intersects with the marginal cost curve ($MC^{CB}|q = \underline{q}$) (a change in z does not imply a change in $\underline{q}$ as long as e has not changed yet, see equation (4.11)). Therefore, the marginal cost/revenue curve becomes steeper implying $\bar{q}$ to rise and K^{max} to fall. Consequently, as Fig. 4.3 shows, aggregate demand and supply shrink such that the effect on e^* is ambiguous.

4.4 Summary

In this chapter, we have presented the base model of this work. First, we considered a single bank which minimizes its total liquidity costs by choosing its optimal central bank borrowing and optimal transactions in the interbank market. Then, we have looked at the banking sector as a whole, assuming that banks differ in their opportunity costs of holding collateral, which is a key feature in all models we will present in this work.

The main result of this chapter can be summarized as follows. If opportunity costs of collateral, which banks need to hold to obtain funds from the central bank, differ between banks, an interbank market will develop. Banks with relatively low opportunity costs will act as intermediaries between the central bank and banks with relatively high costs. The interbank market rate will be higher than the central bank's repo rate, with the spread being determined by total liquidity needs of the banking sector, transaction costs in the interbank market, opportunity costs of holding collateral, and the distribution of the latter across banks.

Finally, it should be noted that we focus on different opportunity costs of holding collateral. However, the crucial point is that banks differ in costs of obtaining funds from the central bank. Different costs of obtaining funds from the central bank may not only result from different opportunity costs of holding collateral, but can also have other reasons such as differences in operating costs.

5

Remuneration of Required Reserves at the Current Repo Rate

5.1 Introduction

In this chapter, we expand the base model by assuming that there are two time periods which cover a reserve maintenance period. For fulfilling their reserve requirements banks can make use of averaging provisions. An important feature of our model is that reserves are remunerated at the end of each period at the current repo rate. As in the base model, the banks can cover their liquidity needs either by borrowing from the central bank or in the interbank market where they can also place liquidity. A further crucial feature of our model is that the banks can borrow in each period from the central bank as well as in the interbank market, and that the maturities of all loans is one period, i.e. the maturities of the central bank credits do not overlap. Within this framework, the banks have to decide on their optimal borrowing from the central bank, their optimal transactions in the interbank market, and on the optimal intertemporal allocation of their required reserve holdings. A main result is that within this model framework, the banks' liquidity management is not influenced by a change in the repo rate within the reserve maintenance period. Independently of a change in the repo rate, reserves are provided smoothly over the maintenance period and borrowing from the central bank corresponds to the central bank's benchmark. Moreover, we show that banks are not affected differently by a monetary impulse in the form of a change in the repo rate. A further result of this chapter is that in this current rate model there is no smoothing of the interbank market rate in the sense that it already increases (decreases) before the repo rate is actually raised (cut).

5.2 Optimal Liquidity Management of a Single Bank

5.2.1 Liquidity Costs

There are two time periods, $t = 1, 2$, which cover a reserve maintenance period. An isolated, price-taking bank is considered which needs liquidity for covering the given autonomous factors A and the given reserve requirements RR imposed by a central bank. Concerning the required reserves, the bank can make use of averaging provisions. The reserve requirement is fulfilled if

$$RR = \frac{R_1 + R_2}{2}, \tag{5.1}$$

with $R_t \geq 0$ being the reserve holdings of the bank in period t.

To cover its liquidity needs, the bank can borrow in each period from the central bank or in the interbank market where it can also place liquidity. In this model, both, central bank loans and interbank market loans, have a maturity of one period.

The loan borrowed from the monetary authority in period t is denoted by K_t, with $K_t \geq 0$. On this loan the bank has to pay the repo rate l_t which is set by the monetary authority. Again, we assume that the bank receives the amount of liquidity it demands from the central bank at this rate. This implies that the central bank always satisfies the bank's demand for reserves. In the Eurosystem's MROs, the Eurosystem's benchmark allotment is the amount of liquidity which allows for smooth provisions of aggregate required reserves over a reserve maintenance period (see p. 13). Following this definition, we define the amount of central bank borrowing in the first period which allows on aggregate for smooth provisions of required reserves over the reserve maintenance period as the central bank's benchmark amount. Consequently, our assumption implies that the central bank will even satisfy the bank's demand for reserves if the aggregate demand for central bank's credits exceeds the central bank's benchmark. In this current rate model, this is not a critical assumption since aggregate liquidity demand always corresponds to the central bank's benchmark (see p. 56). However, in the average rate model and in the overlapping maturities model, which we will present in the next chapters, aggregate liquidity demand can deviate from this benchmark. Therefore, within these models, we will also analyze a bank's optimal liquidity management if the central bank rations liquidity when aggregate liquidity demand exceeds its benchmark amount.

The central bank loan K_t has to be based on adequate collateral. As in the base model, we assume the relevant opportunity cost function to be convex (for the motivation of this assumption see comments on equation (4.1) on p. 34). Postulating a tractable quadratic form, this cost function is given by[1]

$$Q(K_t) = qK_t + \frac{p}{2}K_t^2, \tag{5.2}$$

with the parameters $q \geq 0$ and $p > 0$.

If the bank borrows more funds from the central bank than it needs to cover its own liquidity needs ($K_t > A + R_t$), it will place the excess liquidity at the rate e_t in the interbank market. If, on the other hand, the loan from the central bank is too small to cover the bank's total liquidity needs ($K_t < A + R_t$), it will borrow at the rate e_t in that market. The bank's position in the interbank market is given by

$$B_t = A + R_t - K_t \lesseqqgtr 0. \tag{5.3}$$

When trading in the interbank market the bank faces increasing marginal transaction costs (for the motivation of this assumption see comments on equation (4.3) on p. 35). Analogously to the cost function $Q(K_t)$ we also use the tractable quadratic form so that the transaction cost function is given by

$$Z(B_t(R_t, K_t)) = \frac{z}{2}\left(B_t(R_t, K_t)\right)^2, \tag{5.4}$$

with the parameter $z > 0$.

A further important feature of this model is that holdings of required reserves are remunerated at the end of each period t at the current repo rate l_t. Consequently, net liquidity costs in period t consist of interest payments to the central bank, interest costs or interest revenues resulting from transactions in the interbank market, opportunity costs of holding collateral, transaction costs and interest revenues from holding required reserves:

$$\begin{aligned}
C_t(K_t, R_t) &= K_t l_t + B_t(R_t, K_t)e_t + Q(K_t) \\
&\quad + Z(B_t(R_t, K_t)) - R_t l_t.
\end{aligned} \tag{5.5}$$

As in the base model, we neglect that banks enter the interbank market to balance liquidity imbalances resulting from bank-specific shocks

---

[1] Contrary to the base model, where we only assumed this cost function to be convex, we specify the function by assuming a quadratic form. This simplifies our analysis considerably since it implies that the third derivative of $Q(K_t)$, which occurs in this two-period model, is equal to zero.

to reserves. Furthermore, one should note that in the first period the bank knows the central bank rate l_2 with certainty, i.e. we assume that there are no monetary policy shocks and that the bank forms rational expectations. Introducing uncertainty by incorporating bank-specific liquidity shocks or monetary policy shocks into our model would make our analysis more complex without changing our results.

5.2.2 Optimization Problem

Throughout the remainder of this work, the bank's optimal liquidity management aims at minimizing its net total liquidity costs over the maintenance period, while keeping average reserves to the required level RR, i.e. optimal liquidity management means deciding on

- the optimal intertemporal allocation of reserve holdings (determination of R_1^{opt} and R_2^{opt}),
- the optimal borrowing from the central bank (determination of K_1^{opt} and K_2^{opt}), and
- and optimal transactions in the interbank market (determination of B_1^{opt} and B_2^{opt}).

Disregarding discounting, whose impact is negligible over this short horizon, the bank's objective function becomes

$$\min_{K_t, R_t} \left\{ \sum_{t=1}^{2} C_t(K_t, R_t) \right\}. \tag{5.6}$$

Since the bank can make use of averaging provisions to fulfil its reserve requirements, it faces a simple dynamic optimization problem. Defining V_t as the associated value function, the Bellman equation for the intra-maintenance period optimization problem is given by

$$V_1 = \min_{K_1, R_1} \{C_1(K_1, R_1) + V_2\} \quad \text{subject to} \quad K_t, R_t \geq 0. \tag{5.7}$$

In what follows, we will solve this optimization problem backwards.

5.2.3 Optimal Liquidity Management in the Second Period

According to equation (5.1), we replace R_2 by $(2RR - R_1)$. Then, in the second period we only have to optimize over K_2, and the Lagrangian becomes

$$L(K_2, \lambda_2) = K_2 l_2 + B_2(K_2)e_2 + Q(K_2) + Z(B_2(K_2)) \tag{5.8}$$
$$-(2RR - R_1)l_2 - \lambda_2 K_2$$

and the first order conditions are

$$-e_2 + l_2 + pK_2 + q - zB_2(K_2) - \lambda_2 = 0, \tag{5.9}$$

$$\lambda_2 K_2 = 0, \quad \lambda_2 \geq 0, \quad K_2 \geq 0. \tag{5.10}$$

These first order conditions say that if the bank covers its liquidity needs in the interbank market *and* at the central bank, marginal costs of interbank market funds $(zB_2 + e_2)$ will be equated to marginal costs of central bank funds $(l_2 + pK_2 + q)$. Note, that in this case $\lambda_2 = 0$ since $K_2 > 0$. If the bank places liquidity in the interbank market (again $\lambda_2 = 0$ since $K_2 > 0$), marginal costs of this transaction $(l_2 + pK_2 + q - zB_2)$ will equal its marginal benefits e_2. Note, that in this case $B_2 < 0$. Furthermore, the first order conditions reveal that there is an upper threshold for q given by

$$\bar{q}_2 = e_2 - l_2 + z(A + 2RR - R_1). \tag{5.11}$$

If $q \geq \bar{q}_2$, for all K_2, marginal costs of covering liquidity needs at the central bank will not be lower than in the interbank market, so that the bank will cover its total liquidity needs in that market, i.e. $K_2 = 0$ (we break ties in favour of borrowing in the interbank market). The first order conditions lead to the following result for optimal borrowing from the central bank in the second period:

$$K_2^{opt}(R_1) = \begin{cases} \frac{e_2 - l_2 - q + z(A + 2RR - R_1)}{p + z} & \text{if} \quad q < \bar{q}_2 \\ 0 & \text{if} \quad q \geq \bar{q}_2. \end{cases} \tag{5.12}$$

By inserting K_2^{opt} into C_2, one obtains the minimal net liquidity costs in the second period:

$$V_2(R_1) = K_2^{opt}(R_1)l_2 + B_2(K_2^{opt}(R_1), R_1)e_2 + Q_2(K_2^{opt}(R_1)) \tag{5.13}$$
$$+Z_2(K_2^{opt}(R_1), R_1) - (2RR - R_1)l_2.$$

5.2.4 Optimal Liquidity Management in the First Period

In this model, $R_t \geq 0$ is not a binding constraint, see equations (5.28) and (5.45). Therefore, we neglect this constraint in the Lagrangian which is

$$L(K_1, R_1, \lambda_1) = K_1 l_1 + B_1(K_1, R_1)e_1 + Q(K_1)$$
$$+Z(B_1(K_1, R_1)) - R_1 l_1 - \lambda_1 K_1 + V_2(R_1). \tag{5.14}$$

The first order conditions are[2]

$$-e_1 + l_1 + pK_1 + q - zB_1(K_1, R_1) - \lambda_1 = 0, \tag{5.15}$$

$$e_1 + zB_1(K_1, R_1) - l_1 = e_2 + zB_2(K_2^{opt}(R_1), R_1) - l_2, \tag{5.16}$$

$$\lambda_1 K_1 = 0, \quad \lambda_1 \geq 0, \quad K_1 \geq 0. \tag{5.17}$$

The first order condition for K_1 given by equation (5.15) says analogously to the one given by equation (5.9): if the bank covers its liquidity needs in the interbank market *and* at the central bank, marginal costs of interbank market funds will be equated to marginal costs of central bank funds, and if the bank places liquidity in the interbank market, marginal costs of this transaction will equal its marginal revenue. The first order conditions represented by (5.17) simply reflect the non-negativity constraint for K_1.

The first order condition for R_1 given by equation (5.16) says that an optimal R_1 requires *net* marginal costs of holding required reserves to be the same in both periods. The left hand side captures net marginal costs of holding reserves in the first, the right hand side of holding reserves in the second period. Marginal costs of holding reserves are presented by the first two terms on each side of the equation, the last term on each side captures marginal revenues of holding reserves which result from their remuneration.

---

[2] Equation (5.12) shows that we have to distinguish between two cases when analyzing the bank's optimal liquidity management in the first period. In the first case, the bank borrows liquidity from the monetary authority in the second period, i.e. $q < \bar{q}_2$. In the second case, the bank covers its liquidity needs exclusively in the interbank market, i.e. $q \geq \bar{q}_2$. However, the interpretation of the first order conditions is the same in both cases and we have rewritten the conditions in such a way that their formal presentation is also the same.

5.2.5 Provisional Results

The parameters p and z in the cost functions $Q(K_t)$ and $Z(B_t)$ have been helpful for interpreting the first order conditions. However, for a clearer presentation of our results it is useful to set them equal to one. In doing so, the first order conditions lead to the following provisional results for a bank's optimal liquidity management (these are only provisional results since the results still depend on the interbank market rate e_t which we will determine in a next step):[3]

$$R_1^{opt} = RR - \frac{e_1 - e_2 - l_1 + l_2}{2} \quad \forall q, \tag{5.18}$$

$$R_2^{opt} = RR + \frac{e_1 - e_2 - l_1 + l_2}{2} \quad \forall q, \tag{5.19}$$

$$K_1^{opt} = K_2^{opt} = \begin{cases} \frac{A+RR-q}{2} + \frac{e_1+e_2-l_1-l_2}{4} & \text{if} \quad q < \bar{q} \\ 0 & \text{if} \quad q \geq q, \end{cases} \tag{5.20}$$

$$B_1^{opt} = \begin{cases} \frac{A+RR+q}{2} & \frac{3(e_1-l_1)-(e_2-l_2)}{4} & \text{if} \quad q < \bar{q} \\ A + RR - \frac{(e_1-l_1)-(e_2-l_2)}{2} & \text{if} \quad q \geq \bar{q}, \end{cases} \tag{5.21}$$

and

$$B_2^{opt} = \begin{cases} \frac{A+RR+q}{2} + \frac{(e_1-l_1)-3(e_2-l_2)}{4} & \text{if} \quad q < \bar{q} \\ A + RR + \frac{(e_1-l_1)-(e_2-l_2)}{2} & \text{if} \quad q \geq \bar{q}, \end{cases} \tag{5.22}$$

where

$$\bar{q} = \bar{q}_1 = \bar{q}_2 = A + RR + \frac{e_1 + e_2 - l_1 - l_2}{2}. \tag{5.23}$$

Equations (5.18) and (5.19) represent the bank's optimal intertemporal allocation of required reserves, equation (5.20) its optimal borrowing from the central bank, and equations (5.21) and (5.22) its optimal

---

[3] In order to determine $(K_1^{opt}|q \geq \bar{q}_2)$ and $(R_1^{opt}|q \geq \bar{q}_2)$ we have looked at the marginal bank first, i.e. at the bank for which at $K_2^{opt} = 0$ marginal costs of central bank funds equal marginal costs of interbank market funds $(K_2^{opt}, \lambda_2 = 0)$. In this case, $q = \bar{q}_2 = e_2 - l_2 + z(A + 2RR - R_1)$, see equation (5.11), and one obtains that $(K_1^{opt}|q = \bar{q}_2) = 0$ and $(R_1^{opt}|q = \bar{q}_2) = RR$. It is obvious that for even higher costs of central bank borrowing, i.e. for even higher q, the bank will not borrow from the monetary authority either so that $(K_1^{opt}|q \geq \bar{q}_2) = 0$ and $(R_1^{opt}|q \geq \bar{q}_2) = RR$.

transactions in the interbank market. Equations (5.20) to (5.22) reveal the importance of the bank's opportunity costs of holding collateral. They determine if and when how much liquidity the bank borrows from the monetary authority and how much liquidity it borrows or places in the interbank market. Equation (5.23) gives the upper level of marginal opportunity costs of holding collateral. If $q \geq \bar{q}$, the bank will borrow no liquidity from the central bank but cover its total liquidity needs in the interbank market. Setting the first line of equation (5.20) equal to $(A + R_t)$ and solving for q, one obtains a further threshold for q given by

$$\underline{q}_1 = -(A + RR) + \frac{3(e_1 - l_1) - (e_2 - l_2)}{2} \tag{5.24}$$

and

$$\underline{q}_2 = -(A + RR) - \frac{(e_1 - l_1) - 3(e_2 - l_2)}{2}. \tag{5.25}$$

This threshold $\underline{q}_t$ defines the level of q at which the bank borrows more liquidity from the central bank than it needs to cover its own liquidity needs. If $q < \underline{q}$, marginal costs of borrowing from the central bank will be that low so that the bank will borrow liquidity from the monetary authority in order to place it in the interbank market ($K_t^{opt} > A + R_t$ and $B_t^{opt} < 0$).

Equations (5.18) to (5.25) show that the interbank market rate e_t plays a crucial role for the bank's optimal liquidity management. Therefore, we will first determine the equilibrium value for the interbank market rate first, before discussing the bank's optimal liquidity management in more detail.

5.3 Interbank Market Equilibrium and Final Results

The equilibrium interbank market rate e_t^* is determined by setting liquidity supply equal to demand in the interbank market. We will do so for two cases. In the first more simple case, which we will present in subsection 5.3.1, there are only two groups of price-taking banks. These two groups differ in the banks' level of marginal opportunity costs of holding collateral q. Within each group, the banks are identical. In the second more general case, which we will present in subsection 5.3.2, there is a continuum of banks differing in q. We will structure both subsections as follows. First, we will determine the equilibrium interbank market rate e_t^*. Second, we will insert e_t^* into the provisional results to obtain the final results for the banks' optimal liquidity management. Using these results we will draw conclusions concerning aggregate fulfilling of required reserves (Are they provided smoothly?) and aggregate demand for central bank credits (Does it deviate from the central bank's benchmark?). And finally, we will discuss the impact of monetary policy impulses (Are banks affected differently?).

5.3.1 Two Banks

Equilibrium Interbank Market Rate

For determining the equilibrium interbank market rate, we assume that there are two groups of price-taking banks differing in their level of marginal opportunity costs of holding collateral q. We consider a representative bank for each group, bank A and bank B, with $q^A < \underline{q}_t$ $\forall t$ and $q^B \geq \bar{q}_t$ $\forall t$, i.e. bank A always places liquidity in the interbank market, while bank B always satisfies its total liquidity needs in that market. Then solving

$$B_t^{A,opt} + R_t^{B,opt} - 0 \tag{5.26}$$

for e_t ($B_t^{A,opt}$ is given by the first line of the equations (5.21) and (5.22), $B_t^{B,opt}$ by the second line of these equations), we learn that the equilibrium interbank market rate is given by

$$e_t^* = l_t + q^A + 3(A + RR). \tag{5.27}$$

We will comment on this equilibrium interbank market rate after having determined the final results for the banks' optimal liquidity management.

Optimal Liquidity Management: Final Results

Inserting e_t^* into the intermediate results given by equations (5.18) to (5.22), one obtains the following final results for the banks' optimal liquidity management:

$$R_1^{A,opt} = R_2^{A,opt} = R_1^{B,opt} = R_2^{B,opt} = RR, \tag{5.28}$$

$$K_1^{A,opt} = K_2^{A,opt} = 2(A + RR), \tag{5.29}$$

$$K_1^{B,opt} = K_2^{B,opt} = 0, \tag{5.30}$$

$$B_1^{A,opt} = B_2^{A,opt} = -(A + RR),$$ (5.31)

and

$$B_1^{B,opt} = B_2^{B,opt} = A + RR.$$ (5.32)

The most important result is that an interest rate change neither influences the banks' optimal allocation of required reserves nor bank A's optimal central bank borrowing.[4] Even in case the monetary authority changes the repo rate within the maintenance period, neither bank A nor bank B frontloads or postpones the required reserves, but provides them smoothly over the maintenance period which also implies on aggregate smooth provisions of required reserves. A driving force behind this result is that required reserves are remunerated at the current repo rate. This implies that holding reserves is neutral with regard to interest payments to and interest revenues from the central bank. However, required reserve costs do not only consist of interest payments to the central bank. In addition, bank A faces opportunity costs of holding collateral when borrowing the relevant liquidity from the central bank and bank B faces transaction costs and - since $e_t^* > l_t$ - bank B also faces additional interest costs when borrowing the relevant liquidity in the interbank market. This implies that due to the convex form of the opportunity cost function and of the transaction cost function the banks are not indifferent concerning the intertemporal allocation of their reserve holdings, but they will hold in both periods the same amount of reserves.

The smooth provisions of required reserves imply the liquidity needs of each bank to be the same in both periods so that central bank borrowing as well as interbank market transactions are also the same in both periods. Equations (5.29) and (5.32) reveal that bank A borrows twice as much liquidity from the central bank than it needs to cover its own liquidity needs in order to lend the excess liquidity, which corresponds exactly to bank B's liquidity needs, via the interbank market to bank B.

Moreover, the results reveal that in the current rate model, aggregate central bank borrowing corresponds to the central bank's benchmark amount:[5] Aggregate central bank borrowing is equal to $2(A+RR)$ which is exactly the amount that allows for smooth provisions of required reserve over the reserve maintenance period.

---

[4] That bank B's central bank borrowing is not influenced is obvious since we assumed that $q^B > \bar{q}_t$ so that bank B never borrows from the central bank.

[5] For the definition of this benchmark amount see p. 48.

Equilibrium Interbank Market Rate: Discussion

After having determined the final results for the banks' optimal liquid-ity management, we will comment in more detail on the equilibrium interbank market rate e_t^* given by equation (5.27). We will show that e_t^* reflects bank A's marginal costs of placing liquidity in the interbank market and we will comment on the determinants of e_t^*.

We have shown that independently of a change in the repo rate, bank B provides its required reserves smoothly, i.e. its liquidity needs are given in both periods by $(A + RR)$. Since bank B always covers its total liquidity needs in the interbank market, liquidity demand in that market is absolutely inelastic at point $(A + RR)$, and e_t^* is determined by bank A's marginal costs of placing $(A+RR)$ in the interbank market: Bank A's marginal costs of placing liquidity in the interbank market are given by

$$MC_t^{A,ibm} = l_t + q^A + pK_t^{A,opt} - zB_t^{A,opt}, \tag{5.33}$$

i.e. they consist of marginal interest payments to the central bank (l_t), marginal opportunity costs of holding collateral $(q^A + pK_t^{A,opt})$, and marginal transaction costs $(-zB_t^{A,opt})$. Note that $B_t^{A,opt} < 0$, so that $(-B_t^{A,opt})$ is positive. Setting p and z equal to one and inserting the equilibrium values for $K_t^{A,opt}$ and $B_t^{A,opt}$ given by the equations (5.29) and (5.31), one obtains that

$$MC_t^{A,ibm} = l_t + q^A + 3(A + RR) = e_t^* \tag{5.34}$$

which confirms that the equilibrium interbank market rate is deter-mined by bank A's marginal costs of placing the liquidity $(A + RR)$ in the interbank market.

It is obvious that an increase in one of the marginal cost components given in equation (5.34) implies that the interbank market rate will rise.

An increase in A or RR implies an upsurge in both banks' total liquidity needs. Consequently, bank A borrows more liquidity from the central bank and places more liquidity in the interbank market. Both are combined with increasing marginal costs so that bank A's marginal costs of placing liquidity in the interbank market, and, therefore, e_t^* also increases:

$$\frac{\partial e_t^*}{\partial A} = \frac{\partial e_t^*}{\partial RR} = 3. \tag{5.35}$$

An increase in q^A implies that bank A's marginal costs of borrowing liquidity from the central bank rise so that the equilibrium interbank market also increases:

$$\frac{\partial e_t^*}{\partial q^A} = 1. \tag{5.36}$$

Looking at the consequences of a change in the repo rate on the equilibrium interbank market rate, we distinguish between two cases. In the first case, there is a change in the repo rate at the beginning of the reserve maintenance period so that $l_1 = l_2 = l$. In the second case, the repo rate is changed within the reserve maintenance period so that $l_1 \neq l_2$. In the first case, there is a proportional change in the interbank market rate in both periods:

$$\frac{\partial e_1^*}{\partial l} = \frac{\partial e_2^*}{\partial l} = 1. \tag{5.37}$$

In the second case, the interbank market rate changes in the second period only:

$$\frac{\partial e_1^*}{\partial l_2} = 0 \tag{5.38}$$

and

$$\frac{\partial e_2^*}{\partial l_2} = 1. \tag{5.39}$$

Decisive is that marginal costs of placing liquidity in the interbank market, and, therefore, the equilibrium interbank market rate in period t, depend only on the repo rate of the same period. This means that there is no interest rate smoothing in the sense that the interbank market rate will already slightly decrease (increase) before the central bank actually cuts (raises) the repo rate.

It is worth mentioning that the spread between the interbank market rate and the repo rate $(s_t = e_t^* - l_t)$ remains, independent of a change in the repo rate, the same in both periods so that the sum of the spreads $(\sum_{t=1}^2 s_t)$ is not influenced either by a change in the repo rate. This will not be the case in the average rate and overlapping maturities model which, as we will see, is an important aspect when discussing in how far banks are affected differently by a monetary policy impulse in the form of a change in the repo rate. The implications of a change in the repo rate within the reserve maintenance period for the equilibrium interbank market rate e_t^* and the spread s_t in each model are summarized with the help of a numerical example in the appendix.

Figure 5.1 illustrates the equilibrium in the interbank market and indicates the consequences of an increase in A, RR, l_t, or q^A for the

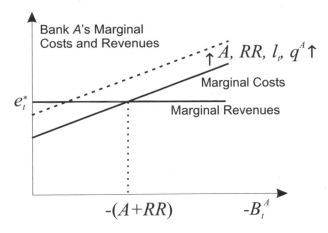

Fig. 5.1: Current Rate Model, Two Banks: Equilibrium in the Interbank Market

equilibrium interbank market rate. The upwards sloping solid line represents bank A's marginal costs of placing liquidity in the interbank market given by equation (5.33). The horizontal line depicts bank A's marginal revenue of placing liquidity in the interbank market which is the interest rate e_t. In equilibrium, bank A's liquidity supply in the interbank market is $[-(A + RR)]$ (see equation (5.31)). Consequently, the equilibrium interbank market rate is given by that horizontal line which intersects the marginal cost curve at the point $[-(A + RR)]$. At this point, bank A's marginal costs of placing liquidity in the interbank market equal its marginal revenues and the interbank market is cleared. The figure indicates that an increase in l_t, q^A, A or RR leads to an increase in the interbank market rate e_t^*: In all four cases the marginal cost curve shifts upwards, and if A or RR increase, there will be in addition a rightward move of the intersection between the marginal cost curve and the marginal revenue curve.

The Impact of Monetary Policy Impulses

Throughout this work, we analyze the impact of monetary policy impulses on the banks' net minimal liquidity costs. If the increase or decrease in these costs differs between banks, they will be affected differently by a monetary policy impulse.

In our model, monetary policy impulses can be initiated by a change in the repo rate or a change in reserve requirements. Concerning the former, we analyze the impact on the banks' net minimal liquidity costs in cases where the repo rate is changed at the beginning of the maintenance period so that $l_1 = l_2 = l$ and in cases where the repo rate is changed within the maintenance period so that $l_1 \neq l_2$. We will see that in this model, in both cases the two banks are not affected differently by the monetary policy impulse.

In case the repo rate is raised or cut at the beginning of the maintenance period, the change in the banks' net minimal liquidity costs is given by

$$\frac{\partial(V_1|l_1 = l_2 = l)^A}{\partial l} = \frac{\partial(V_1|l_1 = l_2 = l)^B}{\partial l} = 2A, \qquad (5.40)$$

in case the repo rate is changed within the reserve maintenance period by

$$(V_1|l_1 = l_2)^A - (V_1|l_1 \neq l_2)^A = (V_1|l_1 = l_2)^B - (V_1|l_1 \neq l_2)^B$$
$$= A(l_1 - l_2), \qquad (5.41)$$

i.e., both banks will face the same increase or decrease in their net minimal liquidity costs. The reason is that the financing of autonomous factors will become more expensive (cheaper) if the repo rate is raised (cut). For bank A it will become more expensive (cheaper) because of the change in the repo rate, for bank B because of the change in the equilibrium interbank market rate. Since both rates increase (decrease) proportionally, both banks are affected to the same extent by this monetary policy impulse. The fact that in both cases the impact of the monetary impulse does not depend on RR but only on A, reveals that holding reserves is neutral with regard to interest payments to and interest revenues from the central bank.

However, holding required reserves is not neutral with regard to *overall* costs and yields: bank A has to bear opportunity costs of holding collateral when borrowing the reserves from the central bank and bank B has to bear transaction costs and additional interest costs when borrowing the reserves in the interbank market since $e_t^* > l_t$. Since these additional costs differ between the two banks, they are affected differently by a monetary policy impulse in the form of a change in reserve requirements. The impact on bank B's minimal liquidity costs is stronger than on bank A's as equations (5.42) and (5.43) confirm:

$$\frac{\partial(V_1|l_1 = l_2)^A}{\partial RR} = -2(A + RR) + 2q^A \qquad (5.42)$$

and

$$\frac{\partial(V_1|l_1 = l_2)^B}{\partial RR} = 14(A + RR) + 2q^A. \qquad (5.43)$$

Let us assume that the central bank raises reserve requirements. Then, both banks have higher liquidity needs, but additional liquidity costs are higher for bank B. Bank B has to bear additional costs because of the increase in the interbank market rate and because it has to bear higher interbank market transaction costs. Bank A on the other hand, also also to bear additional costs because it borrows more liquidity from the central bank to satisfy its own and bank B's increased liquidity needs and because of higher transaction costs in the interbank market, but it also benefits from the increased interbank market rate.

5.3.2 Continuum of Banks

In this section, we leave the relatively simple world of only two banks and determine the equilibrium interbank market rate and the final results for the banks' optimal liquidity management for the more general case of a continuum of banks. The main reason why in this section the analysis becomes more complex is that in the interbank market, liquidity demand is not absolutely inelastic anymore.

Equilibrium Interbank Market Rate

We consider a continuum of measure one of isolated, price-taking banks differing in their level of marginal opportunity costs of holding collateral q. Then, assuming that q is distributed in the interval $[0, q^{max}]$ across banks according to the density function $g(q) = G'(q)$ with $G(0) - 0$, the equilibrium interbank market rate is determined by solving

$$\int_{0}^{\underline{q}_t} (B_t^{opt} | q < \bar{q}_t) g(q) dq + \int_{\underline{q}_t}^{\bar{q}_t} (B_t^{opt} | q < \bar{q}_t) g(q) dq$$
$$+ \int_{\bar{q}_t}^{q^{max}} (B_t^{opt} | q \geq \bar{q}_t) g(q) dq = 0$$

for e_t, where B_t^{opt} is given by equations (5.21) and (5.22). The first term in equation (5.44) represents liquidity supply in the interbank market, while the second and the third term represent liquidity demand. The liquidity demand captured by the second term consists of banks covering a part of their liquidity needs in the interbank market, the last term consists of banks satisfying their total liquidity by borrowing reserves in that market. (This is illustrated by Fig. 5.2. We will comment on this figure in more detail on p. 64 when discussing the final results for the banks' optimal liquidity management.)

To keep matters simple, we assume that q is distributed uniformly across banks, so that $g(q)$ is a constant. Then, solving equation (5.44) for e_t, one obtains for the equilibrium interbank market rate:

$$e_t^* = -(A + RR) + l_t + \sqrt{4q^{max}(A + RR)}. \tag{5.44}$$

We will comment on this equilibrium interbank market rate after having determined the final results for the banks' optimal liquidity management.

Optimal Liquidity Management: Final Results

Inserting the equilibrium value for e_t given by equation (5.44) into the provisional results given by equations (5.18) to (5.25), one obtains the following final results for the banks' optimal liquidity management:

$$R_1^{opt} = R_2^{opt} = RR \forall q, \tag{5.45}$$

$$K_1^{opt} = K_2^{opt} = \begin{cases} \sqrt{q^{max}(A + RR)} - \frac{q}{2} & \text{if} \quad q < \bar{q} \\ 0 & \text{if} \quad q \geq \bar{q}, \end{cases} \tag{5.46}$$

$$B_1^{opt} = B_2^{opt} = \begin{cases} A + RR + \frac{q}{2} - \sqrt{q^{max}(A + RR)} & \text{if} \quad q < \bar{q} \\ A + RR & \text{if} \quad q \geq \bar{q}, \end{cases} \tag{5.47}$$

where $\bar{q}$, the upper threshold for q, is given by

$$\bar{q} = \bar{q}_1 = \bar{q}_2 = \sqrt{4q^{max}(A + RR)}. \tag{5.48}$$

For the lower threshold for q, i.e. for the level at which the bank borrows more reserves from the central bank than it needs to cover its own liquidity needs, one obtains:[6]

$$\underline{q} = \underline{q}_1 = \underline{q}_2 = -2(A + RR) + \sqrt{4q^{max}(A + RR)}. \tag{5.49}$$

As in the two-bank case, the most important result is that the banks' optimal liquidity management is not influenced by a monetary impulse in form of an interest rate change. Equation (5.45) shows that all banks provide their reserve requirements smoothly, no bank postpones or frontloads reserves. As in the two-bank case a driving force behind

---

[6] One obtains $\underline{q}$ either by setting the first line of equation (5.46) equal to $A + RR$ and then solving for q, or by inserting e_t^* given by equation (5.44) into equations (5.24) and (5.25).

this result is the remuneration of reserves in each period at the current repo rate rate (for details see p. 56).

The smooth provisions of reserves imply that the banks' central bank borrowing and their transactions in the interbank market are also the same in both periods, as shown by the equations (5.46) and (5.47). These equations reveal the importance of the parameter q for the banks' liquidity management. It decides whether a bank actually borrows from the central bank, and if so how much, and it decides how much liquidity a bank borrows or places in the interbank market. We illustrate these two equations, and, therefore, the importance of q, by the help of Fig. 5.2. The upper part of the figure illustrates the

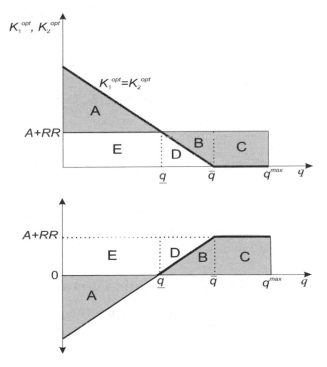

Fig. 5.2: Current Rate Model: Optimal Borrowing from the Central Bank and Optimal Transactions in the Interbank Market

optimal borrowing from the central bank depending on the level of marginal opportunity costs of holding collateral q. Banks which have a lower q than $\underline{q}$ borrow more reserves from the central bank than they need to cover their own liquidity needs in order to place the excess liquidity in the interbank market. Their own liquidity needs correspond to the rectangle E, the amount of liquidity they supply in the interbank market to triangle A. Banks whose level of marginal opportunity costs $\underline{q}$ lies between $\underline{q}$ and $\bar{q}$, cover their liquidity needs at the central bank (triangle D) and in the interbank market (triangle B), while banks with a $q \geq \bar{q}$ borrow their total liquidity needs in the interbank market (rectangle C). Since we have assumed that q is uniformly distributed across banks, at the equilibrium interbank market rate e_t^*, area A, which represents aggregate liquidity supply in the interbank market, is of the same size as area $(B + C)$, which corresponds to aggregate liquidity demand in that market.

The lower part of Fig. 5.2 illustrates explicitly optimal transactions in the interbank market depending on q. Banks with a q smaller than $\underline{q}$ place liquidity in the interbank market, i.e. area A represents aggregate liquidity supply, and banks with a q greater than $\underline{q}$ borrow reserves in that market, i.e. area $(B + C)$ represents aggregate liquidity demand in the interbank market. Consequently, in equilibrium area A and area $(B + C)$ are of the the same size.

Also when considering a continuum of banks, aggregate central bank borrowing, which is given by

$$\int_0^{q^{max}} K_1^{opt} g(q) dq = \int_0^{q^{max}} K_2^{opt} g(q) dq A + RR, \qquad (5.50)$$

allows for smooth provisions of required reserves over the maintenance period, i.e. it does not deviate from the central bank's benchmark (for the definition of the benchmark see p. 48).

Equilibrium Interbank Market Rate: Discussion

In this section, we will comment on the equilibrium interbank market rate given by equation (5.44). We will show that the equilibrium interbank market rate e_t^* reflects the banks' marginal costs of placing liquidity in the interbank market, and we will comment on the determinants of e_t^*.

The banks' marginal costs of placing liquidity in the interbank market are given by

$$MC_t^{ibm} = l_t + q + pK_t^{opt} - zB_t^{opt}. \qquad (5.51)$$

The first three terms represent the marginal costs of borrowing the relevant liquidity from the central bank, the last term the marginal transaction costs. Setting p and z equal to one and inserting the equilibrium values for K_t^{opt} and B_t^{opt} given by the first line of the equations (5.46) and (5.47) one obtains

$$MC_t^{ibm} = -(A + RR) + l_t + \sqrt{4q^{max}(A + RR)} = e_t^* \qquad (5.52)$$

which confirms that e_t^* reflects the banks' marginal costs of placing liquidity in the interbank market.

Equation (5.52) shows that e_t^* is determined by the banks' liquidity needs $(A + RR)$, the repo rate l_t, and the level of marginal opportunity costs of holding collateral of those banks' with the highest level q^{max}.

When looking at the level of marginal opportunity costs first, we see that there is a positive relationship between q^{max} and e_t^*:

$$\frac{\partial e_t^*}{\partial q^{max}} = \frac{\sqrt{A + RR}}{\sqrt{q^{max}}} > 0. \qquad (5.53)$$

An increase in q^{max} leads to a decline in the density of the distribution of q across banks which means that at the current interbank market rate fewer banks are willing to place liquidity in the interbank market (decrease in supply), while more banks want to borrow in that market (increase in demand). Consequently, e_t^* will rise to restore the equilibrium in the interbank market.

An increase in it total liquidity needs also implies an upsurge in e_t^*:[7]

$$\frac{\partial e_t^*}{\partial A} = \frac{\partial e_t^*}{\partial RR} = \frac{\sqrt{q^{max}} - \sqrt{A + RR}}{\sqrt{A + RR}} > 0. \qquad (5.54)$$

If there is an upsurge in the banks' liquidity needs, the banks which place liquidity in the interbank market will borrow more liquidity from the central bank and will place more liquidity in the interbank market - as in the two-bank case. This implies that due to the convex form of the cost functions $Q(\cdot)$ and $Z(\cdot)$ the marginal costs of placing liquidity in the interbank market increases and, therefore, also causes the equilibrium interbank market rate to increase. However, contrary to the two-bank case there is also a negative, although not outweighing

---

[7] Note that $\sqrt{q^{max}} > \sqrt{A + RR}$. This becomes clear when looking at equation (5.49) which represents the lower threshold for q. This lower threshold $\underline{q}_t$ must strictly be greater than zero because otherwise there would be no bank actually supplying liquidity in the interbank market, i.e. an interbank market, and therefore an interbank market rate, would not exist. And if $\underline{q}_t > 0$, $\sqrt{q^{max}} > \sqrt{A + RR}$. In more detail: $\underline{q} > 0 \Rightarrow -2(A+RR) < \sqrt{4q^{max}(A + RR)} \Rightarrow (A + RR)/\sqrt{A + RR} < \sqrt{\underline{q}} \Rightarrow \sqrt{q^{max}} > \sqrt{A + RR}$.

effect of A and RR on e_t^* as shown by equation (5.54). This effect results from the demand side: In the two-bank case, we have assumed that bank B always satisfies its *total* liquidity needs in the interbank market. However, if there is a continuum of banks, an increase in total liquidity needs implies that there are banks which totally cover their liquidity needs in the interbank market before an increase in A or RR occurs, but afterwards they borrow liquidity in the interbank market *and* from the central bank - due to the increasing marginal transaction costs. Formally, this can be seen from equation (5.48) which gives the upper threshold for q. This equation indicates that an increase in A or RR leads to an increase in this threshold, i.e. fewer banks cover their liquidity needs exclusively in the interbank market. This means that an increase in liquidity needs does not imply a proportional increase in liquidity demand in the interbank market as in the two-bank case, but the upsurge is dampened which has - due to the convex form of the transaction cost function - also a dampening effect on the increase in marginal costs of placing liquidity in the interbank market and, therefore, on the increase in e_t^*. Rewriting equation (5.44) by considering the transaction cost parameter z (which we have set equal to one so far) one obtains that

$$e_t^* = -z(A + RR) + l_t + \sqrt{2q^{max}(A + RR)(1 + z)}$$

which confirms that the transaction costs in the interbank market are responsible for the negative effect of total liquidity needs on e_t^* given by the first term in equation (5.44).

When discussing what kind of an impact a change in the repo rate on e_t^* would have, we distinguish between a change in this rate at the beginning and within the reserve maintenance period. Changing the repo rate at the beginning of the reserve maintenance period so that $l_1 = l_2 = l$ implies in both periods a proportional change in e_t^*:

$$\frac{\partial e_1^*}{\partial l} = \frac{\partial e_2^*}{\partial l} = 1. \tag{5.55}$$

In case the repo rate is changed within the reserve maintenance period ($l_1 \neq l_2$), e_t^* will only change in the second period:

$$\frac{\partial e_1^*}{\partial l_2} = 0 \tag{5.56}$$

and

$$\frac{\partial e_2^*}{\partial l_2} = 1. \tag{5.57}$$

These are the same results as in the two-bank case, hence, we refer the reader to detailed comments on p. 58. As in the two-bank
case the spread between the interbank market rate and the repo rate
$(s_t = e_t^* - l_t)$ remains the same in both periods, independent of a change
in the repo rate. Consequently, the sum of the spreads $\sum_{t=1}^{2} s_t$ is not
influenced by a change in the repo rate as well. The appendix summarizes the effects of a change in the repo rate on e_t^* and s_t^* in the various
models presented in this work with the help of a numerical example.

The Impact of Monetary Policy Impulses

As in the two-bank case, a monetary policy impulse can be initiated
by a change in the repo rate or by a change in reserve requirements.

If the central bank changes the repo rate at the beginning of the
reserve maintenance period so that $l_1 = l_2 = l$, the change in minimal
liquidity costs will be given by

$$\frac{\partial(V_1|l_1 = l_2 = l)}{\partial l} = 2A \forall q, \tag{5.58}$$

in case the rate is changed within the maintenance period by

$$(V_1|l_1 = l_2) - (V_1|l_1 \neq l_2) = A(l_1 - l_2)\forall q. \tag{5.59}$$

The equations (5.58) and (5.59) reveal that - as in the two-bank case -
an interest rate cut (increase) implies that minimal liquidity costs decrease (increase) only because holding reserves for autonomous factors
becomes less (more) expensive, i.e. holding reserves for fulfilling reserve
requirements is neutral with regard to interest payments to and revenues from the central bank. Furthermore, the equations show that the
impact of a monetary policy impulse in the form of a repo rate change
is independent of q, i.e. it is the same for all banks.

However, a different picture has to be drawn for a change in reserve
requirements: Holding required reserves is costly, it is not neutral with
regard to overall costs and yields: either a bank faces opportunity costs
of holding collateral when procuring the reserves from the central bank
or it faces transaction costs and additional interest costs $(e_t^* > l_t)$ when
borrowing the liquidity in the interbank market. Since banks differ in
their opportunity costs of holding collateral it is obvious that banks
which borrow from the central bank are affected differently by a monetary policy impulse in the form of a change in reserve requirements,
and that the impact on banks with relatively high opportunity costs is

greater. This result is formally confirmed by equations (5.60) to (5.62):[8]

$$\frac{\partial(V_1|l_1 = l_2)}{\partial RR}$$

$$= \begin{cases} -2(A + RR + q^{max}) + \frac{\sqrt{q^{max}}(q + 6(A + RR))}{\sqrt{A + RR}} & \text{if} \quad q < \bar{q} \\ -2(A + RR) + 6\sqrt{q^{max}(A + RR)} & \text{if} \quad q \geq \bar{q}, \end{cases} \quad (5.60)$$

$$\frac{\partial^2(V_1|l_1 = l_2, q < \bar{q})}{\partial RR \partial q} = \frac{\sqrt{q^{max}}}{\sqrt{A + RR}} > 0, \quad (5.61)$$

$$\frac{\partial(V_1|l_1 = l_2, q \geq \bar{q})}{\partial RR} - \frac{\partial(V_1|l_1 = l_2, q < \bar{q})}{\partial RR}$$

$$= 2q^{max} - \frac{\sqrt{q^{max}}(q|q < \bar{q})}{\sqrt{A + RR}} > 0. \quad (5.62)$$

Equation (5.60) shows that a change in a bank's minimal liquidity costs depends on q, i.e. banks are affected differently by a monetary impulse in the form of a change in reserve requirements. Equation (5.61) demonstrates that if a bank borrows from the central bank, the impact will be greater the higher q is. Furthermore, equation (5.62) reveals that banks which cover their liquidity needs exclusively in the interbank market, i.e. those banks with the highest q, are affected more by a change in reserve requirements than banks which cover their liquidity needs partly or totally by borrowing reserves from the central bank. Figure 5.3 illustrates these results for an increase in reserve requirements. It shows that the resulting increase in minimal net liquidity costs differ across banks and that the banks which have the lowest level of marginal opportunity costs of holding collateral "suffer" the least.

5.4 Summary

In a first step, we have analyzed within a two-period model the liquidity management of a single, price-taking bank. This bank's liquidity needs arise from autonomous factors and reserve requirements imposed by a central bank. It can cover these liquidity needs either by borrowing

---

[8] That $2q^{max} - (\sqrt{q^{max}}(q|q < \bar{q})/\sqrt{A + RR})$ in equation (5.62) is strictly greater than zero becomes clear when inserting for q the upper threshold $\bar{q}$ given by equation (5.48). Then, the expression becomes zero which means that for $q < \bar{q}$, which is relevant in this case, the expression must be positive.

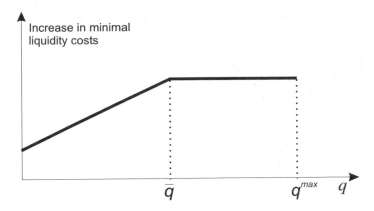

Fig. 5.3: Current Rate Model: Impact of an Increase in Reserve Requirements on Minimal Net Liquidity Costs

from the central bank or in the interbank market, where it can also place liquidity. Besides interest payments, opportunity costs of holding collateral accrue when borrowing from the monetary authority, and transaction costs have to be born when borrowing or placing liquidity in the interbank market. Decisive institutional features of this model - features in which this model differs from the models we will present in the next two chapters - are:

- required reserves are remunerated at the current repo rate at the end of each period, and
- the maturities of central bank credits do not overlap.

The bank minimizes net total liquidity costs over the two periods by choosing the following: optimal intertemporal allocation of required reserves, optimal borrowing from the monetary authority, and optimal transactions in the interbank market.

In a second step, we have determined the equilibrium interbank market rate. We have assumed, as in the base model, that banks differ in their marginal opportunity costs of holding collateral. Then an interbank market emerges where banks with relatively low opportunity costs borrow more reserves from the central bank than they need to cover their own needs. This is done in order to place them in the interbank market, where this supply meets the liquidity demand by banks whose opportunity costs of holding reserves are so high that they prefer to cover their needs partially or totally in the interbank market. We have derived the equilibrium interbank market rate while setting liquidity supply in the interbank market equal to liquidity demand. Inserting the equilibrium interbank market rate into the (provisional) results for the bank's optimal liquidity management, we have derived the following final results:

- Independently of a change in the repo rate, aggregate required reserves are provided smoothly over the maintenance period.
- Independently of a change in the repo rate, aggregate demand for central bank credits, and, therefore, central bank borrowing does not deviate from the central bank's benchmark.
- Banks are not affected differently by a monetary policy impulse in the form of a change in the repo rate.
- Banks are affected differently by a monetary impulse in the form of a change in reserve requirements.
- Holding reserves is neutral with regard to interest payments to and interest revenues from the central bank, but it is not neutral with regard to overall costs and revenues, which implies in this current rate model that banks face different overall net costs of holding required reserves.
- There is no interest rate smoothing in the sense that the interbank market rate will slightly decrease (increase) even before the central bank actually cuts (raises) the repo rate, but there is a constant spread between the interbank market rate and the repo rate over the whole maintenance period.

6

Remuneration of Required Reserves at an Average Rate

6.1 Introduction

In this chapter, we change the current rate model presented in the previous chapter by assuming that reserves are remunerated at the average of the repo rates l_1 and l_2 at the end of the second period instead of at the current repo rate l_t at the end of each period. We will show that under this different assumption concerning the remuneration of required reserves, interest rate changes do influence the banks' optimal liquidity management. If the central bank cuts (raises) the repo rate, banks will postpone (frontload) holdings of required reserves which implies that also on aggregate reserves will be provided unevenly. This again implies that aggregate central bank borrowing will deviate from the benchmark, i.e. underbidding (overbidding) will occur. Furthermore, we will show that banks are not only affected differently by a monetary policy impulse in form of a change in reserve requirements but also by a monetary policy impulse in form of a change in the repo rate. Moreover, it will turn out that the interbank market rate is smoothed in the sense that it will slightly decrease (increase) even before the central bank actually cuts (raises) the repo rate.

6.2 Optimal Liquidity Management of a Single Bank

6.2.1 Liquidity Costs

Again, there are two time periods which cover a reserve maintenance period, and an isolated, price taking bank is considered which has liquidity needs resulting from the given autonomous factors A and the given required reserves RR. The latter can be fulfilled on average over the reserve maintenance period so that

$$RR = \frac{R_1 + R_2}{2}. \tag{6.1}$$

The bank can cover its liquidity needs in the interbank market, where it can also place liquidity, or it can cover its liquidity needs at the central bank. As a start, we assume that the bank receives the amount of liquidity from the central bank it demands at the repo rate l which is set by the monetary authority, i.e. we assume that even if aggregate liquidity demand exceeds the central bank's benchmark amount[1] the central bank will, nevertheless, totally satisfy the liquidity demand. In section 6.3.3 we will analyze the bank's optimal liquidity management assuming that the central bank rations liquidity in this case.

When borrowing liquidity from the monetary authority the bank has to offer adequate collateral. Opportunity costs of holding these collateral are given by

$$Q(K_t) = qK_t + \frac{p}{2}K_t^2, \tag{6.2}$$

with $q \geq 0$ and $p > 0$.

The bank's position in the interbank market is given by

$$B_t = A + R_t - K_t \gtrless 0. \tag{6.3}$$

Independently of whether the bank borrows or lends in the interbank market it faces transaction costs which are

$$Z(B_t(K_t, R_t)) = \frac{z}{2}\left(B_t(K_t, R_t)\right)^2, \tag{6.4}$$

with $z > 0$.

Holdings of required reserves are remunerated at the average of l_1 and l_2 at the end of the second period. Consequently, net liquidity costs in period t are given by:

$$C_t(K_t, R_t) = K_t l_t + B_t e_t + Q(K_t) + Z(B_t)$$
$$-2RR\left(\frac{l_t + l_{t-1}}{2}\right) I_{[t=2]},$$

i.e. they consist of interest payments to the central bank, interest payments or interest yields resulting from transactions in the interbank

---

market, collateral's opportunity costs, transaction costs, minus the remuneration of required reserves. The indicator function $I_{[\cdot]}$ takes a value
of 1 when $t = 2$, and 0 otherwise, reflecting that interests are paid at
the end of the maintenance period. Note that the last term in equation (6.5) shows the crucial difference against the current rate model:
reserves are remunerated at the average of l_1 and l_2 at the end of the
second period.

6.2.2 Optimization Problem

The bank minimizes net total liquidity costs across the maintenance
period by choosing the optimal central bank borrowing and the optimal
intertemporal allocation of required reserves. Consequently, the bank's
objective function becomes

$$\min_{K_t, R_t} \left\{ \sum_{t=1}^{2} C_t(K_t, R_t) \right\}, \tag{6.5}$$

and the Bellman equation for the intra-maintenance period optimization problem is given by

$$V_1 = \min_{K_1, R_1} \{C_1(K_1, R_1) + V_2\} \quad \text{subject to} \quad K_t, R_t \geq 0. \tag{6.6}$$

6.2.3 Optimal Liquidity Management in the Second Period

Again, we solve the optimization problem backwards and look at the
bank's behaviour in the second period first. Replacing R_2 by $(2RR - R_1)$
according to equation (6.1), the Lagrangian becomes

$$\begin{aligned}
(K_2, \lambda_2) &= K_2 l_2 + B_2(K_2)e_2 + Q(K_2) + Z(K_2) \\
&\quad -(RR)(l_1 + l_2) - \lambda_2 K_2.
\end{aligned} \tag{6.7}$$

The term which represents the remuneration of required reserves does
not depend in the current rate model model nor in this average rate
model on K_2. Since it is the remuneration of required reserves which
only distinguishes the two models, the second order conditions in the
second period and, therefore, $K_2^{opt}(R_1)$ are the same (compare equations (5.9) to (5.12)):

$$-e_2 + l_2 + pK_2 + q - zB_2(K_2) - \lambda_2 = 0, \tag{6.8}$$

$$\lambda_2 K_2 = 0, \quad \lambda_2 \geq 0, \quad K_2 \geq 0, \tag{6.9}$$

and

$$K_2^{opt}(R_1) = \begin{cases} \frac{e_2 - l_2 - q + z(A + 2RR - R_1)}{p + z} & \text{if} \quad q < \bar{q}_2 \\ 0 & \text{if} \quad q \geq \bar{q}_2, \end{cases} \tag{6.10}$$

where

$$\bar{q}_2 = e_2 - l_2 + z(A + 2RR - R_1). \tag{6.11}$$

Consequently, minimal net liquidity costs in the second period are given by

$$V_2(R_1) = K_2^{opt}(R_1)l_2 + B_2(K_2^{opt}(R_1), R_1)e_2 + Q_2(K_2^{opt}(R_1)) \atop + Z_2(K_2^{opt}(R_1), R_1) - RR(l_1 + l_2). \tag{6.12}$$

6.2.4 Optimal Liquidity Management in the First Period

The constraint $R_t \geq 0$ will be binding only for a sufficiently large interest rate change. For the sake of simplicity, we, therefore, assume that $|l_1 - l_2| \leq 2RR$. Then, the constraint is not binding[2] hence we do not include it in the Lagrangian which is

$$L(K_1, R_1, \lambda_1) = K_1 l_1 + B_1(K_1, R_1)e_1 + Q(K_1) \atop + Z(B_1(K_1, R_1)) - \lambda_1 K_1 + V_2(R_1) \tag{6.13}$$

and the first order conditions are given by[3]

$$-e_1 + l_1 + pK_1 + q - zB_1(K_1, R_1) - \lambda_1 = 0, \tag{6.14}$$

$$e_1 + zB_1(K_1, R_1) = e_2 + zB_2(K_2^{opt}(R_1), R_1), \tag{6.15}$$

and

$$\lambda_1 K_1 = 0, \quad \lambda_1 \geq 0, \quad K_1 \geq 0. \tag{6.16}$$

---

[2] See equations (6.37), (6.38), (6.42), (6.52), (6.53), (6.60), and (6.61).

[3] Equation (6.10) shows that we have to distinguish between two cases when analyzing the bank's optimal liquidity management in the first period. In the first case, the bank borrows liquidity from the monetary authority in the second period, i.e. $q < \bar{q}_2$. In the second case, the bank covers its liquidity needs exclusively in the interbank market, i.e. $q \geq \bar{q}_2$. However, the interpretation of the first order conditions is the same in both cases and we have rewritten the conditions in such a way that their formal presentation is also the same.

The first order condition for optimal central bank borrowing given by equation (6.14) is the same as in the current rate model (see equation (5.15)). It says that if the bank places liquidity in the interbank market, marginal costs of this transaction will equal its marginal benefits, and if the bank borrows from the central bank and in the interbank market, marginal costs of both alternatives will be the same. Also as in the current rate model, the first order condition for optimal intertemporal allocation of required reserve holdings given by equation (6.15) requires that the net marginal costs of holding reserves must be the same in both periods. However, a difference to the first order condition in the current rate model is that interest yields of holding reserves play no role (see equation (5.16)). The reason is that, due to the remuneration of reserves at the average of l_1 and l_2, marginal revenues of holdings reserves are the same in both periods rendering them irrelevant for intertemporal optimization.

6.2.5 Provisional Results

When presenting the provisional results for the bank's optimal liquidity management (again these are only provisional results because they still depend on the interbank market rate e_t, whose equilibrium value we will determine in the next step), we have to distinguish between a cut and a raise in the repo rate. If there is no interest rate change, obviously the same results for the bank's optimal liquidity management as in the current rate model are obtained. This results from the fact that the only difference to the current rate model is that reserves are remunerated at the average of the repo rates l_1 and l_2 and not at the current repo rate. Consequently, if there is no change in the repo rate, the difference in the method of remunerating required reserves will be irrelevant for the bank's optimal liquidity management. However, if the repo rate is changed, the bank's optimal behaviour will be different from that in the current rate model. It is necessary to distinguish between an interest rate cut and an interest rate increase, i.e. it is not possible to interpret the results in cases of an interest rate cut simply by assuming that $l_1 > l_2$ instead of $l_1 < l_2$, because the upper thresholds $\bar{q}_1$ and $\bar{q}_2$ fall apart. We will comment on this in more detail after having presented the provisional results.

For a clearer presentation we set - as in the current rate model - the parameters p and z equal to one in the cost functions $Q(K_t)$ and $Z(B_t)$. Then, the first order conditions lead to the following results for the bank's optimal liquidity management if the repo rate is cut (the subscript c stands for *cut*):

$$R_{1,c}^{opt} = \begin{cases} RR - \frac{e_1 - e_2 + l_1 - l_2}{2} & \text{if} \quad q < \bar{q}_{1,c} \\ RR - \frac{1}{3}\left(A + RR + 2e_1 - e_2 - l_2 - q\right) \\ \qquad\qquad\qquad\qquad \text{if} \quad \bar{q}_{1,c} \leq q < \bar{q}_{2,c} \\ RR - \frac{e_1 - e_2}{2} & \text{if} \quad \bar{q}_{2,c} \leq q, \end{cases} \tag{6.17}$$

$$R_{2,c}^{opt} = \begin{cases} RR + \frac{e_1 - e_2 + l_1 - l_2}{2} & \text{if} \quad q < \bar{q}_{1,c} \\ RR + \frac{1}{3}\left(A + RR + 2e_1 - e_2 - l_2 - q\right) \\ \qquad\qquad\qquad\qquad \text{if} \quad \bar{q}_{1,c} \leq q < \bar{q}_{2,c} \\ RR + \frac{e_1 - e_2}{2} & \text{if} \quad \bar{q}_{2,c} \leq q, \end{cases} \tag{6.18}$$

$$K_{1,c}^{opt} = \begin{cases} \frac{A + RR - q}{2} + \frac{e_1 + e_2 - 3l_1 + l_2}{4} & \text{if} \quad q < \bar{q}_{1,c} \\ 0 & \text{if} \quad \bar{q}_{1,c} \leq q, \end{cases} \tag{6.19}$$

$$K_{2,c}^{opt} = \begin{cases} \frac{A + RR - q}{2} + \frac{e_1 + e_2 + l_1 - 3l_2}{4} & \text{if} \quad q < \bar{q}_{1,c} \\ \frac{2(A + RR - q)}{3} + \frac{e_1 + e_2 - 2l_2}{3} & \text{if} \quad \bar{q}_{1,c} \leq q < \bar{q}_{2,c} \\ 0 & \text{if} \quad \bar{q}_{2,c} \leq q, \end{cases} \tag{6.20}$$

$$B_{1,c}^{opt} = \begin{cases} \frac{A + RR + q}{2} - \frac{3e_1 - e_2 - l_1 - l_2}{4} & \text{if} \quad q < \bar{q}_{1,c} \\ \frac{2(A + RR) + q}{3} - \frac{2e_1 - e_2 - l_2}{3} & \text{if} \quad \bar{q}_{1,c} \leq q < \bar{q}_{2,c} \\ A + RR - \frac{e_1 - e_2}{2} & \text{if} \quad \bar{q}_{2,c} \leq q, \end{cases} \tag{6.21}$$

and

$$B_{2,c}^{opt} = \begin{cases} \frac{A + RR + q}{2} + \frac{e_1 - 3e_2 + l_1 + l_2}{4} & \text{if} \quad q < \bar{q}_{1,c} \\ \frac{2(A + RR) + q}{3} + \frac{e_1 - 2e_2 + l_2}{3} & \text{if} \quad \bar{q}_{1,c} \leq q < \bar{q}_{2,c} \\ A + RR + \frac{e_1 - e_2}{2} & \text{if} \quad \bar{q}_{2,c} \leq q, \end{cases} \tag{6.22}$$

where

$$\bar{q}_{1,c} = A + RR + \frac{e_1 + e_2 - 3l_1 + l_2}{2} \tag{6.23}$$

and

$$\bar{q}_{2,c} = A + RR + \frac{e_1 + e_2 - 2l_2}{2}. \tag{6.24}$$

If the repo rate is raised, the first order conditions will lead to the following provisional results for the bank's optimal liquidity management (the subscript r stands for *raise*):

$$R_{1,r}^{opt} = \begin{cases} RR - \frac{e_1 - e_2 + l_1 - l_2}{2} & \text{if} \quad q < \bar{q}_{2,r} \\ RR + \frac{1}{3}\left(A + RR - e_1 + 2e_2 - l_1 - q\right) \\ \qquad\qquad\qquad\qquad \text{if} \quad \bar{q}_{2,r} \leq q < \bar{q}_{1,r} \\ RR - \frac{e_1 - e_2}{2} & \text{if} \quad \bar{q}_{1,r} \leq q, \end{cases} \tag{6.25}$$

$$R_{2,r}^{opt} = \begin{cases} RR + \frac{e_1 - e_2 + l_1 - l_2}{2} & \text{if} \quad q < \bar{q}_{2,r} \\ RR - \frac{1}{3}\left(A + RR - e_1 + 2e_2 - l_1 - q\right) \\ \qquad\qquad\qquad\qquad \text{if} \quad \bar{q}_{2,r} \leq q < \bar{q}_{1,r} \\ RR + \frac{e_1 - e_2}{2} & \text{if} \quad \bar{q}_{1,r} \leq q, \end{cases} \tag{6.26}$$

$$K_{1,r}^{opt} = \begin{cases} \frac{A + RR - q}{2} + \frac{e_1 + e_2 - 3l_1 + l_2}{4} & \text{if} \quad q < \bar{q}_{2,r} \\ \frac{2(A + RR - q)}{3} + \frac{e_1 + e_2 - 2l_2}{3} & \text{if} \quad \bar{q}_{2,r} \leq q < \bar{q}_{1,r} \\ 0 & \text{if} \quad \bar{q}_{1,r} \leq q, \end{cases} \tag{6.27}$$

$$K_{2,r}^{opt} = \begin{cases} \frac{A + RR - q}{2} + \frac{e_1 + e_2 + l_1 - 3l_2}{4} & \text{if} \quad q < \bar{q}_{2,r} \\ 0 & \text{if} \quad \bar{q}_{1,r} \leq q, \end{cases} \tag{6.28}$$

$$B_{1,r}^{opt} = \begin{cases} \frac{A + RR + q}{2} - \frac{3e_1 - e_2 - l_1 - l_2}{4} & \text{if} \quad q < \bar{q}_{2,r} \\ \frac{2(A + RR) + q}{3} - \frac{2e_1 - e_2 - l_1}{3} & \text{if} \quad \bar{q}_{2,r} \leq q < \bar{q}_{1,r} \\ A + RR - \frac{e_1 - e_2}{2} & \text{if} \quad \bar{q}_{1,r} \leq q, \end{cases} \tag{6.29}$$

and

$$B_{2,r}^{opt} = \begin{cases} \frac{A + RR + q}{2} + \frac{e_1 - 3e_2 + l_1 + l_2}{4} & \text{if} \quad q < \bar{q}_{2,r} \\ \frac{2(A + RR) + q}{3} + \frac{e_1 - 2e_2 + l_1}{3} & \text{if} \quad \bar{q}_{2,r} \leq q < \bar{q}_{1,r} \\ A + RR + \frac{e_1 - e_2}{2} & \text{if} \quad \bar{q}_{1,r} \leq q, \end{cases} \tag{6.30}$$

where

$$\bar{q}_{1,r} = A + RR + \frac{e_1 + e_2 - 2l_1}{2} \tag{6.31}$$

and

$$\bar{q}_{2,r} = A + RR + \frac{e_1 + e_2 + l_1 - 3l_2}{2}. \tag{6.32}$$

Equations (6.17), (6.18), (6.25), and (6.26) represent the bank's optimal intertemporal allocation of the required reserves, equations (6.19), (6.20),(6.27), and (6.28), its optimal borrowing from the central bank, and equations (6.21), (6.22), (6.29), and (6.30) its optimal transactions in the interbank market. These equations reveal the importance of the level of the bank's opportunity costs of holding collateral q. It determines how much liquidity the bank borrows from the monetary authority and how much liquidity it borrows or places in the interbank market. Contrary to the current rate model, it also influences the optimal intertemporal allocation of the required reserve holdings.

The thresholds $\bar{q}_{t,c}$ and $\bar{q}_{t,r}$ represent again the upper levels for q, i.e. if $q \geq \bar{q}_t$ the bank's marginal costs of borrowing from the central bank will be so high that it will prefer to cover its total liquidity needs in the interbank market. The lower level for q, i.e. the level at which the bank borrows more reserves than it needs to cover its own liquidity needs, is obtained by setting the first line of equation (6.19) equal to $A + (R_{1,c}|q < \bar{q}_{1,c})$ and the first line of equation (6.20) equal to $A + (R_{2,c}|q < \bar{q}_{1,c})$ and solving both equations for q. Then, what is obtained is:[4]

$$\underline{q}_1 = -(A + RR) + \frac{3e_1 - e_2 - l_1 - l_2}{2} \tag{6.33}$$

and

$$\underline{q}_2 = -(A + RR) - \frac{e_1 - 3e_2 + l_1 + l_2}{2}. \tag{6.34}$$

The main difference of these provisional results to those of the current rate model is that if the repo rate is changed, the thresholds $\bar{q}_1$ and $\bar{q}_2$ will fall apart. In the current rate model, independent of an interest rate change, the bank borrows either in both periods or not at all from the central bank, i.e. $\bar{q}_1 = \bar{q}_2$. However, in this average rate model the thresholds fall apart: In case the repo rate is cut the bank may borrow

---

[4] For determining these lower thresholds it is not necessary to distinguish between a decrease and an increase in the repo rate. The *relevant* borrowing from the central bank as well as the relevant holdings of required reserves are the same, i.e. alternatively one could have also used equations (6.25) to (6.28) in order to determine $\underline{q}_1$ and $\underline{q}_2$.

in the second but not in the first period, and vice versa if the repo rate is raised.

The reason for this is that the remuneration of reserves at the average of l_1 and l_2, in cases of an interest rate change, holding reserves will not be neutral with regard to interest payments to and interest revenues from the central bank. However, we will comment on this and other aspects of the bank's optimal liquidity management in more detail when discussing the final results, and we will now use the provisional results to derive the equilibrium interbank market rate.

6.3 Interbank Market Equilibrium and Final Results

One obtains the equilibrium interbank market rate e_t^* by setting liquidity demand in the interbank market equal to liquidity supply and then solving this equation for e_t. As in the current rate model, we will do this by assuming that banks differ in their level of marginal opportunity costs of holding collateral q. Again, we will assume first that there are two groups of banks differing in q and second, that there is a continuum of banks differing in q. In both cases our analysis is structured as in the current rate model: First, we will determine the equilibrium interbank market rate. Second, we will derive the final results for a bank's optimal liquidity management and discuss the results at the aggregate level (Are reserves provided smoothly over the maintenance period? Does the demand for central bank credits deviate from the central bank's benchmark?). Finally, we will analyze the impact of monetary policy impulses on the banks' minimal net liquidity costs (Are banks affected differently?).

6.3.1 Two Banks

Equilibrium Interbank Market Rate

There are two groups of price-taking banks differing in q, represented by the banks A and B, with $q^A < \underline{q}_t$ $\forall t$ and $q^B \geq \bar{q}_t$ $\forall t$, i.e. bank A always places liquidity in the interbank market, while bank B always satisfies its total liquidity needs in that market, i.e. liquidity demand is absolutely inelastic. Then, solving

$$B_t^{A,opt} + B_t^{B,opt} = 0 \tag{6.35}$$

for e_t the equilibrium interbank market rate e_t^* is obtained ($B_t^{A,opt}$ is given by the first line of the equations (6.21) and (6.22), $B_t^{B,opt}$ by the third line of these equations):[5]

$$e_1^* = e_2^* = 3(A + RR) + q^A + \frac{l_1 + l_2}{2}. \tag{6.36}$$

We will comment on the equilibrium interbank market rate after having determined the final results for the bank's optimal liquidity management.

Optimal Liquidity Management: Final Results

Inserting e_t^* into the provisional results given by the first lines (bank A) and bottom lines (bank B) of the equations (6.17) to (6.22), the final results for the banks' optimal liquidity management is obtained:[6]

$$R_1^{A,opt} = RR - \frac{l_1 - l_2}{2}, \tag{6.37}$$

$$R_2^{A,opt} = RR + \frac{l_1 - l_2}{2}, \tag{6.38}$$

$$K_1^{A,opt} = 2(A + RR) - \frac{l_1 - l_2}{2}, \tag{6.39}$$

$$K_2^{A,opt} = 2(A + RR) + \frac{l_1 - l_2}{2}, \tag{6.40}$$

$$B_1^{A,opt} = B_2^{A,opt} = -(A + RR), \tag{6.41}$$

$$R_1^{B,opt} = R_2^{B,opt} = RR, \tag{6.42}$$

and

$$B_1^{B,opt} = B_2^{B,opt} = A + RR. \tag{6.43}$$

The most important result is that, contrary to the current rate model, a change in the repo rate influences the optimal liquidity management

---

[5] Alternatively, the equations (6.29) and (6.30) can be used. The relevant lines are the same.

[6] Alternatively, the equations (6.25) and (6.30) can be used. The relevant lines are the same.

of bank A. If the repo rate is cut, the bank will postpone required reserves ($R_1^{A,opt} < R_2^{A,opt}$), and if the repo rate is raised, it will frontload reserves ($R_1^{A,opt} > R_2^{A,opt}$), i.e. if there is a change in the repo rate bank A provides its required reserves unevenly over the maintenance period (equations (6.37) and (6.38)). The driving force behind this result is that reserves are remunerated at the average of l_1 and l_2. This implies that in case of an interest rate cut, bank A's marginal benefits of holding reserves will decrease in both periods, while its marginal costs of holding reserves will only decrease in the second period. Therefore, intertemporal optimality requires holding more reserves in the second period. Analogously, bank A's marginal benefits of holding reserves will increase in both periods, while its marginal costs of holding reserves will increase in the second period only if the central bank raises the repo rate. Then, intertemporal optimality requires holding more reserves in the first period.

This is not the case for bank B. Equation (6.42) shows that independent of a change in the repo rate, bank B provides its required reserves smoothly over the maintenance period. The reason is that for bank B, marginal interest costs and revenues of holding reserves are the same in both periods, even if the central bank cuts or raises the repo rate: reserves are remunerated at the average of l_1 and l_2, so that the marginal revenues of holding reserves in both periods are $(l_1 + l_2)/2$; and bank B's marginal interest costs are given by c_l^* which is also the same in both periods (see equation (6.36) and comments on p. 83). Consequently, even in case the central bank changes the interest rate, for bank B the difference between the marginal costs and the marginal revenues of holding reserves remains the same in both periods so there is no incentive to postpone or frontload required reserves. On contrary, it is optimal to provide the reserves smoothly: bank B covers its liquidity needs exclusively in the interbank market, and transactions in the interbank market involve increasing marginal transaction costs which implies that it is optimal to transact the same amount in both periods.

Since bank B provides its required reserves smoothly and bank A postpones its reserve holdings if there is an interest rate cut and frontloads them if there is an interest rate increase, it is obvious that aggregate reserves will be provided unevenly if the repo rate is changed.

The uneven provisions of required reserves of bank A are also reflected by its central bank borrowing (see equations (6.39) and (6.40)). If the bank postpones required reserves, i.e. if the repo rate is cut, its liquidity needs in the first period are smaller than in the second period so that $K_1^{A,opt} < K_2^{A,opt}$. Analogously, $K_1^{A,opt} > K_2^{A,opt}$ if the central bank raises the repo rate. Since only bank A borrows from the monetary authority, equation (6.39) reveals that if the repo rate is changed, aggregate central bank borrowing will deviate from the central bank's benchmark. This benchmark is the amount of central bank borrowing which allows for smooth aggregate provisions of required reserves across the maintenance period (see p. 48). In the two-bank case this benchmark is equal to $2(A+RR)$. However, equation (6.39) shows that if an interest rate cut occurs, aggregate central bank borrowing will fall below this benchmark, whereas if the repo rate is raised, aggregate central bank borrowing will exceed the benchmark.

Since bank B provides its required reserves smoothly, its liquidity needs are the same in both periods so obviously the amount of liquidity transacted in the interbank market is with $(A+RR)$ also the same in both periods (equations (6.41) and (6.43)).

Equilibrium Interbank Market Rate: Discussion

After having derived the final results for the banks' optimal liquidity management, we will comment in more detail on the equilibrium interbank market rate e_t^* given by equation (6.36). We will show that e_t^* equals bank A's marginal costs of placing liquidity in the interbank market. Furthermore, we will demonstrate that in this average rate model the interbank market rate is not only smoothed but also always the same in both periods even if the repo rate is not.

Bank A's marginal costs of placing liquidity in the interbank market are given by:

$$MC_t^{A,ibm} = l_t + q^A + pK_t^{A,opt} - zB_t^{A,opt}. \qquad (6.44)$$

The first three terms represent bank A's marginal costs of borrowing the relevant liquidity from the central bank, the last term represents the marginal transaction costs. When setting p and z equal to one and inserting the equilibrium values for $K_t^{A,opt}$ and $B_t^{A,opt}$ given by the equations (6.39), (6.40), and (6.41) the following is obtained

$$MC_t^{A,ibm} = 3(A+RR) + q^A + \frac{l_1 + l_2}{2} = e_t^* \qquad (6.45)$$

which confirms that the equilibrium interbank market rate is determined by bank A's marginal costs of placing $(A+RR)$ in the interbank market. It is obvious that an increase in one of the marginal cost components also implies an increase in e_t^*. Since the impact of a change in A, RR, q^A, or $(l_t|l_1 = l_2)$ on the equilibrium interbank market rate is the same as in the current rate model, we refer the reader to p. 57 concerning these changes and focus our analysis on the impact of a change in the repo rate within the reserve maintenance period $(l_1 \neq l_2)$ on e_t^*. The results of a change in A, RR, q^A, or $(l_t | l_1 = l_2)$ are the same as in the current rate model, because the only difference in the design of this average rate model from the design of the current rate model is that reserves are remunerated at the average of l_1 and l_2 and this difference will obviously not be effective if l_1 is equal to l_2.

Looking at the impact of a change in l_2 on e_t^*, reveals that the interbank market rate is smoothed:

$$\frac{\partial e_1^*}{\partial l_2} = \frac{\partial e_2^*}{\partial l_2} = \frac{1}{2}. \tag{6.46}$$

Equation (6.46) shows that if the central bank raises (cuts) the repo rate in the second period, an increase (decrease) in the interbank market rate in the first period will already have taken place, and the increase (decrease) in the second period is dampened: $\partial e_1^*/\partial l_2 > 0$ and $\partial e_2^*/\partial l_2 < 1$, while in the current rate model $\partial e_1^*/\partial l_2 = 0$ and $\partial e_2^*/\partial l_2 = 1$. The driving force is bank A's frontloading or postponing of the required reserves. Let us assume that the central bank raises the repo rate l_2. Then, bank A frontloads required reserves, and there are two effects influencing e_2^*: Firstly, there is an increasing effect because the marginal costs of borrowing from the central bank increase in the second period due to the upsurge in l_2. Secondly, there is a decreasing effect because bank A frontloads its reserve holdings, i.e. its liquidity needs in period two decrease, so that its central bank borrowing and, therefore, its marginal opportunity costs of holding collateral also decrease. On the other hand, in the first period the frontloading of required reserves has a positive effect on e_1^*, since it implies that bank A's liquidity needs rise so that it borrows more liquidity from the central bank, i.e. its marginal opportunity costs of holding collateral also increase.

Equations (6.36) and (6.46) show that the interbank market rate is not only smoothed but that it is always the same in both periods. The explanation is as follows: The equilibrium interbank market rate reflects bank A's marginal costs of placing liquidity in that market which consist of the marginal costs of borrowing liquidity from the central bank (first three terms in equation (6.44)) and of the marginal transaction costs of placing the liquidity in the interbank market (last term in equation (6.44)). Independently of an interest rate change, the latter are the same in both periods $(z(A + RR) = (A + RR))$. However, in this average rate model the other marginal cost component (marginal costs of borrowing reserves from the central bank), is also always the same in both periods, even if $l_1 \neq l_2$:

The crucial point is that intertemporal optimality requires net marginal costs of holding reserves to be the same in both periods. Bank A's net marginal costs of holding reserves are the marginal costs of borrowing liquidity from the central bank minus the marginal revenues from holding reserves. In this average rate model, the latter are always the same in both periods $((l_1 + l_2)/2)$. Consequently, also the marginal costs of borrowing from the central bank must be the same so that the net marginal costs of holding reserves are identical in both periods. If the repo rate is changed, identical marginal costs of borrowing from the central banks are achieved by frontloading or postponing reserve holdings, since this leads to an increase in marginal opportunity costs of holding collateral in that period in which the repo rate is lower and vice versa in the period in which the repo rate is higher. The shifting of the required reserves into that period with the lower interest rate will take place until the marginal costs of borrowing from the central bank are the same in both periods. This means that both marginal cost components of placing liquidity in the interbank market - costs of borrowing from the central bank and transaction costs in the interbank market - are the same in both periods. Therefore, we can conclude that the interbank market rates must also be identical.[7]

It should be noted that although in each period the change in e_t^* is different from the change in the current rate model, the sum of the changes $(\partial e_1^*/\partial l_2 + \partial e_2^*/\partial l_2)$ is the same. This is important when discussing to what extent banks are affected differently by a monetary policy impulse.

Since in both periods the interbank market rate changes to the same extent, while the repo rate only changes in the second period, it is obvious that a cut or an increase in the repo rate within the reserve maintenance period implies that the spread between the interbank market rate and the central bank rate is no longer the same in both periods. Nevertheless, the sum of the spreads $\sum_{t=1}^{2} s_t$ remains the same (see

---

[7] In the current rate model, things are different: The crucial point is that marginal benefits of holding reserves (l_t) will differ in the two periods if the interest rate is changed. Consequently, intertemporal optimality requires marginal costs of borrowing from the central bank to be different too, so that the net marginal costs of holding reserves are the same in both periods. Obviously, this will be the case if the repo rate is changed (without shifting of reserves). Since the marginal costs of central bank borrowing will differ in both periods if the repo rate is changed, also the marginal costs of placing liquidity in the interbank market and, therefore, the interbank market rates are different in the two periods as well.

the appendix for a numerical example). This is also important when discussing the impact of the monetary policy impulse on the banks' minimal net liquidity costs.

The Impact of Monetary Policy Impulses

With regards to the current rate model, monetary policy impulses can be initiated by an interest rate change or a change in reserve requirements. However, we will only look at the consequences of a change in the repo rate within the reserve maintenance period ($l_1 \neq l_2$) for the banks' liquidity costs since the consequences of a change in the repo rate at the beginning of the reserve maintenance period (implying that $l_1 = l_2$) as well as of a change in reserve requirements are the same as in the current rate model.[8] We have shown that a repo rate change within the maintenance period induces bank A to provide its reserve requirements unevenly over the maintenance period. In order to capture the consequences of how this behaviour impacts the banks' liquidity costs, we will look at the impact of a change in the repo rate on those costs if bank A does not shift its holdings of required reserves first. In this case, the change in the banks' liquidity costs is given by:

$$
\begin{aligned}
&(V_1|l_1 = l_2)^A - \sum_{t=1}^{2}(C_t|l_1 \neq l_2; R_1 = R_2)^A \\
&= (V_1|l_1 = l_2)^B - \sum_{t=1}^{2}(C_t|l_1 \neq l_2; R_1 = R_2)^B = A(l_1 - l_2).
\end{aligned}
\tag{6.47}
$$

The first term of each line represents the bank's minimal liquidity costs if there is no interest rate change. The second term depicts the bank's liquidity costs if the monetary authority changes its rate and if bank A provides its reserve requirements smoothly. Equation (6.47) shows that in this case the impact of a monetary policy impulse in the form of a change in the repo rate on the banks' liquidity costs is the same for both banks. This is not the case if bank A behaves optimally by frontloading or postponing its reserve holdings. Then, the change in the banks' minimal liquidity costs is given by

$$
(V_1|l_1 = l_2)^A - (V_1|l_1 \neq l_2)^A = A(l_1 - l_2) + \frac{(l_1 - l_2)^2}{4}
\tag{6.48}
$$

and

---

[8] The only difference between the current rate model and this average rate model is that reserves are remunerated at the average of l_1 and l_2 which does not play a role if the repo rate is not changed within the reserve maintenance period.

$$(V_1|l_1 = l_2)^B - (V_1|l_1 \neq l_2)^B = A(l_1 - l_2). \tag{6.49}$$

These equations reveal that the banks are affected differently by a monetary impulse in the form of a change in the repo rate. Independent of whether the repo rate is cut or raised, the fraction in equation (6.48) has a positive sign. This means if the repo rate is cut, bank A's minimal liquidity costs decrease more than bank B's and if the monetary authority raises the repo rate, bank A's minimal liquidity costs increase at a lesser rate or even decrease. The reason is obvious: bank A benefits from frontloading or postponing its required reserves.

6.3.2 Continuum of Banks

In this section, we will determine the equilibrium interbank market rate, the final results for the banks' optimal liquidity management, and the impact of monetary policy impulses on the banks' liquidity costs for the more general case of a continuum of banks. As in the current rate model this analysis is more complex because in the interbank market liquidity demand is no longer absolutely inelastic.

Equilibrium Interbank Market Rate

We consider a continuum of measure one of isolated, price-taking banks differing in their level of marginal opportunity costs of holding collateral q. Then, assuming that q is distributed in the interval $[0, q_{max}]$ across banks according to the density function $g(q) = G'(q)$ with $G(0) = 0$, the equilibrium interbank market rate is determined by solving

$$
\begin{aligned}
&\int\limits_{0}^{\underline{q}_t} (B_t^{opt}|q < \bar{q}_t)g(q)dq + \int\limits_{\underline{q}_t}^{\bar{q}_t} (B_t^{opt}|q < \bar{q}_t)g(q)dq \\
&+ \int\limits_{\bar{q}_t}^{q^{max}} (B_t^{opt}|q \geq \bar{q}_t)g(q)dq = 0
\end{aligned}
\tag{6.50}
$$

for e_t, where B_t^{opt} is given by equations (6.21) and (6.22) if the repo rate is cut and by equations (6.29) and (6.30) if the repo rate is raised. The first term in equation (6.50) represents liquidity supply in the interbank market, while the second and the third term represent liquidity demand (for details see the comments on the relevant equation in the current rate model on p. 61). As in the current rate model, we assume q to be distributed uniformly across the banks. Then, solving equation (6.50) for e_t, the equilibrium interbank market rate[9]

$$e_1^* = e_2^*$$
$$= -(A + RR) + \frac{l_1 + l_2}{2} + \sqrt{\frac{-(l_1 - l_2)^2}{2} + 4q^{max}(A + RR)} \qquad (6.51)$$

is obtained. We will comment on the equilibrium interbank market rate in more detail after having determined the final results for the banks' optimal liquidity management.

Final Results for the Optimal Liquidity Management if the Repo Rate Is Cut

For determining the final results for the banks' optimal liquidity management it is necessary to distinguish between a cut and an increase in the repo rate. If there is no change in the repo rate, the same results as in the current rate model will be obtained since the only difference to the model presented in this section is that reserves are remunerated at the current repo rate instead of at the average rate of l_1 and l_2. Obviously, this difference will only be effective if the repo rate is not changed.

Inserting the equilibrium value for e_t given by equation (6.51) into the provisional results given by equations (6.17) to (6.32), the following final results for the banks' optimal liquidity management will be obtained if the central bank cuts the repo rate, i.e. if $l_1 > l_2$:

$$R_{1,c}^{opt} = \begin{cases} RR - \frac{l_1 - l_2}{2} & \text{if} \quad q < \bar{q}_{1,c} \\ RR - \frac{l_1 - l_2}{6} + \frac{q}{3} - \sqrt{\frac{4q^{max}(A+RR)}{9} - \frac{(l_1 - l_2)^2}{18}} \\ \quad \text{if} \quad \bar{q}_{1,c} \leq q < \bar{q}_{2,c} \\ RR & \text{if} \quad \bar{q}_{2,c} \leq q, \end{cases} \qquad (6.52)$$

$$R_{2,c}^{opt} = \begin{cases} RR + \frac{l_1 - l_2}{2} & \text{if} \quad q < \bar{q}_{1,c} \\ RR + \frac{l_1 - l_2}{6} - \frac{q}{3} + \sqrt{\frac{4q^{max}(A+RR)}{9} - \frac{(l_1 - l_2)^2}{18}} \\ \quad \text{if} \quad \bar{q}_{1,c} \leq q < \bar{q}_{2,c} \\ RR & \text{if} \quad \bar{q}_{2,c} \leq q, \end{cases} \qquad (6.53)$$

---

[9] Although the provisional results for B_t^{opt} given by the equations (6.21), (6.22), (6.29), and (6.30) are different for a cut and a raise of the repo rate, the results for the equilibrium interbank market rate are formally the same, so that it is not necessary to distinguish between these two cases when presenting e_t^*.

$$K_{1,c}^{opt} = \begin{cases} -\frac{l_1-l_2}{2} - \frac{q}{2} + \sqrt{q^{max}(A+RR) - \frac{(l_1-l_2)^2}{8}} \\ \quad \text{if} \quad q < \bar{q}_{1,c} \\ 0 \quad \text{if} \quad q \geq \bar{q}_{1,c}, \end{cases} \tag{6.54}$$

$$K_{2,c}^{opt} = \begin{cases} \frac{l_1-l_2}{2} - \frac{q}{2} + \sqrt{q^{max}(A+RR) - \frac{(l_1-l_2)^2}{8}} \\ \quad \text{if} \quad q < \bar{q}_{1,c} \\ \frac{l_1-l_2}{3} - \frac{2q}{3} + \sqrt{\frac{16q^{max}(A+RR)}{9} - \frac{2(l_1-l_2)^2}{9}} \\ \quad \text{if} \quad \bar{q}_{1,c} \leq q < \bar{q}_{2,c} \\ 0 \quad \text{if} \quad \bar{q}_{2,c} \leq q, \end{cases} \tag{6.55}$$

$$B_{1,c}^{opt} = B_{2,c}^{opt} = \begin{cases} A + RR + \frac{q}{2} - \sqrt{q^{max}(A+RR) - \frac{(l_1-l_2)^2}{8}} \\ \quad \text{if} \quad q < \bar{q}_{1,c} \\ A + RR - \frac{l_1-l_2}{6} + \frac{q}{3} - \sqrt{\frac{4q^{max}(A+RR)}{9} - \frac{(l_1-l_2)^2}{18}} \\ \quad \text{if} \quad \bar{q}_{1,c} \leq q < \bar{q}_{2,c} \\ A + RR \quad \text{if} \quad \bar{q}_{2,c} \leq q, \end{cases} \tag{6.56}$$

where $\bar{q}_{t,c}$, the upper threshold for q is given by

$$\bar{q}_{1,c} = -(l_1 - l_2) + \sqrt{4q^{max}(A+RR) - \frac{(l_1-l_2)^2}{2}} \tag{6.57}$$

and

$$\bar{q}_{2,c} = \frac{l_1-l_2}{2} + \sqrt{4q^{max}(A+RR) - \frac{(l_1-l_2)^2}{2}}. \tag{6.58}$$

For the lower threshold for q, i.e. for the level at which the bank borrows more reserves from the central bank than it needs to cover its own liquidity needs, the following is obtained:[10]

$$\underline{q} = \underline{q}_1 = \underline{q}_2 = -2(A+RR) + \sqrt{4q^{max}(A+RR) - \frac{(l_1-l_2)^2}{2}}. \tag{6.59}$$

Looking at the equations given above, the crucial point is that - contrary to the current rate model - the banks' optimal liquidity management is influenced by a cut in the repo rate. We will comment on these final results for the banks' optimal liquidity management with the help of Figs. 6.1 to 6.3.

---

[10] One obtains $\underline{q}_{t,c} = \underline{q}$ either by setting $(K_{t,c}^{opt}|q < \bar{q}_{1,c})$ (see the first line of the equations (6.54) and (6.55)), equal to $A + (R_{t,c}|q < \bar{q}_{t,c})$ and then solving for q, or by inserting e_t^* given by equation (6.51) into the equations (6.33) and (6.34).

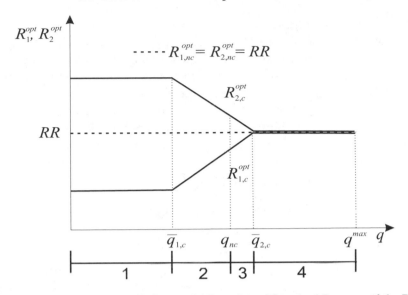

Fig. 6.1: Average Rate Model: Optimal Allocation of Required Reserves if the Repo Rate Is Cut

Optimal Intertemporal Allocation of Required Reserves   We will have a look at the banks' optimal intertemporal allocation of the required reserves first. The crucial point is that if the repo rate is cut, banks with a level of marginal opportunity costs of holding collateral q smaller than $\bar{q}_{2,c}$ will postpone their holdings of the required reserves ($R_{1,c}^{opt} < R_{2,c}^{opt}$), something which implies that on aggregate required reserves are also provided unevenly over the maintenance period. The reason for this is that - as in the two-bank case - the interest rate cut implies that the marginal benefits of holding reserves decrease in both periods, since reserves are remunerated at the average of l_1 and l_2, while the marginal costs decrease in the second period only ($l_1 > l_2$). Consequently, intertemporal optimality requires holding more reserves in the second period. Banks with $q \geq \bar{q}_{2,c}$, i.e. banks which cover their total liquidity needs in both periods in the interbank market, do not frontload required reserves since for them not only the marginal benefits but also the marginal interest costs of holding reserves are the same in both periods because e_1^* is equal to e_2^*. Due to the convex form of the transaction cost function $Z(\cdot)$, they will minimize their net liquidity costs if they provide their reserve requirements smoothly over the maintenance period. Figure 6.1 reveals that the intertemporal allocation of reserves is the same for all banks with $q < \bar{q}_{1,c}$, i.e. the allocation does not change in q, the $R_{t,c}^{opt}$-curves are horizontal. The reason for this is that these banks borrow from the central bank in both periods, so that opportunity costs of holding collateral accrue in both periods, implying that the level of the marginal costs q does not influence the intertemporal allocation. However, for banks which borrow from the monetary authority only in the second period ($\bar{q}_{1,c} < q < \bar{q}_{2,c}$), the optimal intertemporal allocation of reserve holdings changes in q because opportunity costs of holding collateral arise only in the second period. For these banks the cost advantage of fulfilling required reserves unevenly will be the higher, the lower the costs of obtaining funds at the central bank are. Consequently, the difference between $R_{2,c}^{opt}$ and $R_{1,c}^{opt}$ is the higher, the lower q is.

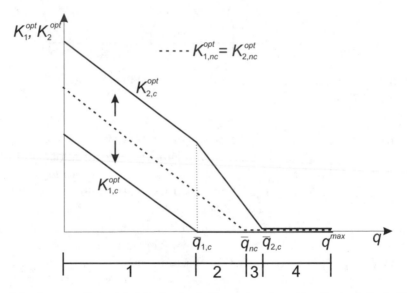

Fig. 6.2: Average Rate Model: Optimal Borrowing from the Central Bank if the Repo Rate Is Cut

Optimal Borrowing from the Monetary Authority   The uneven provisions of required reserves are reflected by the banks' optimal borrowing from the monetary authority. Liquidity needs of those banks postponing required reserve holdings are lower in the first than in the second period. This implies that, contrary to the current rate model, their central bank borrowing is not the same in both periods, but it is lower in the first than in the second period. This is illustrated by Fig. 6.2. The dotted line represents optimal borrowing if there is no interest rate change. The solid lines illustrate optimal borrowing from the central bank if the repo rate is cut. If the repo rate is cut, the banks with a relatively low level of marginal opportunity costs of holding collateral $(q < \bar{q}_{2,c})$ will postpone holdings of required reserves. Consequently, the liquidity needs of these banks are smaller in the first than in the second period, which implies that in the first period, they borrow fewer reserves when compared to the second period $(K_{1,c}^{opt} < K_{2,c}^{opt})$. The reduced liquidity needs in the first and the increased liquidity needs in the second period also imply that the upper thresholds fall apart: There are banks which borrow from the central bank in the second period although they do not do so in the first, i.e. $\bar{q}_{2,c} > \bar{q}_{1,c}$. The negative relationship between $R_{2,c}^{opt}$ and q in case $\bar{q}_{1,c} < q < \bar{q}_{2,c}$ is also reflected by the $K_{2,c}^{opt}$-curve: its slope becomes steeper within this interval, i.e. depending on q the decrease in central bank borrowing becomes stronger. Since the interest rate cut does not imply a change in the total liquidity needs of the banking sector over the whole reserve maintenance period (we consider a continuum of measure one of banks which implies that independent of an interest rate change these liquidity needs are $2(A + RR)$) smooth provisions of aggregate required reserves require aggregate central bank borrowing in the first period to be $(A + RR)$. In Fig. 6.2 this benchmark is represented by the dotted line. The figure demonstrates that if the repo rate is cut, aggregate central bank borrowing in the first period will fall below this benchmark, i.e. it will be too small to allow on aggregate for smooth provisions of required reserves over the reserve maintenance period.

Optimal Transactions in the Interbank Market   The banks' optimal transactions in the interbank market are illustrated by Fig. 6.3. The dotted line shows the optimal transactions if there is no interest rate change. The solid line depicts optimal interbank market transactions if the central bank changes the repo rate. The figure demonstrates that if the repo rate is cut, the transaction volume in the interbank market decreases in both periods. For the first period the reason is simply that due to the postponement of required reserve holdings, the liquidity needs of the banking sector have decreased. On the other hand, in the second period aggregate demand and supply in the interbank market also decrease despite the increased liquidity needs of the banking sector. This is a consequence of a larger spread between e_2 and l_2.[11] This

---

[11] The spread between e_2^* and l_2 is larger if the repo rate is cut than if it is left unchanged. We will comment on this in more detail on p. 98 when discussing the behaviour of the equilibrium interbank market rate within the reserve mainte-

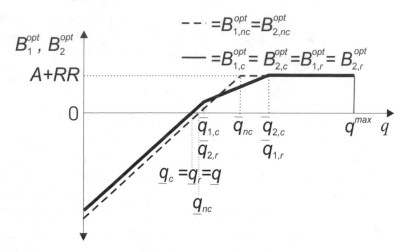

Fig. 6.3: Average Rate Model: Optimal Transactions in the Interbank Market

larger spread indicates that intermediation has become more expensive. Central bank borrowing has become relatively cheaper when compared to borrowing in the interbank market. Consequently, in the second period a kind of disintermediation takes place. Finally, we will comment on the slope of $B_{t,c}^{opt}(q)$. If $q < \bar{q}_{1,c}$, $B_{t,c}^{opt}(q)$ will increase in q, because when banks place liquidity in the interbank market, the marginal costs for doing so increase in q, so that their investment in the interbank market $(-B_{t,c}^{opt})$ depends negatively on q. For banks borrowing in the interbank market, a rising q implies an increase in marginal costs of central bank borrowing so that they prefer to cover a higher portion of their liquidity needs in the interbank market, i.e. their borrowing in the interbank market $(B_{t,c}^{opt})$ depends positively on q. This effect will be dampened if $\bar{q}_{1,c} \leq q < \bar{q}_{2,c}$. Concerning the borrowing in the second period, this dampening effect is due to the fact that the amount of reserves which is frontloaded decreases in q in this interval (see Fig. 6.1), so that also the liquidity needs decrease. Concerning the borrowing in the first period, this dampening effect can be explained as follows. As long as $q < \bar{q}_{1,c}$, $R_{1,c}^{opt}$ does not change in q, i.e. liquidity needs do not change. However, since in this interval $K_{1,c}^{opt}$ decreases in q, $B_{1,c}^{opt}$ must increase. If $\bar{q}_{1,c} \leq q < \bar{q}_{2,c}$, $R_{1,c}^{opt}$ will increase in q while $K_{1,c}^{opt}$ will be equal to zero. Consequently, in this interval $B_{1,c}$ must also increase.

---

nance period. Table A.1 given in the appendix summarizes the reaction of the equilibrium interbank market rate and, therefore, of the spread between e_t^* and l_t to a change in the repo rate for each model.

However, since the increase in $R_{1,c}^{opt}$ in the interval $[\bar{q}_{1,c}, \bar{q}_{2,c}[$ is smaller than the decrease in $K_{1,c}^{opt}$ in the interval $[0, \bar{q}_{1,c}[$, the slope of $B_{1,c}^{opt}$ is also smaller.[12]

Final Results for the Optimal Liquidity Management if the Repo Rate Is Raised

Inserting the equilibrium value for the interbank market rate e_t^* given by equation (6.51) into the provisional results for the banks' optimal liquidity management given by the equations (6.25) to (6.32), the following results for the banks' optimal liquidity management will be obtained if the repo rate is raised:

$$
R_{1,r}^{opt} = \begin{cases} RR - \frac{l_1-l_2}{2} & \text{if } q < \bar{q}_{2,r} \\ RR - \frac{l_1-l_2}{6} - \frac{q}{3} + \sqrt{\frac{4q^{max}(A+RR)}{9} - \frac{(l_1-l_2)^2}{18}} \\ \qquad \text{if } \bar{q}_{2,r} \le q < \bar{q}_{1,r} \\ RR & \text{if } \bar{q}_{1,r} \le q, \end{cases} \tag{6.60}
$$

$$
R_{2,r}^{opt} = \begin{cases} RR + \frac{l_1-l_2}{2} & \text{if } q < \bar{q}_{2,r} \\ RR + \frac{l_1-l_2}{6} + \frac{q}{3} - \sqrt{\frac{4q^{max}(A+RR)}{9} - \frac{(l_1-l_2)^2}{18}} \\ \qquad \text{if } \bar{q}_{2,r} \le q < \bar{q}_{1,r} \\ RR & \text{if } \bar{q}_{1,r} \le q, \end{cases} \tag{6.61}
$$

$$
K_{1,r}^{opt} = \begin{cases} -\frac{l_1-l_2}{2} - \frac{q}{2} + \sqrt{q^{max}(A+RR) - \frac{(l_1-l_2)^2}{8}} \\ \qquad \text{if } q < \bar{q}_{2,r} \\ -\frac{l_1-l_2}{3} - \frac{2q}{3} + \sqrt{\frac{16q^{max}(A+RR)}{9} - \frac{2(l_1-l_2)^2}{9}} \\ \qquad \text{if } \bar{q}_{2,r} \le q < \bar{q}_{1,r} \\ 0 \text{ if } \bar{q}_{1,r} \le q, \end{cases} \tag{6.62}
$$

$$
K_{2,r}^{opt} = \begin{cases} \frac{l_1-l_2}{2} - \frac{q}{2} + \sqrt{q^{max}(A+RR) - \frac{(l_1-l_2)^2}{8}} & \text{if } q < \bar{q}_{2,r} \\ 0 & \text{if } q \ge \bar{q}_{2,r}, \end{cases} \tag{6.63}
$$

---

[12] The slope of the $K_{1,c}^{opt}$-curve is equal to $-1/2$ if $q < \bar{q}_{1,c}$ as shown in equation (6.54). The slope of the $R_{1,c}^{opt}$-curve is equal to $1/3$ if $\bar{q}_{1,c} \le q < \bar{q}_{2,c}$ as shown in equation (6.52).

$$B_{1,r}^{opt} = B_{2,r}^{opt} = \begin{cases} A + RR + \frac{q}{2} - \sqrt{q^{max}(A+RR) - \frac{(l_1-l_2)^2}{8}} \\ \quad \text{if} \quad q < \bar{q}_{2,r} \\ A + RR + \frac{l_1-l_2}{6} + \frac{q}{3} - \sqrt{\frac{4q^{max}(A+RR)}{9} - \frac{(l_1-l_2)^2}{18}} \quad (6.64) \\ \quad \text{if} \quad \bar{q}_{2,r} \le q < \bar{q}_{1,r} \\ A + RR \quad \text{if} \quad q \ge \bar{q}_{1,r}, \end{cases}$$

where $\bar{q}$, the upper threshold for q is given by

$$\bar{q}_{1,r} = \frac{-(l_1 - l_2)}{2} + \sqrt{4q^{max}(A+RR) - \frac{(l_1-l_2)^2}{2}} \qquad (6.65)$$

and

$$\bar{q}_{2,r} = (l_1 - l_2) + \sqrt{4q^{max}(A+RR) - \frac{(l_1-l_2)^2}{2}}. \qquad (6.66)$$

The lower threshold for q, i.e. the level at which a bank borrows more reserves from the central bank than it needs to cover its own needs in order to place them in the interbank market, is formally the same as in the case where the interest rate decreases given by equation (6.59). As in the case of interest rate decreasing, we will interpret these results graphically.

Optimal Intertemporal Allocation of Required Reserves   Figure 6.4 illustrates the banks' optimal intertemporal allocation of the required reserves if the central bank raises the repo rate. The figure shows that, analogously to the case where the interest rate decreases, banks with a relatively low q will frontload holdings of required reserves ($R_{1,c}^{opt} > R_{2,c}^{opt}$) which implies that also on aggregate reserves are provided unevenly over the maintenance period if the central bank raises the repo rate. The reason for this is that the marginal costs of holding reserves only increase in the second period, while marginal benefits increase in both periods due to the remuneration of reserves at the average rate.

Optimal Borrowing from the Monetary Authority   The uneven provisions of required reserves are reflected by the banks' central bank borrowing which is shown by Fig. 6.5. Liquidity needs of those banks frontloading their reserve holdings are higher in the first than in the second period so that for these banks $K_{1,r}^{opt} > K_{2,r}^{opt}$. Furthermore, analogously to the case where the central bank decreases the repo rate, the

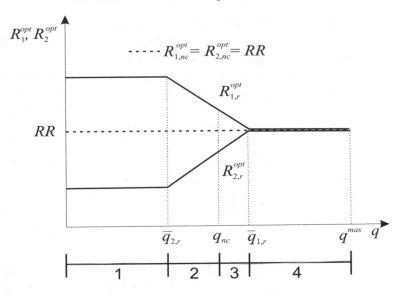

Fig. 6.4: Average Rate Model: Optimal Allocation of Required Reserves if the Repo Rate Is Raised

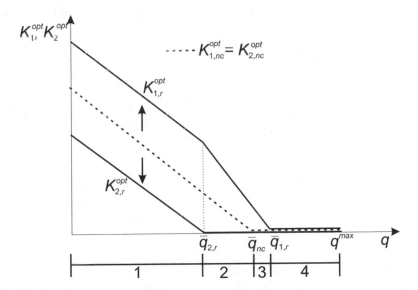

Fig. 6.5: Average Rate Model: Optimal Borrowing from the Central Bank if the Repo Rate Is Raised

upper thresholds fall apart. Due to the increased liquidity needs in the first period, there are banks which borrow liquidity from the central bank in the first but do not so in the second period ($\bar{q}_{1,r} > \bar{q}_{2,r}$). This reveals that - in comparison to the case of the interest rate decreasing - the thresholds fall apart the other way around (note that $\bar{q}_{1,c} < \bar{q}_{2,c}$). An increase in the repo rate does not imply a change in total liquidity needs of the banking sector over the whole reserve maintenance period. Since we have assumed a continuum of measure one of banks, liquidity needs are still equal to $2(A + RR)$ so that the smooth provisions of reserves require aggregate central bank borrowing in the first period to be equal to $(A+RR)$. Consequently, Fig. 6.5 illustrates that if the repo rate is raised, aggregate central bank borrowing in the first period will exceed the cental bank's benchmark depicted by the dotted line.

Optimal Transactions in the Interbank Market   The graphical presentation of the banks' optimal transactions in the interbank market is - apart from the upper thresholds $\bar{q}_t$ - identical to the one in the case where the interest rate decreases given by Fig. 6.3. The figure shows that the transaction volume in the interbank market will also decrease if the repo rate is raised. In the second period, this is again simply the consequence of the banking sector's decreased liquidity needs due to a shift of required reserves into the first period. In the first period, analogously to the second period of the case of the interest rate decreasing, a kind of disintermediation takes place due to a larger spread between e_1^* and l_1.[13] The interpretation of the slope of $B_{t,r}^{opt}$ is analogous to the one of $B_{t,r}^{opt}$ given on p. 92.

Equilibrium Interbank Market Rate: Discussion

In this section, we will discuss the equilibrium interbank market rate e_t^* given by equation (6.51) in more detail. We will show that e_t^* reflects the banks' marginal costs of placing liquidity in the interbank market. Furthermore, we will demonstrate that, contrary to the current rate model, the interbank market rate will be smoothed and that the sum of the spreads between the interbank market rate and the repo rate $\sum_{t=1}^{2} s_t$ will decrease if the repo rate is changed.

---

[13] For details concerning the disintermediation see p. 91. On the spread we will comment in more detail on p. 98 when discussing the behaviour of the equilibrium interbank market rate within the maintenance period. Table A.1 given in the appendix summarizes the reaction of the equilibrium interbank market rate and, therefore, of the spread between e_t^* and l_t to a change in the repo rate in each model.

Marginal Costs of Placing Liquidity in the Interbank Market
Marginal costs of placing liquidity in the interbank market are given by

$$MC_t^{ibm} = l_t + q + pK_t^{opt} - zB_t^{opt}. \tag{6.67}$$

The first three terms represent a bank's marginal costs of borrowing the relevant liquidity from the central bank, and the last term represents its marginal transaction costs. Setting p and z equal to one and inserting the equilibrium values for K_t^{opt} and B_t^{opt} given by the first line of the equations (6.54), (6.55), and (6.56) the following is obtained:[14]

$$MC_t^{ibm} = -(A + RR) + \frac{l_1 + l_2}{2} + \sqrt{\frac{-(l_1 - l_2)^2}{2} + 4q^{max}(A + RR)}$$

$$= e_t^*. \tag{6.68}$$

Consequently, equation (6.68) confirms that the equilibrium interbank market rate reflects the banks' marginal costs of placing liquidity in the interbank market. And it is obvious that an increase in one of the marginal cost components implies that the equilibrium interbank market rate will rise. The impact of a change in A, RR, q^{max}, or l_t at the beginning of the maintenance period, so that $l_1 = l_2$, on e_t^* is the same as in the current rate model. Therefore, we refer the reader to p. 65 concerning the impact of a change in these variables on e_t^* and focus our analysis on the impact of a change in the repo rate within the reserve maintenance period.[15]

Interest Rate Smoothing   When looking at the impact of a change in l_2 on e_t^*, it reveals that the interbank market rate is smoothed:

$$\frac{\partial e_1^*}{\partial l_2} = \frac{\partial e_2^*}{\partial l_2} = \frac{1}{2} + \frac{l_1 - l_2}{2\sqrt{\frac{-(l_1-l_2)^2}{2} + 4q^{max}(A + RR)}} > 0. \tag{6.69}$$

Equation (6.69) shows that the derivative of e_1^* as well as of e_2^* with respect to l_2 is strictly greater than zero[16] so that an increase (decrease)

---

[14] Alternatively, one can also use the equations (6.62), (6.63), and (6.64) since for banks which place liquidity in the interbank market the formal results for B_t^{opt} and R_t^{opt} are the same independent of whether the repo rate is cut or raised.

[15] The only difference to the design of the current rate model is that reserves are remunerated at the average of l_1 and l_2 instead of at the current repo rate. And if the repo rate is not changed, so that $l_1 = l_2$, obviously this difference will not be effective.

[16] Even in case $l_1 < l_2$ the expression is strictly greater than zero because it means that $l_1 - l_2 + \sqrt{-(l_1 - l_2)^2/2 + 4q^{max}(A + RR)} > 0$ and $l_1 - l_2 + \sqrt{-(l_1 - l_2)^2/2 + 4q^{max}(A + RR)} = \bar{q}_{2,r} > 0$.

in l_2 implies that the equilibrium interbank market rate increases (decreases) in *both* periods. As in the two-bank case the remuneration of reserves at the average of l_1 and l_2 implies that the interbank market rate is not only smoothed but also always the same in both periods. For details concerning the smoothing of the interbank market rate and why the interbank market rate is not only smoothed but why it is always the same in both periods, we refer the reader to the relevant comments in the two-bank case on p. 83.

Negative Effect on the Equilibrium Interbank Market Rate
When comparing the partial derivatives of e_t^* with respect to l_2 with the relevant partial derivatives in the two-bank case given by equation (6.46) it shows that the increase in e_t^* as a result of an increase in l_2 is dampened, while a decrease as a result of a decrease in l_2 is reinforced. The reason for this is that in the simple two-bank case total transactions in the interbank market are always equal to $(A + RR)$, whereas if there is a continuum of banks total transactions in that market will decrease if the repo rate is changed (see pages 91 and 96 for details). This decrease in total transactions implies that the marginal transaction costs decrease due to the convex form of the transaction cost function. This again means that the marginal costs of placing liquidity in the interbank market will also decrease. Since e_t^* equals the banks' marginal costs of placing liquidity in the interbank market, the decreased volume of total transactions in the interbank market explains the additional negative impact on e_t^* if the repo rate is cut and the negative effect on e_t^* if the repo rate is raised. This negative effect on e_t^* implies that the sum of the changes in e_t^* over the whole maintenance period $(\partial e_1^*/\partial l_2 + \partial e_2^*/\partial l_2)$ is larger if the repo rate is cut and smaller if the repo rate is raised in comparison to the current rate model, but also in comparison to the two-bank case.[17] The postponing/frontloading of reserves is the cause for the reduced transactions in the interbank market, and, therefore, also causes the negative effect on e_t^* (see pages 91 and 96). Consequently, the banks which actually do not frontload or postpone reserves also benefit from the reserve shifting of the other banks. They have lower interest costs. This is an important aspect when analyzing to what extent banks are affected differently by a monetary policy impulse.

---

[17] The appendix summarizes the effects of a change in the repo rate on e_t^* and s_t^* in the various models presented in this work by the help of a numerical example.

Spread between the Interbank Market Rate and the Repo Rate The smoothing of the interbank market rate implies that the spread between the interbank market rate and the repo rate is not the same in both periods as in the current rate model, but if the repo rate is raised (cut) the spread is smaller (higher) in the second period. However, in the current rate model and in the two-bank case the sum of the spreads between the interbank market rate and the repo rate will not change if the repo rate is cut or raised. In this model, the sum of the spreads will become smaller due to the negative effect on e_t^* as described in the previous paragraph.[18] This is important when discussing the impact of this monetary impulse on the banks' minimal net liquidity costs which we will do next.

The Impact of Monetary Policy Impulses

We will only look at the impact of a change in the repo rate within the reserve maintenance period on the banks' minimal liquidity costs. We are doing this because the impact of a change in the repo rate at the beginning of the reserve maintenance period as well as of a change in reserve requirements is the same as in the current rate model, so with regards to the impact of these monetary policy impulses we refer the reader to p. 67.

We have shown that an interest rate change within the reserve maintenance period induces the banks which cover their liquidity needs, at least partially, by borrowing reserves from the central bank to postpone or frontload their reserve holdings. For analyzing the consequences of this shifting of required reserves for the banks' liquidity costs, we will first look at the change in the banks' net liquidity costs, triggered by a change in the repo rate, if the banks do not frontload or postpone their reserves. This change in net liquidity costs is given by

$$(V_1|l_1 = l_2) - \sum_{t=1}^{2}(C_t|l_1 \neq l_2; R_1 = R_2) = A(l_l - l_2)\forall q. \quad (6.70)$$

The first term represents a bank's minimal net liquidity costs if there is no interest rate change. The second term depicts a bank's net liquidity costs if the monetary authority changes its rate but in situations where all banks provide their reserve requirements smoothly. Equation (6.70) reveals that if the banks do not shift their holdings of required reserves, the increase or decrease in liquidity costs will be the same

---

[18] The appendix summarizes the effects of a change in the repo rate on e_t^* and s_t^* in the various models presented in this work by the help of a numerical example.

for all banks, independent of the bank specific q. This will not be the case if banks behave optimally by shifting their reserve holdings if the central bank changes the repo rate. In what follows, we will show that liquidity costs will then increase less if the central bank raises the repo rate, and that they will decrease more if an interest rate cut occurs. Moreover, we will show that the extent of this cost advantage depends on q. When analyzing the impact of a change in the repo rate on the banks' minimal liquidity costs, we distinguish between four groups of banks. First, we will give the formal results, then we will interpret the results graphically.

First Group   The banks which are in the first group borrow liquidity from the central bank in both periods independent of an interest rate change (see section 1 in Figs. 6.2 and 6.5). The change in their minimal net liquidity costs is given by

$$
\begin{aligned}
(V_1|l_1 = l_2, q < \bar{q}_{nc}) - (V_1|l_1 > l_2; q < \bar{q}_{1,c}) &= A(l_1 - l_2) \\
+ (2(A + RR) + q)\left(\bar{q}_{nc} - \bar{q}_{1,c} - (l_1 - l_2)\right)
\end{aligned}
\tag{6.71}
$$

in case the repo rate is cut and by

$$
\begin{aligned}
(V_1|l_1 = l_2, q < \bar{q}_{nc}) - (V_1|l_1 < l_2; q < \bar{q}_{2,r}) &= A(l_1 - l_2) \\
+ (2(A + RR) + q)\left(\bar{q}_{nc} - \bar{q}_{2,r} + (l_1 - l_2)\right)
\end{aligned}
\tag{6.72}
$$

in case the repo rate is raised.

Second Group   The banks of the second group will borrow in both periods from the central bank if the repo rate is left unchanged, but they will only borrow from the monetary authority in one period if the repo rate is raised or cut (see section 2 in Figs. 6.2 and 6.5). The change in these banks' net liquidity costs is given by

$$
\begin{aligned}
&(V_1|l_1 = l_2; q < \bar{q}_{nc}) - (V_1|l_1 > l_2; \bar{q}_{1,c} \leq q < \bar{q}_{nc}) = A(l_1 - l_2) \\
&+ \frac{3(l_1-l_2)^2 + 4(3(A+RR)+\bar{q}_{1,c})(l_1-l_2) + 8(3(A+RR)+q)(\bar{q}_{nc}-\bar{q}_{2,c}) - 2(q-\bar{q}_{nc})^2}{12}
\end{aligned}
\tag{6.73}
$$

and

$$
\begin{aligned}
&(V_1|l_1 = l_2; q < \bar{q}_{nc}) - (V_1|l_1 < l_2; \bar{q}_{2,r} \leq q < \bar{q}_{nc}) = A(l_1 - l_2) \\
&+ \frac{3(l_1-l_2)^2 - 4(3(A+RR)+\bar{q}_{2,r})(l_1-l_2) + 8(3(A+RR)+q)(\bar{q}_{nc}-\bar{q}_{1,r}) - 2(q-\bar{q}_{nc})^2}{12}.
\end{aligned}
\tag{6.74}
$$

Third Group   In the third group, where the banks will not borrow in any period from the central bank if there is not an interest rate change, and only in one period if the repo rate is cut or raised (see section 3 in Figs. 6.2 and 6.5), the change in minimal net liquidity costs is

$$(V_1|l_1 = l_2; q \geq \bar{q}_{nc}) - (V_1|l_1 > l_2; \bar{q}_{nc} \leq q < \bar{q}_{2,c}) = A(l_1 - l_2)$$
$$+ \frac{3(l_1-l_2)^2 + 4(3(A+RR)+\bar{q}_{1,c})(l_1-l_2) + 8(3(A+RR)+q)(\bar{q}_{nc}-\bar{q}_{2,c}) + 4(q-\bar{q}_{nc})^2}{12} \tag{6.75}$$

and

$$(V_1|l_1 = l_2; q \geq \bar{q}_{nc}) - (V_1|l_1 < l_2; \bar{q}_{nc} \leq q < \bar{q}_{1,r}) = A(l_1 - l_2)$$
$$+ \frac{3(l_1-l_2)^2 - 4(3(A+RR)+\bar{q}_{2,r})(l_1-l_2) + 8(3(A+RR)+q)(\bar{q}_{nc}-\bar{q}_{1,r}) + 4(q-\bar{q}_{nc})^2}{12}. \tag{6.76}$$

Fourth Group   Banks which are in the fourth group do not borrow liquidity from the central bank in any period independent of whether the repo rate is changed or not (section 4 in Figs. 6.2 and 6.5). If the repo rate is changed, the change in minimal net liquidity costs of these banks will be given by

$$(V_1|l_1 = l_2; q \geq q_{nc}) - (V_1|l_1 > l_2; q \geq \bar{q}_{2,c}) = A(l_1 - l_2)$$
$$+ 2(A + RR)(\bar{q}_{nc} - \bar{q}_{1,c} - (l_1 - l_2)) \tag{6.77}$$

and

$$(V_1|l_1 = l_2; q \geq \bar{q}_{nc}) - (V_1|l_1 < l_2; q \geq \bar{q}_{1,r}) = A(l_1 - l_2)$$
$$+ 2(A + RR)(\bar{q}_{nc} - \bar{q}_{2,r} + (l_1 - l_2)). \tag{6.78}$$

The comparison of equations (6.71) to (6.78) with equation (6.70) reveals that *all* banks benefit from the shifting of reserves, even those banks which actually do not frontload or postpone their holdings of required reserves: Independent of a cut or an increase in the repo rate, the second line in the equations (6.71) to (6.78) has a positive sign, i.e. if the central bank cuts its rate, there will be a further decline in liquidity costs, and if the central bank raises its interest rate, the increase in liquidity costs will be dampened or even overcompensated. However, the equations also show that the cost advantage depends on q which means that banks are affected differently by a monetary impulse in the form of a change in the repo rate. We will analyze this cost advantage in more detail by the help of Fig. 6.6.

The figure shows that within the first group, the banks with a relatively high q benefit more from the shifting of reserves, although all of them frontload/postpone the same amount. This is the result of the

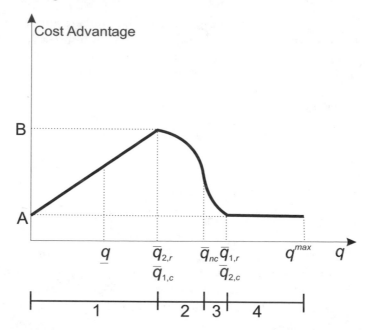

Fig. 6.6: Average Rate Model: Cost Advantage of Frontloading/Postponing Required Reserves

negative effect on e_t^* and, therefore, of the decreased sum of spreads between the interbank market rate and the repo rate $\sum_{t=1}^{2} s_t$ as described on p. 98. In this first group, there are banks which place liquidity in the interbank market ($q < \underline{q}$) and which borrow in this market ($q > \underline{q}$). For the former, the decreased sum of the spreads implies that over the whole period net revenues of placing liquidity in the interbank market decrease. For the latter the decreased sum of the spreads means that borrowing liquidity in the interbank market becomes relatively cheaper. Since the amount of liquidity a bank places in the interbank market depends negatively on q and since the amount a bank borrows in the interbank market depends positively on q, the cost advantage is increasing in q in the interval $[0, \bar{q}_{2,r}]$ and in the interval $[0, \bar{q}_{1,c}]$ respectively.

The negative effect on e_t^* as described on p. 98, implies that the sum of the changes in e_t^* over the whole maintenance period will be larger if the repo rate is cut and smaller if the repo rate is raised (for details see also p. 98). This means that the banks in the fourth group, which do not frontload or postpone reserves, also benefit from the reserve shifting of the other banks: They face lower interest costs (note that this negative effect on e_t^* is the result of the reserve shifting of the other banks).

Since the group-four banks cover their total liquidity needs exclusively in the interbank market, i.e. they do not borrow any liquidity directly from the central bank, their cost advantage does not change in q.

The cost advantage of those banks, on the other hand, which borrow liquidity from the central bank only in one period decreases in q, since the amount of reserves they frontload or postpone decreases in q (see Figs. 6.1 and 6.4). However, Fig. 6.6 shows that the cost advantage of group-two banks decreases more slowly than the advantage of group-three banks. The explanation is as follows: For determining the impact of a change in the repo rate on the banks' minimal net liquidity costs, and, therefore, for determining the cost advantage of the reserve shifting, we have looked at the difference between the banks' minimal net liquidity costs without and with a change in the repo rate $(V_1|l_1 = l_2) - (V_1|l_1 \neq l_2)$. Responsible for the different development of the cost advantage in group two and group three as revealed by Fig. 6.6 is a different $(V_1|l_1 = l_2)$. If the repo rate is not changed, the group-two banks borrow liquidity from the central bank so that in this case their minimal net liquidity costs increase in q:

$$\frac{\partial(V_1|l_1 = l_2; q < \bar{q}_{nc})}{\partial q} \qquad \bar{q}_{nc} \quad q > 0. \tag{6.79}$$

Group-three banks, on the other hand, do not borrow liquidity from the central bank in this case, so that their minimal liquidity costs will not depend on q if the repo rate is not changed:

$$\frac{\partial(V_1|l_1 = l_2; q \geq \bar{q}_{nc})}{\partial q} = 0. \tag{6.80}$$

However, if the repo rate is changed the banks of both groups borrow from the central bank so that in this case the minimal liquidity costs of the banks in both groups increase in q:

$$\frac{\partial(V_1|l_1 > l_2; \bar{q}_{1,c} \leq q < \bar{q}_{2,c})}{\partial q} = \frac{2}{3}(\bar{q}_{2,c} - q) > 0 \tag{6.81}$$

and

$$\frac{\partial(V_1|l_1 > l_2; \bar{q}_{2,r} \leq q < \bar{q}_{1,r})}{\partial q} = \frac{2}{3}(\bar{q}_{1,r} - q) > 0. \tag{6.82}$$

Consequently, the cost advantage of group-three banks decreases faster in q than it does in group-two banks.

6.3.3 Rationing

So far, we have assumed that the central bank always totally satisfies the banks' demand for reserves, even if the aggregated demand exceeds the central bank's benchmark amount. However, in the euro area, the ECB will normally ration liquidity in form of a pro-rata allotment of the individual bank bids if total bids exceeds the ECB's benchmark allotment (European Central Bank, 2004c, p. 80). Therefore, this subsection analyzes the banks' optimal liquidity management assuming that the central bank never provides more liquidity than its benchmark amount, i.e. that it will ration liquidity if the demand exceeds its benchmark. Since this will only be the case if the central bank is going to *raise* the repo rate, we can restrict our analysis to this scenario. Furthermore, for the sake of simplicity, we restrict our analysis to the two-bank case.

In the two-bank case, the central bank's benchmark amount is $2(A + RR)$, i.e. $K_1^A = \min[K_1^{A,opt}, 2(A + RR)]$. When solving the average rate model under the rationing assumption, for the banks' optimal liquidity management the following will be obtained if the repo rate is raised ($l_1 < l_2$):

$$K_1^A = K_2^{A,opt} = 2(A + RR), \tag{6.83}$$

$$B_1^{A,opt} = B_2^{A,opt} = -(A + RR), \tag{6.84}$$

$$K_1^{B,opt} = K_2^{B,opt} = 0, \tag{6.85}$$

$$B_1^{B,opt} = B_2^{B,opt} = A + RR, \tag{6.86}$$

$$R_1^{A,opt} = R_2^{A,opt} = R_1^{B,opt} = R_2^{B,opt} = RR. \tag{6.87}$$

These results show that in both periods the benchmark amount of liquidity is provided via bank A to the banking sector, that in both periods the same amount of liquidity ($A + RR$) is transacted in the interbank market, and that on aggregate reserves are provided smoothly over the reserve maintenance period despite an increase in the repo rate.

However, the extent to which the banks are affected differently by the monetary policy impulse is higher when compared to the non-rationing case: If there is no rationing, bank A's liquidity costs will increase less than bank B's if the repo rate is raised because it benefits from the frontloading of its reserve holdings (see p. 85). If, on the other hand, the central bank rations liquidity, bank B faces even additional liquidity costs while bank A's liquidity costs actually decrease:

$$V_1^A(l_2 = l_1) - V_1^A(l_1 < l_2) = -(l_1 - l_2)RR > 0 \qquad (6.88)$$

$$V_1^B(l_2 = l_1) - V_1^B(l_1 < l_2) = (l_1 - l_2)(2A + RR) < 0. \qquad (6.89)$$

Equation (6.88) shows that bank A's minimal liquidity costs are higher if the repo rate is not raised, i.e. bank A actually benefits from the monetary policy impulse. Bank B's minimal liquidity costs, on the other hand, will increase if the repo rate is raised as shown by equation (6.89), and the comparison with equation (6.49) reveals that this increase is even higher than in the non-rationing case. Consequently, the extent to which the banks are affected differently is higher than in the non-rationing case. The reason for this is that the rationing implies an additional increase in the interbank market rate from which bank A as a lender benefits and bank B as a borrower suffers. The explanation for the additional increase in the market rate is as follows. The interbank market rate reflects bank A's marginal costs of placing liquidity in the interbank market which consist inter alia of interest payments to the central bank, and the rationing implies an additional increase in the marginal interest payments to the central bank since in both periods, they are determined only by the (higher) repo rate l_2:[19]

$$e_1^* = e_2^* = l_2 + q_i + 3(A + RR) = MC^A. \qquad (6.90)$$

The intuition for this result is as follows. If bank A wants to place additional liquidity in the interbank market in the first period, it cannot borrow the necessary liquidity from the central bank because of the rationing. Consequently, bank A has to reduce its reserve holdings R_1^A. However, this implies that bank A has to hold more reserves in the second period to fulfil its reserve requirements, which again implies that it has to borrow more reserves from the central bank in the second period - at the higher rate l_2. Formally, the additional increase in the interbank market rate due to the rationing can be seen by comparing the differentiation of the interbank market rate with respect to l_2 with and without rationing. Without rationing $\partial e_t^*/\partial l_2 = 0.5 \forall t$ (see equation (6.46)), with rationing $\partial e_t^*/\partial l_2 = 1 \forall t$.

---

[19] If the central bank does not ration liquidity, marginal interest payments, and therefore the interbank market rate, will be determined by the average of l_1 and l_2 as shown by equation (6.36).

6.4 Summary

As in Chap. 5, we have considered a two-period model in which we have first analyzed the optimal liquidity management of a single, price-taking bank. Decisive institutional features of this model - features in which this model differs from the other models presented in this work - are:

- required reserves are remunerated at the average of the repo rates valid in the current reserve maintenance period, and
- the maturities of central bank loans do not overlap.

The bank minimizes net total liquidity costs across the two periods by choosing the optimal intertemporal allocation of required reserves, the optimal borrowing from the monetary authority, and optimal transactions in the interbank market. After having solved this optimization problem, we have assumed that the banking sector is heterogenous. Banks differ in their marginal costs of obtaining funds from the central bank causing an interbank market to emerge. When setting liquidity supply in the interbank market equal to liquidity demand, we have derived the equilibrium interbank market rate and have obtained the following results (for a more detailed summary of the model framework, we refer the reader to the summary of the current rate model given on p. 68):

- If the repo rate is raised within the reserve maintenance period, the demand for central bank credits in the first period will exceed the central bank's benchmark. If the central bank totally satisfies this demand, holdings of required reserves will be frontloaded. If the central bank rations liquidity by providing only its benchmark amount, reserves will be provided evenly across the maintenance period.
- If the repo rate is cut within the reserve maintenance period, central bank borrowing in the first period will fall below the central bank's benchmark and holdings of required reserves will be postponed.
- If the central bank changes the repo rate within the reserve maintenance period, banks will be affected differently by this monetary policy impulse. If the central bank rations liquidity, the extent to which banks are affected differently will be higher than in the non-rationing case.
- Banks are affected differently by a monetary impulse in form of a change in reserve requirements.
- Holding reserves is neither neutral with regard to interest costs and yields initiated by the central bank nor with regard to overall costs

and yields which implies that banks face different overall costs of holding required reserves

- There is an interest rate smoothing in the sense that the interbank market rate will already decrease (increase) before the central bank actually cuts (raises) the repo rate.

7

Overlapping Maturities of Central Bank Credits

7.1 Introduction

In this chapter, we change the average rate model presented in the previous chapter by assuming that there are overlapping maturities of central bank credits. We will show that the overlapping maturities imply that central bank borrowing will deviate even more from the central bank's benchmark amount and that even more required reserves will be postponed if the repo rate is cut. If the repo rate is raised, the overlapping maturities *may* imply that central bank borrowing deviates even more from the central bank's benchmark amount and that even more required reserves are frontloaded. Furthermore, we will show that banks are affected differently by a monetary policy impulse if the repo rate is cut and that they *may* be affected differently if the repo rate is raised. Moreover, we will demonstrate that the overlapping maturities may prevent a smoothing of the interbank market rate.

This overlapping maturities model framework is the most complex of those presented in this work. Therefore, it is important to keep in mind the structure of the analysis. As in the previous chapter, we will first present the optimal liquidity management of a single bank. This liquidity management includes the bank's decision on its optimal borrowing from the central bank, its optimal transactions in the interbank market, and its optimal intertemporal allocation of reserve requirements. To determine the equilibrium interbank market rate, we first consider only two banks and then a continuum of banks differing in their costs of borrowing liquidity directly from the central bank. For each case, we analyze whether a change in the repo rate implies a deviation of the aggregate demand for central bank credits from the central bank's benchmark, whether it implies that on aggregate required reserves are provided unevenly over the maintenance period, and to what extent banks are affected differently by this monetary policy impulse. We compare the outcome of this analysis with the outcome of the analysis in the average rate model.

We model the overlapping maturities of the central bank credits by considering a two-period model. There are two time periods, $t = 1, 2$, and we assume that in each period the banks can borrow liquidity from the central bank. The first-period credit has a two-period maturity, which results in overlapping maturities of central bank credits. For the sake of simplicity, we assume the stock of central bank credits at the beginning of the first period to be zero ($K_0 = 0$). If the repo rate is raised, our results are not robust to this simplifying assumption, so in the last section of this chapter, we will skip this assumption and analyze the bank's optimal liquidity management and the behaviour of the interbank market rate in case $K_0 > 0$ for the relatively simple two-bank case.

7.2 Optimal Liquidity Management of a Single Bank

7.2.1 Liquidity Costs

Again, there are two time periods which cover a reserve maintenance period and an isolated, price-taking bank has liquidity needs resulting from autonomous factors A and required reserves RR, which can be fulfilled on average over the reserve maintenance period so that

$$RR = \frac{R_1 + R_2}{2}. \tag{7.1}$$

The bank can cover its liquidity needs at the central bank or in the interbank market where it can also place liquidity. A crucial feature of this model is that the maturities of two subsequent central bank credit operations overlap so that the bank's stock of central bank credits in period t is given by

$$RK_t = K_{t-1} + K_t, \tag{7.2}$$

given $K_0 = 0$. The overlapping maturities imply that the opportunity costs of holding collateral become

$$Q(K_{t-1}, K_t) = q(K_{t-1} + K_t) + \frac{p}{2}(K_{t-1} + K_t)^2, \tag{7.3}$$

i.e., the opportunity costs of holding collateral in period t now also depend on the central bank credit granted in period $t - 1$. The reason for this is that assets used as collateral in period $t - 1$ cannot be used as such in period t due to the overlapping maturities. Consequently, for a central bank credit granted in period t additional eligible assets must be held at the dispense of other assets which have - due to the assumed hierarchical order of the bank's assets described on p. 34 - higher rates of return. Consequently, for $K_{t-1} > 0$ the *level* of marginal opportunity costs of holding collateral in t is higher when compared to the case where the maturities do not overlap (it is $q + pK_{t-1}$ instead of q).

The overlapping maturities also imply a change in the interbank market position which is

$$B_t(K_{t-1}, K_t, R_t) = A + R_t - RK_t \lesseqgtr 0, \tag{7.4}$$

implying that the interbank market transaction costs in period t also depend on K_{t-1}:

$$Z(B_t(K_{t-1}, K_t, R_t)) = \frac{z}{2}(B_t(K_{t-1}, K_t, R_t))^2. \tag{7.5}$$

As in the previously presented models, net liquidity costs in period t consist of interest payments to the central bank, interest costs or revenues from transactions in the interbank market, opportunity costs of holding collateral, and transactions costs minus interest yields from holding required reserves. As in the average rate model, reserves are remunerated at the average of l_1 and l_2 at the end of the second period. (The indicator function $I_{[\cdot]}$ in equation (7.6) takes a value of 1 when $t = 2$, and 0 otherwise.) Equation (7.6) shows that due to the overlapping maturities net liquidity costs in period t now also depend on the liquidity borrowed from the central bank in period $t - 1$:

$$\begin{aligned} C_t(K_{t-1}, K_t, R_t) &= K_{t-1}l_{t-1} + K_t l_t + B_t(K_{t-1}, K_t, R_t)e_t \\ &+ Q(K_{t-1}, K_t) + Z(B_t(K_{t-1}, K_t, R_t)) - RR(l_t + l_{t-1})I_{[t=2]}. \end{aligned} \tag{7.6}$$

7.2.2 Optimization Problem

The bank minimizes these net liquidity costs over the maintenance period by choosing the optimal intertemporal allocation of required reserves and optimal liquidity borrowing from the central bank, i.e. the bank's objective function is

$$\min_{K_t, R_t} \left\{ \sum_{t=1}^{2} C_t(K_{t-1}, K_t, R_t) \right\}. \tag{7.7}$$

The bank can make use of averaging provisions to fulfil its reserve requirements and the maturities of the central bank credits overlap. Consequently, the bank faces a dynamic optimization problem. Defining V_t as the associated value function, the Bellman equation is given by

$$V_1 = \min_{K_1, R_1} \{C_1(K_1, R_1) + V_2\} \quad \text{subject to} \quad K_t, R_t \geq 0. \tag{7.8}$$

Again, this optimization problem is solved backwards by looking at the bank's optimal liquidity management in the second period first.

7.2.3 Optimal Liquidity Management in the Second Period

Replacing R_2 by $2RR - R_1$, the Lagrangian in period two is

$$
\begin{aligned}
L(K_2, \lambda_2) = & K_1 l_1 + K_2 l_2 + B_2(K_1, K_2, R_1)e_2 + Q(K_1, K_2) \\
& + Z(B_2(K_1, K_2, R_1)) - RR(l_1 + l_2) - \lambda_2 K_2
\end{aligned} \tag{7.9}
$$

and the first order conditions are:

$$-e_2 + l_2 + p(K_1 + K_2) + q - zB_2(K_1, K_2, R_1) - \lambda_2 = 0, \tag{7.10}$$

$$\lambda_2 K_2 = 0, \quad \lambda_2 \geq 0, \quad K_2 \geq 0. \tag{7.11}$$

The interpretation of the first order conditions is the same as in the previously presented models. Equation (7.10) says that if the bank places liquidity in the interbank market, the marginal costs of this transaction will equal its marginal benefits, and if the bank borrows from the central bank and in the interbank market, marginal costs of both alternatives will be the same.

The first order conditions lead to the following optimal central bank borrowing in the second period:

$$K_2^{opt}(K_1, R_1) = \begin{cases} \dfrac{e_2 - l_2 - pK_1 - q + z(A + 2RR - K_1 - R_1)}{p + z} > 0 \\ \qquad \text{if} \quad q + pK_1 < m \\ 0 \quad \text{if} \quad q + pK_1 \geq m, \end{cases} \tag{7.12}$$

where

$$m = e_2 - l_2 + z(A + 2RR - R_1 - K_1).$$

Crucial is that the overlapping maturities imply that K_2^{opt} depends on K_1. It is obvious that K_1 influences K_2^{opt} negatively.

By inserting K_2^{opt} into $C_2(\cdot)$ the minimal net liquidity costs in the second period are obtained:

$$V_2(K_1, R_1) = K_1 l_1 + K_2^{opt}(K_1, R_1) l_2$$
$$+ B_2(K_2^{opt}(K_1, R_1), K_1, R_1) e_2 + Q(K_2^{opt}(K_1, R_1), K_1) \quad (7.13)$$
$$+ Z(B_2(K_2^{opt}(K_1, R_1), K_1, R_1)) - RR(l_1 + l_2).$$

7.2.4 Optimal Liquidity Management in the First Period

The non-negativity constraint for R_t is binding only for a sufficiently large decrease in the repo rate. Therefore, for the sake of simplicity we assume that $|l_1 - l_2| < RR$. Then, the constraint is not binding[1] and can be neglected in the Lagrangian which is then given by

$$L(K_1, R_1, \lambda_1) = K_1 l_1 + B_1(K_1, R_1) e_1 + Q(K_1)$$
$$+ Z(B_1(K_1, R_1)) - \lambda_1 K_1 + V_2(R_1, K_1). \quad (7.14)$$

We derive the first order conditions for two cases: first, for $K_2^{opt} > 0$ and second, for $K_2^{opt} = 0$. In the first case, i.e. for relatively low marginal opportunity costs of holding collateral ($q + pK_1 < m$), the Lagrangian leads to the following first order conditions:

$$-e_1 + 2l_1 - l_2 + pK_1 + q - zB_1(K_1, R_1) - \lambda_1 = 0, \quad (7.15)$$

$$e_1 + zB_1(K_1, R_1) = e_2 + zB_2(K_2^{opt}(K_1, R_1), R_1), \quad (7.16)$$

$$\lambda_1 K_1 = 0, \quad \lambda_1 \geq 0, \quad K_1 > 0. \quad (7.17)$$

In the second case, i.e. for relatively high marginal opportunity costs of holding collateral ($q + pK_1 \geq m$), the first order conditions are given by

$$-\frac{e_1 + e_2}{2} + l_1 + pK_1 + q - z(A + RR - K_1) - \lambda_1 = 0, \quad (7.18)$$

$$e_1 + zB_1(R_1) = e_2 + zB_2(R_1), \quad (7.19)$$

---

[1] See equations (7.42), (7.48), (7.49), (7.50), (7.67), (7.74), (7.75), (7.99), (7.100), and (7.104).

$$\lambda_1 K_1 = 0, \quad \lambda_1 \geq 0, \quad K_1 \geq 0. \tag{7.20}$$

The interpretation of these first order conditions is the same as in the previously presented models. The first order conditions given by the equations (7.15) and (7.18) say that if the bank covers its liquidity needs in the interbank market and at the central bank, the marginal costs of interbank market funds will be equated to the marginal costs of central bank funds, and if the bank places liquidity in the interbank market, the marginal costs of this transaction will equal its marginal revenues. The equations (7.16) and (7.19) show that the optimal allocation of required reserves requires net marginal costs of holding reserves to be the same in both periods. However, the overlapping maturities imply that formally the first order conditions differ from those in the average rate model. The decisive difference is that in this overlapping-maturities model optimal central bank borrowing in the first period depends on second-period interest rates (see equations (7.15) and (7.18)). The reason for this is that the maturity of the period-one central bank credit lasts into the second period. Therefore, also the interest rates of that period must be taken into account when determining the optimal K_1. Even if the bank does not borrow from the monetary authority in the second period because of its relatively high opportunity costs of holding collateral, it must take into account the interbank market rate in the second period e_2.

7.2.5 Provisional Results

When presenting the provisional results for the bank's optimal liquidity management we distinguish between two cases. In the first case, the repo rate is left unchanged or is raised. In the second case, the repo rate is cut. For a clearer presentation we set - as in the previous models - the parameters p and z equal to one in the cost functions $Q(\cdot)$ and $Z(\cdot)$.

In the case where repo rate is left unchanged or is raised, the first order conditions lead to the following provisional results for the bank's optimal liquidity management (r stands for *raise*, nc for *no change*):

$$R_{1,r}^{opt} = R_{1,nc}^{opt} = RR - \frac{e_1 - e_2}{2} \forall q, \tag{7.21}$$

$$R_{2,r}^{opt} = R_{2,nc}^{opt} = RR + \frac{e_1 - e_2}{2} \forall q, \tag{7.22}$$

$$K_{1,r}^{opt} = K_{1,nc}^{opt} = \begin{cases} \frac{A+RR-q}{2} + \frac{e_1+e_2-2l_1}{4} & \text{if} \quad q < \bar{q}_{1,r} \\ 0 & \text{if} \quad \bar{q}_{1,r} \leq q, \end{cases} \quad (7.23)$$

$$K_{2,r}^{opt} = K_{2,nc}^{opt} = 0 \forall q, \quad (7.24)$$

$$B_{1,r}^{opt} = B_{1,nc}^{opt} = \begin{cases} \frac{A+RR+q}{2} - \frac{3e_1-e_2-2l_1}{4} & \text{if} \quad q < \bar{q}_{1,r} \\ A + RR - \frac{e_1-e_2}{2} & \text{if} \quad \bar{q}_{1,r} \leq q, \end{cases} \quad (7.25)$$

$$B_{2,r}^{opt} = B_{2,nc}^{opt} = \begin{cases} \frac{A+RR+q}{2} + \frac{e_1-3e_2+2l_1}{4} & \text{if} \quad q < \bar{q}_{1,r} \\ A + RR + \frac{e_1-e_2}{2} & \text{if} \quad \bar{q}_{1,r} \leq q, \end{cases} \quad (7.26)$$

where

$$\bar{q}_{1,r} = \bar{q}_{1,nc} = e_1 - l_1 + A + RR - \frac{e_1 - e_2}{2}. \quad (7.27)$$

The lower thresholds for q are given by[2]

$$\underline{q}_{1,r} = \underline{q}_{1,nc} = e_1 - l_1 - (A + RR) + \frac{e_1 - e_2}{2} \quad (7.28)$$

and

$$\underline{q}_{2,r} = \underline{q}_{2,nc} = e_2 - l_1 - (A + RR) - \frac{e_1 - e_2}{2}. \quad (7.29)$$

If the central bank cuts the repo rate, the following provisional results for the bank's optimal liquidity management will be obtained (c stands for *cut*):

$$R_{1,c}^{opt} = \begin{cases} RR - \frac{e_1-e_2}{2} - l_1 + l_2 & \text{if} \quad q < \bar{q}_{1,c} \\ RR - \frac{1}{3}\left(A + RR + 2e_1 - e_2 - l_2 - q\right) & \\ \qquad \text{if} \quad \bar{q}_{1,c} \leq q < \bar{q}_{2,c} \\ RR - \frac{e_1-e_2}{2} & \text{if} \quad \bar{q}_{2,c} \leq q, \end{cases} \quad (7.30)$$

---

[2] Note that the derivation of the threshold $\underline{q}_2$ differs from the one in the previous chapters. Due to the overlapping maturities one obtains $\underline{q}_2$ by solving $(K_{1,r}^{opt}|q < \bar{q}_{1,r}) + K_{2,r}^{opt} = A + R_{2,r}^{opt}$ for q.

$$R_{2,c}^{opt} = \begin{cases} RR + \frac{e_1 - e_2}{2} + l_1 - l_2 & \text{if} \quad q < \bar{q}_{1,c} \\ RR + \frac{1}{3}\left(A + RR + 2e_1 - e_2 - l_2 - q\right) \\ \qquad\qquad\qquad\qquad \text{if} \quad \bar{q}_{1,c} \leq q < \bar{q}_{2,c} \\ RR + \frac{e_1 - e_2}{2} & \text{if} \quad \bar{q}_{2,c} \leq q, \end{cases} \tag{7.31}$$

$$K_{1,c}^{opt} = \begin{cases} \frac{A + RR - q}{2} + \frac{e_1 + e_2 - 4(2l_1 - l_2)}{4} & \text{if} \quad q < \bar{q}_{1,c} \\ 0 & \text{if} \quad \bar{q}_{1,c} \leq q, \end{cases} \tag{7.32}$$

$$K_{2,c}^{opt} = \begin{cases} 2(l_1 - l_2) & \text{if} \quad q < \bar{q}_{1,c} \\ \frac{2(A + RR - q)}{3} + \frac{e_1 + e_2 - 2l_2}{3} & \text{if} \quad \bar{q}_{1,c} \leq q < \bar{q}_{2,c} \\ 0 & \text{if} \quad \bar{q}_{2,c} \leq q, \end{cases} \tag{7.33}$$

$$B_{1,c}^{opt} = \begin{cases} \frac{A + RR + q}{2} - \frac{3e_1 - e_2 - 2l_1}{4} & \text{if} \quad q < \bar{q}_{1,c} \\ \frac{2(A + RR) + q}{3} - \frac{2e_1 - e_2 - l_2}{3} & \text{if} \quad \bar{q}_{1,c} \leq q < \bar{q}_{2,c} \\ A + RR - \frac{e_1 - e_2}{2} & \text{if} \quad \bar{q}_{2,c} \leq q, \end{cases} \tag{7.34}$$

$$B_{2,c}^{opt} = \begin{cases} \frac{A + RR + q}{2} + \frac{e_1 - 3e_2 + 2l_1}{4} & \text{if} \quad q < \bar{q}_{1,c} \\ \frac{2(A + RR) + q)}{3} + \frac{e_1 - 2e_2 + l_2}{3} & \text{if} \quad \bar{q}_{1,c} \leq q < \bar{q}_{2,c} \\ A + RR + \frac{e_1 - e_2}{2} & \text{if} \quad \bar{q}_{2,c} \leq q, \end{cases} \tag{7.35}$$

where

$$\bar{q}_{1,c} = A + RR + \frac{e_1 + e_2 - 4(2l_1 - l_2)}{2} \tag{7.36}$$

and

$$\bar{q}_{2,c} = A + RR + \frac{e_1 - e_2 - 2l_2}{2}. \tag{7.37}$$

The lower thresholds are given by:[3]

---

[3] Note that the derivation of the threshold $\underline{q}_{2,c}$ differs from the one in the previous chapters. Due to the overlapping maturities $\underline{q}_{2,c}$ is obtained by solving $(K_{1,c}^{opt}|q < \bar{q}_{1,c}) + (K_{2,c}^{opt}|q < \bar{q}_{1,c}) = A + (R_{2,c}^{opt}|q < \bar{q}_{1,c})$ for q. Note that in the second period, the bank will not borrow more funds from the central bank than it needs to cover its own liquidity needs if it does not borrow from the central bank in

$$\underline{q}_{1,c} = -(A + RR) + \frac{3e_1 - e_2 - 2l_1}{2} \tag{7.38}$$

and

$$\underline{q}_{2,c} = -(A + RR) - \frac{e_1 - 3e_2 + 2l_1}{2}. \tag{7.39}$$

The comparison of these provisional results with those of the average rate model reveals that a main impact of the overlapping maturities on a bank's optimal liquidity management is that independent of whether the interest rate is raised or is left unchanged, the bank does not borrow any liquidity from the central bank in the second period, K_2^{opt} is equal to zero for all q. Equation (7.33) shows that if the repo rate is cut, the bank may borrow from the monetary authority in the second period despite the overlapping maturities. Furthermore, the equation shows that the bank may even borrow from the central bank in the second period although it does not do so in the first, i.e. the upper thresholds $\bar{q}_{1,c}$ and $q_{2,c}$ fall apart.

We will comment in more detail on the impact of the overlapping maturities on the bank's optimal liquidity management when discussing the final results and use now the provisional results to derive the equilibrium interbank market rate.

7.3 Equilibrium in the Interbank Market and Final Results

As in the previously presented models, we derive the equilibrium interbank market rate and the final results for the bank's optimal liquidity management for the rather simple two-bank case before presenting the results for the more general case where there is a continuum of banks differing in q.

---

the first period. Solving $(K_{2,c}|\bar{q}_{1,c} \leq q < \bar{q}_{2,c}) = A + (R_{2,c}|\bar{q}_{1,c} \leq q < \bar{q}_{2,c})$ for q leads to $q = -2(A + RR) - e_1 + 2e_2 - l_2$. However, for this threshold to exist, $-2(A + RR) - e_1 + 2e_2 - l_2$ must be greater than $\bar{q}_{1,c}$, since the bank does not demand funds in the first period. Rearranging $-2(A + RR) - e_1 + 2e_2 - l_2 > \bar{q}_{1,c}$ reveals that this implies that $(l_1 - l_2) > (A + RR) + (e_1 - e_2)/2$. However, this violates our assumption that $(l_1 - l_2) < RR$ (see p. 113).

7.3.1 Two Banks

Equilibrium Interbank Market Rate

Again, there are two groups of price-taking banks differing in q, represented by the banks A and B, with $q^A < \underline{q}_t$ $\forall t$ and $q^B \geq \bar{q}_t$ $\forall t$. Then, solving

$$B_t^{A,opt} + B_t^{B,opt} = 0 \tag{7.40}$$

for e_t, the equilibrium interbank market rate e_t^* is obtained ($B_t^{A,opt}$ is given by the first line of the equations (7.34) and (7.35), $B_t^{B,opt}$ by the third line of these equations):[4]

$$e_1^* = e_2^* = 3(A + RR) + q^A + l_1. \tag{7.41}$$

We will comment on this equilibrium interbank market rate after having derived and discussed the final results for the the banks' optimal liquidity management which we will do next.

Optimal Liquidity Management: Final Results

When inserting the equilibrium interbank market rate given by equation (7.41) into the equations (7.21) to (7.26),[5] the following final results for the banks' optimal liquidity management will be obtained if the central bank does not change the repo rate or if the central bank raises the repo rate (in the former case simply set l_1 equal to l_2):

$$R_{1,nc,r}^{A,opt} = R_{2,nc,r}^{A,opt} = R_{1,nc,r}^{B,opt} = R_{2,nc,r}^{B,opt} = RR, \tag{7.42}$$

$$K_{1,nc,r}^{A,opt} = 2(A + RR), \tag{7.43}$$

$$K_{2,nc,r}^{A,opt} = 0, \tag{7.44}$$

$$K_{1,nc,r}^{B,opt} = K_{2,nc,r}^{B,opt} = 0, \tag{7.45}$$

---

[4] Alternatively, one can use the equations (7.25) and (7.26) since in this simple two-bank case the provisional results for an interest rate cut and for an interest rate increase are formally the same.

[5] If there are two lines, one has to insert e_t^* into the first line for bank A and into the second line for bank B.

$$B_{1,nc,r}^{A,opt} = B_{2,nc,r}^{A,opt} = -(A + RR), \tag{7.46}$$

and

$$B_{1,nc,r}^{B,opt} = B_{2,nc,r}^{B,opt} = A + RR. \tag{7.47}$$

The most interesting result is that an increase in the repo rate within the reserve maintenance period has no impact on the banks' optimal liquidity management, i.e despite the remuneration of reserves at the average of l_1 and l_2 - which has been the cause for bank A's frontloading of required reserves in the previously presented model - both banks provide their reserve requirements smoothly across the maintenance period. The reason for this is that the banks also have the relatively cheap first-period liquidity in the second period at their disposal (due to the overlapping maturities) and that there is no central bank credit which expires in the second period since we have assumed K_0 to be zero. Therefore, total liquidity needs of both periods can be covered with the relatively cheap first-period liquidity so that both banks have no incentive to frontload their reserve holdings despite the interest rate increase. This implies that at the aggregate level reserves are also provided smoothly.

These smooth provisions of required reserves obviously imply that aggregate central bank borrowing in the first period corresponds to the central bank's benchmark amount despite the interest rate increase.[6] In this simple two-bank case this benchmark is equal to $2(A + RR)$ and equation (7.43) reveals that bank A, which is by assumption the only bank which demands liquidity at the monetary authority, borrows exactly this amount.

As already mentioned above, crucial for these results (smooth provisions of required reserves and no deviation of aggregate central bank borrowing from the benchmark even if the central bank increases the repo rate) is the assumption that K_0 is equal to zero. This assumption implies that at the end of the first period no central bank credit expires. Consequently, fresh liquidity is actually not needed. We will skip this assumption and discuss the consequences for the banks' optimal liquidity management in section 7.3.3. Skipping the assumption is no problem in the relatively simple two-bank case. However, when considering a continuum of heterogenous banks, the model gets too complex since one has to make additional assumptions concerning K_0. To capture the effects of expiring central bank credits within the reserve maintenance period for a continuum of heterogenous banks one

---

[6] For the definition of the benchmark amount see p. 48.

should employ a model with more than two periods. However, in this work we will stick to our two-period model and will only discuss in section 7.3.3 the consequences of expiring central bank credits within the reserve maintenance period for the two-bank case.

If the repo rate is cut, the banks' optimal liquidity management will be given by

$$R_{1,c}^{A,opt} = RR - (l_1 - l_2), \qquad (7.48)$$

$$R_{2,c}^{A,opt} = RR + (l_1 - l_2), \qquad (7.49)$$

$$R_{1,c}^{B,opt} = R_{2,c}^{B,opt} = RR, \qquad (7.50)$$

$$K_{1,c}^{A,opt} = 2(A + RR) - (l_1 - l_2), \qquad (7.51)$$

$$K_{2,c}^{A,opt} = 2(l_1 - l_2), \qquad (7.52)$$

$$K_{1,c}^{B,opt} = K_{2,c}^{B,opt} = 0, \qquad (7.53)$$

$$B_{1,c}^{A,opt} = B_{2,c}^{A,opt} = -(A + RR), \qquad (7.54)$$

and

$$B_{1,c}^{B,opt} = B_{2,c}^{B,opt} = A + RR. \qquad (7.55)$$

Equations (7.48) to (7.50) reveal that bank A postpones its reserve holdings while bank B provides them smoothly across the maintenance period. Bank A postpones its reserve holdings for two reasons. The first reason is the same as in the average rate model: Due to the remuneration of reserves at the average of l_1 and l_2, bank A's marginal revenues of holding reserves decrease in both periods, while its marginal costs only decrease in the second period (if the bank borrows from the monetary authority in the second period which it will do as we show below). Therefore, intertemporal optimality requires holding more reserves in the second period. The second reason for bank A's postponing of the required reserves is that the maturity of the relatively expensive first-period credit lasts into the second period which implies that the fewer reserves bank A holds in the first period, the lower its liquidity needs are in the first and the higher they are in the second period, i.e. it can benefit more from the interest rate decrease in the second period. Since this second reason does not exist in the average rate model, it is obvious that the overlapping maturities reinforce the uneven provisions of required reserves of bank A. Formally, this reinforcement effect can be seen by comparing equations (7.48) and (7.49) with the relevant equations in the average rate model (6.37) and (6.38).

For bank B it is optimal to provide its required reserve smoothly despite the change in the repo rate. The reasons are that the bank's marginal interest costs as well as its marginal revenues are the same in both periods and that transactions in the interbank market involve increasing marginal costs.[7]

Since bank B provides its required reserves smoothly and since bank A postpones even more reserves than in the average rate model, it is obvious that at the aggregate level, reserves will also not be provided smoothly if the repo rate is cut and in addition the overlapping maturities reinforce this problem.

The uneven provisions of required reserves of bank A are also reflected by its central bank borrowing (see equations (7.51) and (7.52)). Bank A's liquidity needs in the first period are smaller than in the second period due to the postponing of the required reserves. Consequently, bank A borrows liquidity from the monetary authority in the second period despite the overlapping maturities which implies that aggregate central bank borrowing in the first period falls below the central bank's benchmark which is equal to $2(A + RR)$ in this simple two-bank case.[8]

Equilibrium Interbank Market Rate: Discussion

In this section, we will comment on the equilibrium interbank market rate e_t^* given by equation (7.41). We will show that e_t^* reflects bank A's marginal costs of placing liquidity in the interbank market. Furthermore, we will explain why a change in the repo rate resulting in $l_1 \neq l_2$ has no influence on the equilibrium interbank market rate during that reserve maintenance period.

Marginal Costs of Placing Liquidity in the Interbank Market
If *the repo rate is raised or left unchanged,* bank A's marginal costs of placing liquidity in the interbank market are given by:

---

[7] The bank's marginal interest costs are the same in both periods since $e_1^* = e_2^*$, and the bank's marginal revenues are the same because reserves are remunerated at the average of l_1 and l_2.

[8] For the definition of the central bank's benchmark see p. 48.

$$MC_{1,nc,r}^{A,ibm} = MC_{2,nc,r}^{A,ibm} = l_1 + q^A + pK_{1,nc,r}^{A,opt} - zB_{t,nc,r}^{A,opt}. \qquad (7.56)$$

The first three terms on the right hand side of equation (7.56) represent bank A's marginal costs of borrowing the relevant liquidity from the central bank and the last term represents the marginal transaction costs of placing the liquidity in the interbank market. If the repo rate is left unchanged or if the repo rate is raised, bank A will not borrow any liquidity from the central bank in the second period. Consequently, l_2 does not influence its marginal costs. When setting p and z equal to one and inserting the equilibrium values for $K_{1,nc,r}^{A,opt}$ and $B_{t,nc,r}^{A,opt}$ given by the equations (7.43) and (7.46) into equation (7.56) gives

$$MC_{1,nc,r}^{A,ibm} = MC_{2,nc,r}^{A,ibm} = 3(A + RR) + q^A + l_1 = e_t^* \qquad (7.57)$$

which confirms that the interbank market rate reflects bank A's marginal costs of placing liquidity in the interbank market.

If *the repo rate is cut*, i.e. if case bank A borrows from the monetary authority in the second period, its marginal costs of placing liquidity in the interbank market will be given by

$$MC_{1,c}^{A,ibm} = l_1 + (l_1 - l_2) + q^A + pK_{1,c}^{A,opt} - zB_{1,c}^{A,opt} \qquad (7.58)$$

in the first period and by

$$MC_{2,c}^{A,ibm} = l_2 + q^A + p(K_{1,c}^{A,opt} + K_{2,c}^{A,opt}) - zB_{2,c}^{A,opt} \qquad (7.59)$$

in the second period. Equation (7.58) shows that the repo rate of the second period l_2 influences already bank A's marginal costs of placing liquidity in the interbank market in the first period. The obvious reason is the two-period maturity of $K_{1,c}^{A,opt}$: If bank A borrows in the first period liquidity from the central bank to place it in the interbank market, it must consider that this reduces its profit in the second period when it can borrow liquidity from the central bank at a lower rate. Furthermore, equations (7.58) and (7.59) show that due to the cut in the repo rate, bank A's marginal *interest* costs are higher in the first period than in the second period.[9] However, this cost advantage in the second period (disadvantage in the first period) is exactly compensated by higher (lower) opportunity costs of holding collateral in the second

---

[9] If one compares the equations (7.58) and (7.59) with the equation (6.44) in the average rate model, it can be seen that the overlapping maturities imply that the difference in marginal interest costs between the two periods is even higher. In the average rate model the difference is $(l_1 - l_2)$, in this model it is $(2l_1 - l_2)$. The reason for this is that the overlapping maturities imply that in the second period bank A still has to pay the relatively high interest rate l_1.

(first) period: Setting p and z equal to one and inserting the equilibrium values for $K_{t,c}^{A,opt}$ and $B_{t,c}^{A,opt}$ given by the equations (7.51), (7.52), and (7.54) into the equations (7.58) and (7.58) gives t

$$MC_{1,c}^{A,ibm} = MC_{2,c}^{A,ibm} = 3(A + RR) + q^A + l_1 = e_t^* \qquad (7.60)$$

which shows that the repo rate reflects bank A's marginal costs of placing liquidity in the interbank market and that these costs are the same in both periods despite different repo rates. Obviously, an increase in one of the marginal cost components implies an increase in e_t^*. The impact of a change in A, RR, q^A, or in the repo rate at the beginning of the maintenance period ($l_1 = l_2 = l$) on the equilibrium interbank market rate is the same as in the current rate model. Therefore, we refer the reader to p. 57 concerning the analysis of these changes and focus now on the impact of a change in the repo rate within the reserve maintenance period ($l_1 \neq l_2$).

Change in the Repo Rate   An interesting point is that a change in the repo rate within the reserve maintenance period has no impact on the equilibrium interbank market rate during that reserve maintenance period:

$$\frac{\partial e_1^*}{\partial l_2} = \frac{\partial e_2^*}{\partial l_2} = 0. \qquad (7.61)$$

If the repo rate is raised ($l_1 < l_2$), this is an obvious result since bank A does not borrow liquidity from the monetary authority at the rate l_2 so that it does not influence its marginal costs of placing liquidity in the interbank market.

If there is an interest rate cut, the driving force behind this result is that the optimal intertemporal allocation of the required reserves implies that net marginal costs of holding reserves are the same in both periods. These net marginal costs consist of interest payments to the central bank and opportunity costs of holding collateral minus interest yields. The latter are the same in both periods due to the remuneration of reserves at the average of l_1 and l_2. Consequently, the sum out of interest payments to the central bank and opportunity costs of holding collateral must also be the same in both periods. Since marginal interest payments differ, the compensation takes place via the opportunity costs of holding collateral which are higher in the second period because bank A's stock of central bank credit is higher in that period (it is $K_{1,c}^{A,opt}$ in the first and $(K_{1,c}^{A,opt} + K_{2,c}^{A,opt})$ in the second period). Intertemporal optimality requires that bank A postpones so many reserves that in the first period the higher interest costs are exactly compensated by lower opportunity costs of holding collateral and vice versa in the second period. Also in this context it becomes clear that overlapping maturities reinforce the problem that required reserves are provided unevenly over the maintenance period: Since in this overlapping maturities model the difference in marginal interest costs between the two periods is higher than in the average rate model (see footnote 9 on p. 122), more reserves must be postponed to achieve intertemporal optimality.[10] In the average rate model, the decline in marginal opportunity costs of holding collateral in the first period implies a decrease in e_1^* (although the repo rate is not changed until the second period). However, in this overlapping maturities model, the decline in marginal opportunity costs of holding collateral does not lead to a decrease in e_1^* because this cost advantage is compensated by higher marginal interest costs resulting from the two-period maturity of K_1 (see equation (7.58)).

Since the interbank market rate does not change in any period, whereas the repo rate only changes in the second period, it is obvious that a cut or an increase in the repo rate within the reserve maintenance period implies that the spread between the interbank market rate and the central bank rate is no longer the same in both periods. However, the sum of the spreads $\sum_{t=1}^{2} s_t$ is also no longer the same. If the repo rate is cut, it will increase; if the repo rate is raised, it will decline (see the appendix for a numerical example).

Impact of Monetary Policy Impulses

Again, we only consider an interest rate change within the reserve maintenance period as a monetary policy impulse. This is done because the consequences of an interest rate change at the beginning of the maintenance period ($l_1 = l_2$), as well as a change in reserve requirements are the same as in the current rate model and in the average rate model.

If the repo rate is changed within the reserve maintenance period ($l_1 \neq l_2$), the impact on the banks' minimal liquidity costs will be given by

$$(V_1|l_1 = l_2)^A - (V_1|l_1 < l_2)^A =$$
$$(V_1|l_1 = l_2)^B - (V_1|l_1 \neq l_2)^B = -RR(l_1 - l_2) \tag{7.62}$$

and

---

[10] For a more detailed analysis on the equality of e_1^* and e_2^* see the discussion of the equilibrium interbank market rate in the average rate model on p. 83.

$$(V_1|l_1 = l_2)^A - (V_1|l_1 > l_2)^A = -RR(l_1 - l_2) + (l_1 - l_2)^2. \quad (7.63)$$

Equation (7.62) shows that if the repo rate is raised, both banks will *benefit* from this monetary policy impulse to the same extent. This is because their interest yields increase due to the remuneration of reserves at the average of l_1 and l_2, while their interest costs do not change: Bank A also covers its liquidity needs in the second period with the relatively cheap first-period central bank credit because of the two-period maturity of $K_1^{A,opt}$. Bank B's interest costs do not change since the equilibrium interbank market rate remains the same in both periods. However, by a monetary policy impulse in form of an interest rate cut, bank A and bank B will be affected differently since only bank A benefits from the postponing of its required reserves.

When comparing bank A's cost advantage from its reserve shifting in the average rate model with this cost advantage in the overlapping maturities model,[11] it is revealed that the overlapping maturities reinforce the problem that banks are affected differently by a monetary policy impulse in form of an interest rate cut. The reason for this is that the overlapping maturities imply that bank A postpones even more reserves, so that its cost advantage increases as well.

7.3.2 Continuum of Banks

Analogously to the previously presented models, we will next derive and discuss next the equilibrium interbank market rate and the final results for the banks' optimal liquidity management for the more general case where there is a continuum of banks.

Equilibrium Interbank Market Rate

We consider a continuum of measure one of isolated, price-taking banks differing in their level of marginal opportunity costs of holding collateral q. Then, assuming that q is distributed in the interval $[0, q_{max}]$ across banks according to the density function $g(q) = G'(q)$ with $G(0) = 0$, the equilibrium interbank market rate is determined by solving

---

[11] In the average rate model, this cost advantage is represented by the last term in equation (6.48). In the overlapping maturities model, this cost advantage is represented by the last term in equation (7.63).

$$\int_0^{q_t}(B_t^{opt}|q<\bar{q}_t)g(q)dq + \int_{q_t}^{\bar{q}_t}(B_t^{opt}|q<\bar{q}_t)g(q)dq$$
$$+ \int_{\bar{q}_t}^{q^{max}}(B_t^{opt}|q\geq\bar{q}_t)g(q)dq = 0 \tag{7.64}$$

for e_t, where B_t^{opt} will be given by equations (7.34) and (7.35) if the repo rate is cut and by equations (7.25) and (7.26) if the repo rate is raised. The first term in equation (7.64) represents liquidity supply in the interbank market, while the second and the third term represent liquidity demand (for details see the comments on the relevant equation in the benchmark model on p. 61).

As in the previously presented models, we assume q to be distributed uniformly across banks. Then, solving equation (7.64) for e_t

$$e_{1,nc,r}^* = e_{2,nc,r}^* = -(A+RR)+l_1+\sqrt{4q^{max}(A+RR)}, \tag{7.65}$$

if the repo rate is raised or if it is left unchanged. If the repo rate is cut,

$$e_{1,c}^* = e_{2,c}^*$$
$$= -(A+RR)+l_1+\sqrt{-2(l_1-l_2)^2+4q^{max}(A+RR)}. \tag{7.66}$$

We will comment on these equilibrium interbank market rates after having determined the final results for the banks' optimal liquidity management.

Final Results for the Optimal Liquidity Management if the Repo Rate Is Raised or Left Unchanged

Presenting the final results for the banks' optimal liquidity management, we distinguish between the case where the repo rate is left unchanged or raised and the case where the repo rate is cut. We will have a look at the former first.

For determining the final results for the banks' optimal liquidity management if the repo rate is raised or left unchanged, the equilibrium interbank market rate given by equation (7.65) has to be inserted into the provisional results given by the equations (7.21) to (7.29). Then the following is obtained (nc stands for no change, r for raise):

$$R_{1,nc,r}^{opt} = R_{2,nc,r}^{opt} = RR\forall q, \tag{7.67}$$

$$K_{1,nc,r}^{opt} = \begin{cases} -\frac{q}{2} + \sqrt{q^{max}(A+RR)} & \text{if} \quad q < \bar{q}_{nc,r} \\ 0 & \text{if} \quad q \geq \bar{q}_{nc,r}, \end{cases} \qquad (7.68)$$

$$K_{2,nc,r}^{opt} = 0 \forall q, \qquad (7.69)$$

$$B_{1,nc,r}^{opt} = B_{2,nc,r}^{opt} \begin{cases} A + RR + \frac{q}{2} - \sqrt{q^{max}(A+RR)} \\ \qquad \text{if} \quad q < \bar{q}_{nc,r} \\ A + RR \quad \text{if} \quad q \geq \bar{q}_{nc,r}, \end{cases} \qquad (7.70)$$

where $\bar{q}_{nc,r}$, the upper threshold for q, is given by

$$\bar{q}_{nc,r} = \sqrt{4q^{max}(A+RR)}. \qquad (7.71)$$

For the lower threshold for q, i.e. for the level at which the bank borrows more reserves from the central bank than it needs to cover its own liquidity needs, the following is obtained:

$$\underline{q} = \underline{q}_{1,nc,r} = \underline{q}_{2,nc,r} = -2(A+RR) + \sqrt{4q^{max}(A+RR)}. \quad (7.72)$$

We will comment on these results with the help of Figs. 7.1 and 7.2.

Optimal Allocation of Required Reserves   Figure 7.1 illustrates the banks' optimal borrowing from the central bank and their optimal allocation of required reserves. As in the two-bank case, no bank will frontload its required reserve holdings. Consequently, at the aggregate level reserves are also provided smoothly across the reserve maintenance period even if the repo rate is raised. There are two reasons for this. The first reason is that the overlapping maturities imply that in the second period the banks can also cover their liquidity needs with the relatively cheap liquidity borrowed from the central bank in the first period. The second reason is that, despite the overlapping maturities, no central bank credit expires in the second period, due to the assumption that for all banks K_0 is equal to zero. This assumption implies that there is no additional liquidity needed in the second period. In both periods, the total liquidity needs of the banking sector can be covered with the relatively cheap first-period liquidity. (We will skip this assumption and discuss the consequences for the banks' optimal liquidity management in section 7.3.3.)

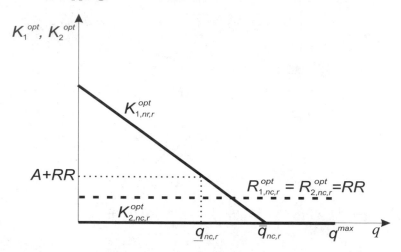

Fig. 7.1: Overlapping Maturities Model: Optimal Allocation of Required Reserves and Optimal Borrowing from the Central Bank if the Repo Rate Is Raised or Left Unchanged

Optimal Borrowing from the Central Bank   Figure 7.1 illustrates that optimal central bank borrowing in the first period implies that banks with q smaller than $\underline{q}_{1,nc,r}$ borrow more reserves from the central bank than they need to cover their own liquidity needs in order to place the excess liquidity in the interbank market. Banks with $\underline{q}_{1,nc,r} < q < \bar{q}_{1,nc,r}$ cover their liquidity needs at the central bank and in the interbank market, and banks with $q \geq \bar{q}_{1,nc,r}$ prefer to cover their total liquidity needs in the interbank market. Consequently, aggregate central bank borrowing in the first period is given by

$$\int_0^{q^{max}} K_1^{opt} g(q) dq = A + RR. \tag{7.73}$$

Obviously, this aggregate central bank borrowing in the first period allows for smooth aggregate provisions of required reserves over the maintenance period, i.e. it corresponds to the central bank's benchmark.[12] Since the maturity of $K_{1,nc,r}$ lasts into the second period, and since liquidity needs do not change (reserves are provided smoothly, autonomous factors are assumed to be A in both periods, and no central bank credit expires in the second period), no bank borrows from the central bank in the second period, i.e. $K_{2,nc,r} = 0$ for all q.

---

[12] For the definition of this benchmark see p. 48.

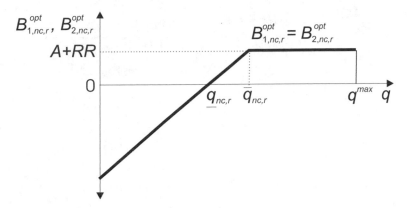

Fig. 7.2: Overlapping Maturities Model: Optimal Transactions in the Interbank Market if the Repo Rate Is Raised or Left Unchanged

Optimal Transactions in the Interbank Market Figure 7.2 illustrates the banks' optimal transactions in the interbank market. As in the current rate model banks with $q < \underline{q}_{1,nc,r}$ place liquidity in the interbank market, while banks with $q > \underline{q}_{1,nc,r}$ cover their liquidity needs either partially or totally in that market. The only difference to the current rate model is that - due to the overlapping maturities - the liquidity supply in the interbank market in the second period results from central bank credits which have already be granted in the first period.

Final Results for the Optimal Liquidity Management if the Repo Rate Is Cut

If the repo rate is cut, the final results for the banks' optimal liquidity management will be more complex. They are (c stands for cut):

$$
R_{1,c}^{opt} = \begin{cases} RR - (l_1 - l_2) & \text{if } q < \bar{q}_{1,c} \\[2mm] RR - \frac{l_1 - l_2}{3} + \frac{q}{3} - \sqrt{\frac{4q^{max}(A+RR)}{9} - \frac{2(l_1 - l_2)^2}{9}} \\ \quad \text{if } \bar{q}_{1,c} \le q < \bar{q}_{2,c} \\[2mm] RR & \text{if } \bar{q}_{2,c} \le q, \end{cases} \tag{7.74}
$$

$$R_{2,c}^{opt} = \begin{cases} RR + (l_1 - l_2) & \text{if} \quad q < \bar{q}_{1,c} \\ RR + \frac{l_1 - l_2}{3} - \frac{q}{3} + \sqrt{\frac{4q^{max}(A+RR)}{9} - \frac{2(l_1-l_2)^2}{9}} \\ \qquad \text{if} \quad \bar{q}_{1,c} \leq q < \bar{q}_{2,c} \\ RR & \text{if} \quad \bar{q}_{2,c} \leq q, \end{cases} \quad (7.75)$$

$$K_{1,c}^{opt} = \begin{cases} -(l_1 - l_2) - \frac{q}{2} + \sqrt{q^{max}(A + RR) - \frac{(l_1-l_2)^2}{2}} \\ \qquad \text{if} \quad q < \bar{q}_{1,c} \\ 0 \quad \text{if} \quad q \geq \bar{q}_{1,c}, \end{cases} \quad (7.76)$$

$$K_{2,c}^{opt} = \begin{cases} 2(l_1 - l_2) & \text{if} \quad q < \bar{q}_{1,c} \\ \dfrac{2\left(l_1 - l_2 - q + 2\sqrt{q^{max}(A+RR) - \frac{(l_1-l_2)^2}{2}}\right)}{3} & \text{if} \quad \bar{q}_{1,c} \leq q < \bar{q}_{2,c} \\ 0 & \text{if} \quad \bar{q}_{2,c} \leq q, \end{cases} \quad (7.77)$$

$$B_{1,c}^{opt} = B_{2,c}^{opt} = \begin{cases} A + RR + \frac{q}{2} - \sqrt{q^{max}(A + RR) - \frac{(l_1-l_2)^2}{2}} \\ \qquad \text{if} \quad q < \bar{q}_{1,c} \\ A + RR - \frac{l_1-l_2}{3} + \frac{q}{3} - \sqrt{\frac{4q^{max}(A+RR)}{9} - \frac{2(l_1-l_2)^2}{9}} \quad (7.78) \\ \qquad \text{if} \quad \bar{q}_{1,c} \leq q < \bar{q}_{2,c} \\ A + RR \quad \text{if} \quad q \geq \bar{q}_{2,c}, \end{cases}$$

where $\bar{q}_{t,c}$, the upper threshold for q is given by

$$\bar{q}_{1,c} = -2(l_1 - l_2) + \sqrt{4q^{max}(A + RR) - 2(l_1 - l_2)^2} \quad (7.79)$$

and

$$\bar{q}_{2,c} = l_1 - l_2 + \sqrt{4q^{max}(A + RR) - 2(l_1 - l_2)^2}. \quad (7.80)$$

The lower threshold for q, i.e. for the level at which the bank borrows more reserves from the central bank than it needs to cover its own liquidity needs, is given by[13]

$$\underline{q} = \underline{q}_{1,c} = \underline{q}_{2,c} = -2(A + RR) + \sqrt{4q^{max}(A + RR) - 2(l_1 - l_2)^2}. \quad (7.81)$$

As in the case where the interest rate is raised or left unchanged, we will illustrate these results graphically.

---

[13] The lower threshold $\underline{q}_{t,c}$ is obtained either by setting $(K_{t,c}^{opt}|q < \bar{q}_{1,c})$ (first line of the equations (6.54) and (6.55)) equal to $A + (R_{t,c}|q < \bar{q}_{t,c})$ and then solving for q, or by inserting e_t^* given by equation (6.51) into equations (6.33) and (6.34).

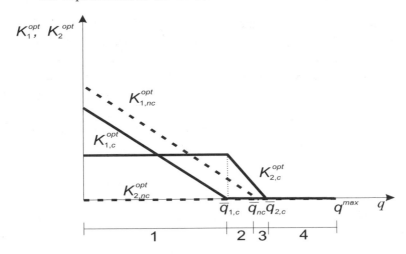

Fig. 7.3: Overlapping Maturities Model: Optimal Borrowing from the Central Bank if the Repo Rate Is Cut

Optimal Borrowing from the Central Bank   Figure 7.3 illustrates optimal borrowing from the central bank. The dotted lines represent optimal borrowing if there is no interest rate change, the thick solid lines show optimal borrowing if the repo rate is cut. Two features are immediately apparent. First, the interest rate cut implies that optimal central bank borrowing in the first period declines, and second, optimal central bank borrowing in the second period is different from zero. The reason for this is that the interest rate cut implies that banks can cover liquidity needs in the second period at a lower rate, which means that it is profitable to postpone reserve holdings as Fig. 7.4 shows. Consequently, compared to the case in which the repo rate is left unchanged, banks need less liquidity in the first period, but more in the second period. The figure reveals that fewer banks actually borrow liquidity from the central bank and those still borrowing borrow less liquidity. This implies that aggregate borrowing from the monetary authority in the first period falls below the central bank's benchmark which corresponds to the amount borrowed if the repo rate is left unchanged, since that amount allows for smooth aggregate provisions of the required reserves (dotted line in Fig. 7.3). It is worth mentioning that the deviation from the central bank's benchmark is even stronger than in the average rate model.[14] The reason for this is that the over-

---

[14] $(K_{1,c}^{opt,average}|q=0) > (K_{1,c}^{opt,overlapping}|q=0)$ and $\bar{q}_{1,c}^{overlapping} < \bar{q}_{1,c}^{average}$ as the equations (6.54), (6.57), (7.76), and (7.79) reveal. Since the slope of the $K_{1,c}^{opt}$-curves is the same in both models it is obvious that first-period aggregate central

lapping maturities imply that at the aggregate level an even higher amount of reserves is postponed as shown below. Next we will have a closer look at the slope of $K_{2,c}^{opt}(q)$. If the bank borrows from the central bank in both periods, i.e. if $q < \bar{q}_{1,c}$, the horizontal line indicates that $K_{2,c}^{opt}$ does not change in q. The reason being that when deciding on how to cover period-two liquidity needs, the bank compares the marginal costs of the period-two central bank credit with those of the period-one central bank credit because the maturity of the latter lasts into the second period. However, since q accrues in both alternatives, it does not influence the bank's decision. This is not the case, when deciding on how to cover period-one liquidity needs. Then, the two alternatives to be compared are borrowing from the central bank versus borrowing in the interbank market, and a decreasing q makes borrowing from the central bank less attractive, i.e. $K_{2,c}^{opt}$ is decreasing in q. The same argument holds when the bank borrows liquidity from the central bank only in the second period ($\bar{q}_{1,c} \leq q < \bar{q}_{2,c}$). Then, the alternative is also borrowing in the interbank market which again means that a decreasing q makes central bank borrowing less beneficial so that there is also a negative slope. Furthermore, the slope given by $\partial K_{2,c}^{opt}/\partial q$ for $q < \bar{q}_{2,c}$ is steeper than the one given by $\partial K_{1,c}/\partial q$ for $q < \bar{q}_{1,c}$ because liquidity needs decrease in the interval $[\bar{q}_{1,c}, \bar{q}_{2,c}]$ due to a decreasing $R_{2,c}^{opt}$ as Fig. 7.4 illustrates.

Optimal Allocation of Required Reserves   In Fig. 7.4, the thin solid lines represent the optimal allocation of required reserves in the average rate model, the thick solid lines illustrate the optimal allocation in the overlapping maturities model. The dotted line refers to the benchmark case. The figure illustrates that *at the aggregate level* the overlapping maturities reinforce the postponement of the required reserve holdings. Looking at Fig. 7.4, we will comment on the optimal allocation of required reserves in more detail, by answering the following three questions and by discussing the slope of the $R_t^{opt}(q)$-curves.

Why will the overlapping maturities reinforce the problem of uneven provisions of required reserves if $q < \bar{q}_{1,c}$?   Banks with $q < \bar{q}_{1,c}$ borrow liquidity from the central bank in both periods. This implies that they have two reasons for postponing their reserves. The first reason is the same as in the average rate model. Due to the remuneration of reserves at the average of l_1 and l_2 their marginal

---

bank borrowing in the average rate model exceeds the one in the overlapping maturities model.

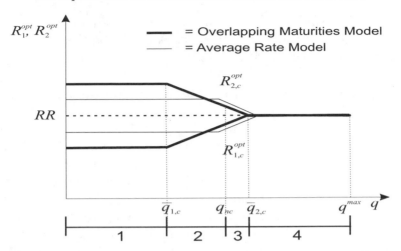

Fig. 7.4: Overlapping Maturities Model: Optimal Allocation of Required Reserves if the Repo Rate Is Cut

revenues of holding reserves will decrease in both periods while their marginal costs will only decrease in the second period. Consequently, optimal intertemporal behaviour requires holding more reserves in the second than in the first period. The second reason is that the maturity of the relatively expensive first-period credit lasts into the second period. This implies that for these banks ($q < \bar{q}_{1,c}$) it is beneficial to postpone *even more* reserves since this reduces the liquidity needs in the first period, so that the banks have to borrow less first-period liquidity from the central bank. Since the second reason does not exist in the average rate model, the overlapping maturities reinforce the problem of uneven provisions of the required reserves.

Why will banks fulfil their reserve requirements smoothly if $q \geq \bar{q}_{2,c}$? Banks with $q \geq \bar{q}_{2,c}$ borrow liquidity in neither period from the central bank, but they cover their total liquidity needs in both periods in the interbank market. Intertemporal optimality requires *net* marginal costs of holding collateral to be the same in both periods, and for these banks this requirement will be fulfilled if R_1 equals R_2: The banks' marginal revenues of holding reserves are the same in both periods due to their remuneration at the average of l_1 and l_2. Their marginal costs consist of interest payments in the interbank market and transaction costs. The former are also the same in both periods since e_1^* equals e_2^*. Consequently, transaction costs must also be the same in both periods which is achieved by transacting the same amount in both periods due to the convex form of the transaction cost function. This means that liquidity needs of these banks must be the same in both periods which implies that R_1^{opt} must equal R_2^{opt}.

Why may the postponing effect be dampened in the interval $[\bar{q}_{1,c}, \bar{q}_{2,c}]$**?**   Banks with $\bar{q}_{1,c} \leq q < \bar{q}_{2,c}$ borrow liquidity from the central bank in the second period only. Figure 7.4 shows that in this interval the overlapping maturities do not imply that all banks postpone more reserves but that there are also banks which actually postpone fewer. However, the latter is not unambiguous. In this interval it *may* be that the overlapping maturities imply that some banks postpone fewer reserves as illustrated with the figure, but it may also be the case that all banks in this interval postpone more reserves. The crucial point is that the effect of the overlapping maturities on e_2^* and, therefore, on the spread between e_2^* and l_2 is not unambiguous (see pages 137 to 138 for details). If the spread is higher in the average rate model, central bank borrowing will be relatively cheaper than in the overlapping maturities model. This means that in the average rate model there are banks which will borrow more reserves from the central bank in order to postpone a higher amount of reserves and more banks will borrow reserves from the central bank in order to postpone reserves ($\bar{q}_{2,c}^{average} > \bar{q}_{2,c}^{overlapping}$). In this case, which is illustrated in the figure, the postponing effect is stronger in the average rate model. If, on the other hand, the spread between e_2^* and l_2 is higher in the overlapping maturities model, analogously the postponing effect will be stronger in that model. However, even if in the interval $[\bar{q}_{1,c}^{average}, \bar{q}_{2,c}^{average}]$ the postponing effect is dampened, on aggregate the overlapping maturities will still reinforce the postponing of the required reserves. In the first period, aggregate central bank borrowing as well as total transactions in the interbank market are smaller than in the average rate model (see pages 131 and 135). Consequently, the total liquidity needs of the banking sector are smaller in this overlapping maturities model. The only reason this can be is that at the aggregate level more reserves are postponed.

Slope of the $R_t^{opt}(q)$**-curves.**   If $q < \bar{q}_{1,c}$, the bank will borrow from the central bank in both periods, i.e. q accrues in both periods, so that the optimal intertemporal allocation of reserves does not change in q. If $q \geq \bar{q}_{2,c}$, the bank will not borrow from the central period in any period, so that in this case the optimal intertemporal allocation of reserves also does not change in q. However, if $\bar{q}_{1,c} < q \leq \bar{q}_{2,c}$, the bank will borrow from the monetary authority only in the second period, i.e. opportunity costs of holding collateral only accrue in the second period and, therefore, have an impact on the optimal allocation. The lower q is the more liquidity the bank borrows from the monetary authority, implying that $R_{2,c}^{opt}$ increases and that $R_{1,c}^{opt}$ decreases in q.

Optimal Transactions in the Interbank Market   Figure 7.5 illustrates the banks' optimal transactions in the interbank market in case the repo rate is cut. The figure shows that in both periods the

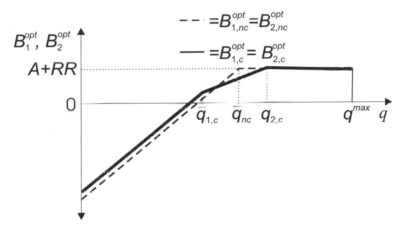

Fig. 7.5: Overlapping Maturities Model: Optimal Transactions in the Interbank Market if the Repo Rate Is Cut

volume of transactions is smaller when compared to a situation where the repo rate is left unchanged. In the first period, this is simply due to the reduced liquidity needs of the banking sector, a consequence of postponing reserves. In the second period, the postponing implies that intermediation becomes more expensive so that, as in the average rate model, a disintermediation takes place (see p. 91 for details). When comparing the optimal transactions in the interbank market with those in the average rate model, we find that the overlapping maturities imply that the decline in transaction volumes is even stronger.[15] The reason is that at the aggregate level, in this overlapping maturities model, more

---

[15] In the average rate model, the absolute value of interbank market transactions at point $q = 0$ is higher than in the overlapping maturities model: $[(|B_t^{opt,overlapping}|)|q = 0] < [(|B_t^{opt,average}|)|q = 0]$ and $q_{t,c}^{overlapping} < q_{t,c}^{average}$ as the equations (6.56), (6.59), (6.56), and (7.81) reveal. Since the slope of the $B_{t,c}^{opt}$-curves is the same in both models it is obvious that the total transaction

reserves are postponed. This means that in the first period, liquidity needs are even smaller and in the second period intermediation is even more expensive.

Equilibrium Interbank Market Rate: Discussion

In this section, we will discuss the equilibrium interbank market rate e_t^* given by the equations (7.65) and (7.66) in more detail. We will show that e_t^* reflects the banks' marginal costs of placing liquidity in the interbank market. Furthermore, we will demonstrate that the interbank market rate will be smoothed and that the sum of the spreads between the interbank market rate and the repo rate $\sum_{t=1}^{2} s_t$ will decrease if the repo rate is changed.

Marginal Costs of Placing Liquidity in the Interbank Market
If the repo rate is raised or is left unchanged, banks will not borrow any liquidity from the central bank in the second period. Therefore, the banks' marginal costs of placing liquidity in the interbank market do not depend on l_2, they are given by

$$MC_{t,r}^{ibm} = l_1 + q + pK_{1,nc,r}^{opt} - zB_{t,nc,r}^{opt}. \qquad (7.82)$$

If the repo rate is cut, the banks which place liquidity in the interbank market will borrow from the central bank in the second period so that l_2 influences their marginal costs. The maturity of the first-period credit lasts into the second period which implies that l_2 influences the banks' marginal costs of placing liquidity in the interbank market not only in the second but also in the first period (for details, see comments in the two-bank case on p. 122). In the first period, the banks' marginal costs of placing liquidity in the interbank market are given by

$$MC_{1,c}^{ibm} = (2l_1 - l_2) + q + pK_{1,c}^{opt} - zB_{1,c}^{opt}, \qquad (7.83)$$

and in the second period by

$$MC_{2,c}^{ibm} = l_2 + q + p(K_{1,c}^{opt} + K_{2,c}^{opt}) - zB_{2,c}^{opt}. \qquad (7.84)$$

The first three terms represent the banks' marginal costs of borrowing the relevant liquidity from the central bank, the last term represents the marginal transaction costs. Setting p and z equal to one and inserting the equilibrium values for $K_{1,nc,r}^{opt}$, $B_{t,nc,r}^{opt}$, $K_{t,c}^{opt}$ and $B_{2,c}^{opt}$ given by the

---

volumes in the average rate model exceed those in the overlapping maturities model.

first line of the equations (7.68), (7.70), (7.76), (7.77), and (7.78), the following is obtained

$$MC_{t,nc,r}^{ibm} = -(A + RR) + l_1 + \sqrt{4q^{max}(A + RR)} = e_{t,nc,r}^* \quad (7.85)$$

and that

$$MC_{t,c}^{ibm} = -(A + RR) + l_1 + \sqrt{-2(l_1 - l_2)^2 + 4q^{max}(A + RR)} = e_{t,c}^* \quad (7.86)$$

which confirms that e_t^* reflects the banks' marginal costs of placing liquidity in the interbank market. The equations (7.85) and (7.86) show that for $l_1 = l_2$ the expression for e_t^* is the same as in the current rate model (see equation (5.52)). Consequently, the impact of a change in A, RR, q^{max}, or l_t at the beginning of the maintenance period so that $l_1 = l_2$ on e_t^* is also the same, so concerning the analysis of the impact of a change in these variables on e_t^* we refer the reader to p. 65 and focus on the case where the repo rate is cut within the reserve maintenance period so that $l_1 \neq l_2$.

The Impact of a Change in the Repo Rate within the Reserve Maintenance Period   If the repo rate is raised, banks do not borrow any liquidity from the central bank at the rate l_2. Consequently, the interbank market rate is not affected by this change in the repo rate in *that* reserve maintenance period. (In section 7.3.3 we will show that this result will change if we skip our assumption that K_0 is equal to zero.) The more interesting case is the impact of a cut in the repo rate on the equilibrium interbank market rate. Looking at equation (7.86) reveals the following. First, contrary to the two-bank case, l_2 will influence the interbank market rates (compare equations (7.61) and (7.87)). Second, a decrease in the repo rate implies a decrease in e_1^* and e_2^* to the same extent:

$$\frac{\partial c_{1,c}^*}{\partial l_2} = \frac{\partial e_{2,c}^*}{\partial l_2} = \frac{l_1 - l_2}{\sqrt{\frac{-(l_1-l_2)^2}{2} + q^{max}(A + RR)}} > 0, \quad (7.87)$$

i.e., the equilibrium interbank market rate is smoothed. Third, it is ambiguous whether the decrease in e_t^* is stronger in the average rate model or in the overlapping maturities model (compare equations (6.69) and (7.87)). The driving force behind the second aspect is again that reserves are remunerated at the average of l_1 and l_2, so we refer the reader for details to p. 83 and comment only on the first aspect and on the third aspect. The difference to the two-bank case is due to the fact that if a continuum of banks is considered, the total volume of interbank market transactions will decrease (see p. 135). This has, due to the convex form of the transaction cost function, a negative impact on the banks' marginal costs of placing liquidity in the interbank market and, therefore, on the equilibrium interbank market rate. The negative effect on e_t^* leads us to the third aspect. In the overlapping maturities model, e_t^* will only decrease because of this marginal transaction cost effect. In the average rate model, there is an additional effect. The equilibrium interbank market rate will also decrease because marginal interest payments to the central bank decrease. Since this marginal interest cost effect does not exist in the overlapping maturities model[16] and since the marginal transaction cost effect is higher in that model,[17] it is ambiguous in which model the overall decrease in e_t^* will be stronger if the repo rate is cut. If the difference in the transaction cost effect is relatively high, while the marginal interest cost effect is relatively small, the decrease in e_t^* will be stronger in the overlapping maturities model and vice versa. Due to the convex form of the transaction cost function, the difference in the marginal transaction cost effect will be relatively high if total liquidity needs $(A + RR)$ are relatively high. The marginal interest cost effect will be relatively high if there is a relatively strong decrease in the repo rate. Consequently, if liquidity needs $(A + RR)$ are relatively high and if the change in the repo rate $(l_1 - l_2)$ is relatively small, the decline in the interbank market rate rate will be stronger in the overlapping maturities. Formally, this result is confirmed by a comparison of the equations (6.69) and (7.87), and it is illustrated by the numerical example given in the appendix. Since the described negative effect on e_t^* is a result of the postponement of reserves (if it were not for the postponement of reserves, there would not be a decline in total transactions in the interbank market and, therefore, in marginal transaction costs), banks which actually do not postpone reserves by themselves also benefit from the reserve shifting of the other banks. They face lower interest costs.

Spread between the Interbank Market Rate and the Repo Rate   If the repo rate is raised so that $l_1 < l_2$, the equilibrium interbank market rate will not change in that reserve maintenance period. This implies that the spread between the equilibrium interbank market

---

[16] Compare the second term on the right hand side of the equations (6.68) and (7.86).

[17] The marginal transaction cost effect is higher in the overlapping maturities model because the decline in the total volume of transactions in the interbank market is stronger which is a result of the higher amount of reserves postponed in the overlapping maturities model (see pages 91 and 135.)

rate and the repo rate remains the same in the first period but that it increases in the second period. Consequently, the sum of the spreads $(s_1 + s_2)$ increases (see the appendix for a numerical example). We have shown that if the repo rate is cut so that $l_1 > l_2$, the equilibrium interbank market rate will decrease in both periods. This decrease in e_t^* only results from the postponement of reserves since this implies a reduction in total transactions in the interbank market and, therefore, in marginal transaction costs of placing liquidity in the interbank market. If it were not for the postponement of reserves, aggregate central bank borrowing in the first period would be equal to $(A + RR)$, and in the second period it would be equal to zero. Moreover, the banks' marginal costs of placing liquidity in the interbank market and, therefore, e_t^* would be the same as if the repo rate had not been changed as given by equation (7.85), i.e. the equilibrium interbank market rate would not change in that maintenance period despite the change in the repo rate. However, due to the postponement of reserves the e_t^* decreases in both periods, i.e. the postponing of reserves also implies that the spread between the interbank market rate and, therefore, also the sum of the spreads $(s_1 + s_2)$ decrease. The numerical example given in the appendix illustrates this result. The result that the postponing of reserves reduces the sum of the spreads is important when discussing to what extent banks are affected differently by a monetary policy impulse in form of a cut in the repo rate which we will do in the next section.

The Impact of Monetary Policy Impulses

Again monetary policy impulses can be initiated by an interest rate change or a change in reserve requirements. The impact of a change in reserve requirements as well as of a change in the repo rate at the beginning of the maintenance period so that $l_1 = l_2$ on the banks' liquidity costs is the same as in the current rate model. Hence, we will focus on the impact of an interest rate change within the maintenance period.

If the repo rate is raised, all banks will provide their reserves smoothly. This implies that the change in the banks' net minimal liquidity costs is the same for all banks. It is given by

$$(V_1 | l_1 = l_2) - (V_1 | l_1 < l_2) = -RR(l_1 - l_2) > 0 \forall q. \qquad (7.88)$$

Equation (7.88) shows that all banks *benefit* from the increase in the repo rate in that reserve maintenance period. The reason for this is, that in the second period no bank borrows relatively expensive liquidity from the central bank, i.e. their liquidity costs do not increase, while their revenues increase due to the remuneration of their reserve holdings at the average of l_1 and l_2.

However, if the repo rate is cut, banks will be affected differently by the monetary policy impulse since their benefits from postponing reserves differ. If reserves are not postponed, all banks will be affected in the same way:

$$(V_1|l_1 = l_2) - \sum_{t=1}^{2}(C_t|l_1 \neq l_2; R_1 = R_2) = -RR(l_l - l_2)\forall q. \quad (7.89)$$

The first term represents minimal net liquidity costs if the repo rate is not changed, the second shows total net liquidity costs if the repo rate is cut, but where banks nevertheless provide their reserves smoothly. Equation (7.89) reveals that in this case all banks "suffer" in that maintenance period from the interest rate cut. The reason for this is that no bank borrows any liquidity from the central bank in the second period due to the two-period maturity of $K_{1,c}^{opt}$. This means that despite the cut in the repo rate their liquidity costs do not change but only their benefits. The latter decrease due to the remuneration at the average of l_1 and l_2. The result given by equation (7.89) allows us to determine the banks' cost advantage from postponing reserves. As in the average rate model, we divide the banks into four groups. We will present the results formally first before commenting on them in more detail with the help of Fig. 7.6.

First Group   The banks of the first group will borrow liquidity in both periods from the central bank if the repo rate is cut, and they will borrow from the central bank in the first period only if the repo rate is left unchanged (see section 1 in Fig. 7.3). The change in their minimal liquidity costs is given by

$$(V_1|l_1 = l_2, q < \bar{q}_{nc}) - (V_1|l_1 > l_2; q < \bar{q}_{1,c})$$
$$= -R(l_1 - l_2) \qquad (7.90)$$
$$+ (2(A + RR) + q)(\bar{q}_{nc} - \bar{q}_{1,c} - 2(l_1 - l_2)).$$

Second Group   The second group will borrow from the central bank in the first period if the repo rate is not changed, but if the repo rate is cut, they will demand liquidity from the monetary authority only in the second period (see section 2 in Fig. 7.3). The change in their minimal liquidity costs is given by

$$(V_1|l_1 = l_2; q < \bar{q}_{nc}) - (V_1|l_1 > l_2; \bar{q}_{1,c} \leq q < \bar{q}_{nc})$$
$$= -RR(l_1 - l_2)$$
$$+(l_1 - l_2)^2 \tag{7.91}$$
$$+\frac{4(3(A+RR)+\bar{q}_{1,c})(l_1-l_2)+4(3(A+RR)+q)(\bar{q}_{nc}-\bar{q}_{2,c})-(q-\bar{q}_{nc})^2}{6}.$$

Third Group   The third group will not borrow from the central bank in any period if the repo rate is left unchanged, but if the rate is cut, they will borrow in the second period (see section 3 in Fig. 7.3). The change in their minimal liquidity costs is given by

$$(V_1|l_1 = l_2; q \geq \bar{q}_{nc}) - (V_1|l_1 > l_2; \bar{q}_{nc} \leq q < \bar{q}_{2,c})$$
$$= -RR(l_1 - l_2)$$
$$+(l_1 - l_2)^2 \tag{7.92}$$
$$+\frac{2(3(A+RR)+\bar{q}_{1,c})(l_1-l_2)+2(3(A+RR)+q)(\bar{q}_{nc}-\bar{q}_{2,c})+(q-\bar{q}_{nc})^2}{3}.$$

Fourth Group   And finally, the fourth group will not borrow in any period from the central bank independently of a change in the repo rate. The change in the minimal liquidity costs of this group is given by

$$(V_1|l_1 = l_2; q \geq \bar{q}_{nc}) - (V_1|l_1 > l_2; q \geq \bar{q}_{2,c})$$
$$= -RR(l_1 - l_2) \tag{7.93}$$
$$+2(A + RR)(\bar{q}_{nc} - q_{1,c} - 2(l_1 - l_2)).$$

The comparison of the results given by the equations (7.90) to (7.93) with the one given by equation (7.89) shows that all banks benefit from the postponement of required reserve holdings, even those banks which actually do not postpone reserves (the third line and - if existent - the fourth line of the equations from (7.90) to (7.93) have a positive sign). However, the equations also show that this cost advantage depends on q which implies that banks are affected differently by a monetary policy impulse in form of an interest rate cut. We analyze the cost advantage in more detail with the help of Fig. 7.6.

The banks in the first group benefit for two reasons from the postponing of their required reserves. First, due to the remuneration of reserves at the average of l_1 and l_2, the postponing of reserves into the second period implies for these banks that holding reserves generates net interest revenues. Second, due to the overlapping maturities, postponing reserves for them means a further reduction in interest payments

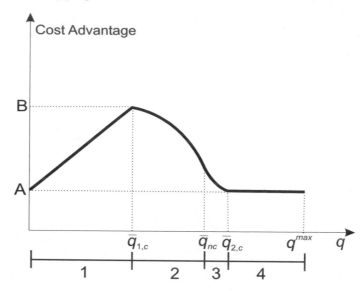

Fig. 7.6: Overlapping Maturities Model: Advantage of Postponing Required Reserves

to the central bank, because they can replace in the second period a part of the relatively expensive first-period credit with the relatively cheap second period credit. Although within this group all banks postpone the same amount of reserves, the banks with a relatively high q benefit more from the postponement of reserves. The reason is - as in the average rate model - the reduced sum of the spreads $(s_1 + s_2)$.[18]

In this overlapping maturities model, the equilibrium interbank market rate would not change if the banks did not postpone their reserve holdings (for details see pages 137 and 138). However, cost minimizing behaviour requires the postponement of reserves which leads to a decline in the interbank market rate. This decrease in the interbank market rate implies that the group-four banks also benefit from the reserve shifting, although they do not postpone reserves themselves. Since the banks in this group do not borrow from the monetary authority in any period, their cost advantage does not change in q.

The banks in the second and third group, on the other hand, borrow from the central bank only in the second period. In these groups the amount of postponed reserves is decreasing in q (see Fig. 7.4). The

---

[18] For an explanation as to why the sum of the spreads $(s_1 + s_2)$ is reduced in this overlapping maturities model, see p. 138. For details as to why a reduced sum of the spreads implies that the cost advantage from postponing reserves increases in q, we refer the reader to p. 101.

fewer reserves are postponed the smaller is the cost advantage of the reserve shifting. This explains the negative slope of the cost advantage curve for these two groups. The reason for the different slope of the cost advantage curve in these two groups is the same as in the average rate model so with regards to this aspect the reader is referred to p. 103.

What has been shown so far is that in the overlapping maturities model as well as in the average rate model banks are affected differently by a monetary policy impulse in form of a cut in the repo rate. A remaining interesting point to analyze is in which model the problem is bigger, i.e. whether the overlapping maturities reinforce this problem. We measure this problem with the difference in the cost advantages between those banks which benefit the most and those which benefit the least from the postponement of reserves. We denote this difference in the cost advantages by DCA. In Figs. 6.6 and 7.6 this difference is given by the distance $\overline{AB}$. The banks which benefit most from postponing the required reserves are those which have a q which is equal to $\bar{q}_{1,c}$: They postpone the highest amount of required reserves without borrowing relatively expensive liquidity from the central bank in the first period. The banks of the fourth group benefit the least from postponing the reserves. They do not postpone reserves themselves, they benefit only from the decreased interbank market rate. For both types of banks the cost advantage is higher in the overlapping maturities model than in the average rate model. In order to determine whether the problem that banks are affected differently by the monetary policy impulse is reinforced by the overlapping maturities, we analyze for which of the two types of banks the additional cost advantage is higher. If it is higher for the $\bar{q}_{1,c}$-banks, the problem is reinforced; if it is higher for the group-four banks, it will be dampened. However, when comparing the additional cost advantage for both types of banks it shows that it is ambiguous for which type it is higher. The additional cost advantage of the group-four banks results from the stronger relevant decrease in e_t^* in the overlapping maturities model than in the average rate model. The *relevant* decrease in e_t^* is the decrease due to the postponing of reserves.[19] The additional cost advantage of the $\bar{q}_{1,c}$-banks results from this stronger decrease in e_t^* too, but they benefit less from this effect

---

[19] In both models, the interbank market rate will decrease if the repo rate is cut and it is ambiguous in which model the total decrease will be stronger. However, the decrease in e_t^* which is due to the postponement of reserves, is the transaction cost effect and this effect is unambiguously stronger in the overlapping maturities model. In the average rate model, there will also be a decline in the interbank market rate because marginal interest payments to the central banks decrease,

because contrary to the group-four banks they do not cover their total liquidity needs in the interbank market. However, in addition to the decrease in e_t^* they benefit from postponing a higher amount of reserves (see Fig. 7.4 which illustrates that the amount of reserves which is postponed by the $\bar{q}_{1,c}$-banks is higher in the overlapping maturities model than in the average rate model).

Consequently, if the decrease in e_t^*, which is due to the postponing of reserves, is relatively strong and if the cut in the repo rate is relatively small, the additional cost advantage in the overlapping maturities model will be higher for the group-four banks than for the $\bar{q}_{1,c}$-banks. In this case, the problem that banks are affected differently by a monetary policy impulse in the form of an interest rate cut will be dampened in the overlapping maturities model. The distance $\overline{AB}$ in the Figs. 6.6 and 7.6 will be longer in the average rate model. However, if the decrease in e_t^*, which results from the postponing of reserves, is relatively small and if the cut in the repo rate is relatively large, the additional cost advantage in the overlapping maturities model will be higher for $\bar{q}_{1,c}$-banks. In this case the problem that banks are affected differently by the monetary policy impulse will be reinforced in the overlapping maturities model. The distance $\overline{AB}$ in the Figs. 6.6 and 7.6 will be smaller in the average rate model.

The decrease in e_t^* due to the postponing of reserves will be strong if there is a strong decrease in the marginal transaction costs of placing liquidity in the interbank market. This will be the case if total liquidity needs $(A + RR)$ are relatively high, which is a result of the convex form of the transaction cost function. Consequently, the problem that banks are affected differently by the monetary policy impulse will be dampened in the overlapping maturities model if total liquidity needs are relatively high and if the change in the repo rate is relatively small and vice versa. This result is confirmed by equation (7.94):[20]

$$DCA^{overl.} - DCA^{average}$$

$$= \bar{q}_{1,c}^{overl.}\left(\bar{q}_{nc} - \sqrt{4q^{max}(A + RR) - 2(l_1 - l_2)^2}\right)$$

$$-\bar{q}_{1,c}^{average}\left(\bar{q}_{nc} - \sqrt{4q^{max}(A + RR) - \frac{(l_1-l_2)^2}{2}}\right) \gtreqless 0.$$

$$(7.94)$$

---

but this decrease in e_t^* is not related to the postponement of reserves. For details see pages 137 to 138.

[20] In equation (7.94), $\bar{q}_{1,c}^{overl.} < \bar{q}_{1,c}^{average}$ but $(\bar{q}_{nc}-\sqrt{4q^{max}(A + RR) - 2(l_1 - l_2)^2}) > (\bar{q}_{nc} - \sqrt{4q^{max}(A + RR) - \frac{(l_1-l_2)^2}{2}})$.

7.3.3 Expiring Central Bank Credits within the Reserve Maintenance Period

Introduction

Finally, we will analyze the consequences for the banks' optimal liquidity management if a central bank credit expires within the reserve maintenance period, i.e. we will skip the assumption that K_0 is equal to zero for all banks. We have argued that this assumption implies that all banks will provide their reserve requirements smoothly and that the banks' borrowing from the central bank will not deviate from the central bank's benchmark despite an increase in the repo rate (see p. 119). Due to the two-period maturity of K_1, the banks can cover their total liquidity needs in both periods with the relatively cheap first-period central bank credits, i.e. they have no incentive to frontload reserves. However, this will not be the case if $K_0 > 0$ expires after the first period. Then, a new loan has to be taken out from the central bank - at the higher rate. We will show that this implies frontloading of reserves and a deviation of central bank borrowing from the central bank's benchmark.

Equilibrium Interbank Market Rate

We will restrict our analysis to the relatively simple two-bank case. Analyzing the banks' optimal liquidity management with overlapping maturities and expiring central bank credits within the reserve maintenance period for a continuum of heterogenous banks should be done in a model where the maintenance period consists of more than two periods. Otherwise so many assumptions concerning K_0 have to be made which make the model too complex. In the case of only two representative banks, A and B, we will simply assume that $0 < K_0^A \leq 2(A + RR)$ and that $K_0^B = 0$. The assumption $K_0^A \leq 2(A + RR)$ means that there is no excess liquidity in the banking sector which has to be absorbed by the central bank. Concerning the banks' central bank borrowing in the first and second period, we will assume again that $q^A < \underline{q}_t$ and that $q^B \geq \bar{q}_t$ for all t, i.e. bank A always places liquidity in the interbank market and bank B always covers its total liquidity needs in that market. Solving the banks' optimization problem in the same way as in section 7.2 and aggregating over the banks' optimal transactions in the interbank market, for the equilibrium interbank market rate

$$e_1^* = e_2^* = 3(A + RR) + q^A + l_1 \qquad (7.95)$$

is obtained. Comparing equation (7.95) with equation (7.40) reveals that the assumptions concerning K_0 have no impact on the equilibrium interbank market rate. It is the same independent of whether K_0 is equal to zero for all banks or whether it is strictly greater than zero for bank A and equal to zero for bank B. The reason is that bank A's marginal costs of placing liquidity in the interbank market, which are reflected by the equilibrium interbank market rate, are independent of K_0 as well as of l_0. In the first period, these costs are given by

$$MC_1^{A,ibm} = (l_1 + (l_1 - l_2)) + q^A + p(K_0^A + K_1^{A,opt}) - zB_1^{A,opt} \quad (7.96)$$

and in the second period by

$$MC_2^{A,ibm} = l_2 + q^A + p(K_1^{A,opt} + K_2^{A,opt}) - zB_2^{A,opt}. \quad (7.97)$$

The first term on the right hand side of these equations reflects bank A's marginal interest payments to the central bank,[21] the second and third term represent bank A's marginal opportunity costs of holding collateral, and the last term shows its marginal transaction costs of placing liquidity in the interbank market. The equations show that l_0 does not influence bank A's marginal costs of placing liquidity in the interbank market in either period. However, equation (7.96) shows that K_0^A influences marginal opportunity costs of holding collateral in the first period. This happens because the maturity of K_0^A lasts into the first period, so that assets used as collateral for K_0^A cannot be used as such in the first period for K_1^A (see the comments on equation (7.3) on p. 111 for more details). However, since $K_0^A > 0$ reduces $K_1^{A,opt}$ exactly by this amount (see equation (7.101)), for bank A's total marginal opportunity costs of holding collateral it plays no role whether the liquidity it places in the interbank market has been borrowed in the first period or borrowed before from the central bank, i.e. whether it is K_1^A-liquidity or K_0^A-liquidity. Setting p and z equal to one and inserting the results for $K_t^{A,opt}$ and $B_t^{A,opt}$ given by the equations (7.101) to (7.103) into the equations (7.96) and (7.97) leads to

$$MC_1^{A,ibm} = MC_2^{A,ibm} = 3(A + RR) + q^A + l_1 = e_t^* \quad (7.98)$$

which confirms that bank A's marginal costs of placing liquidity in the interbank market, and, therefore, the equilibrium interbank market rate, do not depend on the assumptions concerning K_0. Consequently, the determinants of e_t^* are also the same and we refer the

---

[21] Due to the two-period maturity of K_1^A, the interest rate of the second period also has to be taken into account when determining the marginal costs of placing liquidity in the interbank market, see p. 122 for details.

reader concerning the analysis of the impact of a change in A, RR, q^A or $(l_t | l_1 = l_2)$ to the pages 57 and 123.

However, we will comment on the impact of a change in the repo rate within the reserve maintenance period $(l_1 \neq l_2)$, i.e. we will briefly discuss why such a change in the repo rate left the equilibrium interbank market rate unchanged in that reserve maintenance period. In the $(K_0 = 0)$-case, the driving force behind this result is that the optimal bank behaviour requires the net marginal costs of holding reserves to be the same in both periods. So if the repo rate is cut, bank A will postpone so many reserves until in the first (second) period the higher (lower) marginal interest costs are exactly compensated by lower (higher) opportunity costs of holding collateral (see p. 123 for details). In this $(K_0^A) > 0$-case, the same argument will hold if the repo rate is cut. If the repo rate is raised, e_t^* will be independent of l_2 in the $(K_0 = 0)$-case because bank A borrows no liquidity from the central bank at that rate so that its marginal costs of placing liquidity in the interbank market also do not depend on l_2. In the $(K_0 > 0)$–case, this argument does not hold in general, because as equation (7.102) shows, bank A may borrow from the central bank at that rate. However, then the argument given for the interest rate cut holds analogously. If the repo rate is raised, Bank A will frontload so many reserves until in the first (second) period the lower (higher) marginal interest costs are exactly compensated by higher (lower) opportunity costs of holding collateral (for details see analogously the discussion for an interest rate cut given on p. 123).

Optimal Liquidity Management

For the banks' optimal liquidity management he following final results are obtained:

$$R_1^{A,opt} = RR - (l_1 - l_2),\tag{7.99}$$

$$R_2^{A,opt} = RR + (l_1 - l_2),\tag{7.100}$$

$$K_1^{A,opt} = 2(A + RR) - K_0^A - (l_1 - l_2),\tag{7.101}$$

$$K_2^{A,opt} = \begin{cases} K_0^A + 2(l_1 - l_2) \\ \quad \text{if } l_1 \geq l_2 \text{ or if } l_1 < l_2 \text{ and } K_0^A > |2(l_1 - l_2)| \\ 0 \quad \text{if } l_1 < l_2 \text{ and } K_0^A \leq |2(l_1 - l_2)|, \end{cases}\tag{7.102}$$

$$B_1^{A,opt} = B_2^{A,opt} = -RR - A, \tag{7.103}$$

$$R_1^{B,opt} = R_2^{B,opt} = RR, \tag{7.104}$$

$$K_1^{B,opt} = K_2^{B,opt} = 0, \tag{7.105}$$

and

$$B_1^{B,opt} = B_2^{B,opt} = A + RR. \tag{7.106}$$

If the repo rate is left unchanged or cut, the results will be the same as in the case where K_0 is assumed to be zero for all banks: If the repo rate is left unchanged, all banks will provide their reserve requirements smoothly and aggregate central bank borrowing will not deviate from the central bank's benchmark. If the repo rate is cut, bank A will postpone its holdings of required reserves and aggregate central bank borrowing falls below the central bank's benchmark. The only difference is that K_1^A is smaller and that K_2^A is bigger by the amount of K_0^A. Therefore, we refer the reader to section 7.3.1 for a more detailed analysis of these two cases and focus our analysis on the case where the repo rate is raised. In section 7.3.1, we have shown that the ($K_0 = 0$)-assumption implies that all banks provide their reserve requirements smoothly and that aggregate central bank borrowing corresponds to the central bank's benchmark despite an increase in the repo rate (see p. 119). In what follows, we demonstrate that assuming ($K_0^A > 0$) implies that reserves will be frontloaded and that aggregate demand for central bank credits will exceed the central bank's benchmark if the central bank raises the repo rate. The reason for this is the expiration of K_0^A at the end of the first period implies that if reserves are provided smoothly, liquidity needs in the second period cannot be covered totally with the relatively cheap liquidity borrowed from the central bank in the first period. The consequence is that bank A reduces its liquidity needs in the second period by frontloading the required reserves ($R_1^{A,opt} > R_2^{B,opt}$). Obviously, this implies that bank A borrows in the first period more liquidity from the central bank than it needs to fulfil its reserve requirements smoothly. Bank B does not frontload reserves. Its net marginal costs of holding reserves consist of marginal interest costs from its transactions in the interbank market, marginal transaction costs and marginal interest revenues. Its marginal interest costs as well as its marginal interest revenues of holding reserves are already the same in both periods (the interbank market rate is the same in both periods and reserves are remunerated at the average of l_1 and l_2 in both periods). Consequently, its marginal transaction costs must also be the same in both periods, which will only be achieved if reserves are provided smoothly because of the convex form of the transaction cost function. Since bank A frontloads its holdings of required reserves and bank B provides its required reserves smoothly over the reserve maintenance period, it is obvious that on aggregate required reserves are not provided smoothly and that aggregate central bank borrowing in the first period exceeds the central bank's benchmark amount.

Impact of Monetary Policy Impulses

Finally, we will have a look at the impact of a change in the repo rate on the banks' minimal net liquidity costs. The banks' change in these costs if the repo rate is cut or raised is given by

$$(V_1|l_1 = l_2)^A - (V_1|l_1 \neq l_2)^A$$
$$= -RR(l_1 - l_2) + K_0(l_1 - l_2) + (l_1 - l_2)^2 \qquad (7.107)$$

and

$$(V_1|l_1 = l_2)^B - (V_1|l_1 \neq l_2)^B = -RR(l_1 - l_2). \qquad (7.108)$$

The equations (7.107) and (7.108) reveal that if the repo rate is cut $(l_1 > l_2)$, the banks will be affected differently. Bank B faces, as in the case in which K_0 is equal to zero for all banks, higher net liquidity costs because its interest costs do not change (the interbank market rate remains the same), while its interest revenues decrease due to the remuneration of reserves at the average of l_1 and l_2. Bank A, on the other hand, also has lower interest revenues due to the remuneration at the average rate, but it also benefits from the interest rate cut for two reasons. First, as in the case in which K_0 is equal to zero for all banks, from postponing reserves (last term in equation (7.107)), and second from the expiration of K_0^A at the end of the first period (second term on the right hand side of equation (7.107)). The latter implies that bank A covers its liquidity needs in the second period with relatively cheap liquidity borrowed from the central bank in that period. Since this effect does not exist in the case where K_0 is equal to zero, the assumption $K_0^A > 0$ reinforces the problem that banks are affected differently by a monetary policy impulse in form of a cut in the repo rate (compare the equations (7.107) and (7.63)).

For discussing to what extent banks are affected differently by an increase in the repo rate, we make the plausible assumption that $K_0^A >$

$|l_1 - l_2|$. In this case, bank B unambiguously benefits from this monetary policy impulse since its liquidity costs do not change (the interbank market rates remain the same in that maintenance period), while its revenues increase due to the remuneration of the reserves at the average of l_1 and l_2. Bank A, on the other hand, additionally benefits from the frontloading of reserves (last term in equation (7.107)). However, the expiration of K_0^A in the second period implies a cost disadvantage for bank A (second term on the right hand side of equation (7.107)), because bank A has to take out a new loan from the central bank in the second period at the higher interest rate l_2. Since this effect on bank A's liquidity costs outweighs the effect from the reserve shifting, bank A benefits less than bank B from the monetary policy impulse or faces even additional costs. Since in case K_0^A is equal to zero, banks are not affected differently by a monetary policy impulse in form of an increase in the repo rate (see section 7.3.1), it is $K_0^A > 0$ which implies that banks are affected differently.

Summary

The following list summarizes the effects of the assumption that K_0^A is strictly greater than zero instead of that K_0 is equal to zero for all banks:

- The equilibrium interbank market rate is not influenced by the assumptions concerning K_0.
- As in the case where no central bank credit expires within the reserve maintenance period reserves will be provided smoothly and aggregate central bank borrowing will correspond to the central bank's benchmark if the repo rate is left unchanged.
- As in the case where no central bank credit expires within the reserve maintenance period, reserves will be postponed and aggregate central bank borrowing will fall below the central bank's benchmark in the first period if the repo rate is cut.
- Contrary to the case where no central bank credit expires within the reserve maintenance period, reserves will be frontloaded and aggregate central bank borrowing will exceed the central bank's benchmark in the first period if the repo rate is raised.
- The extent to which banks are affected differently by a monetary policy impulse in the form of a cut in the repo rate will be reinforced if $K_0^A > 0$.
- If $K_0^A > 0$ banks are affected differently by a monetary policy impulse in the form of an increase in the repo rate.

- As in the case where no central bank credit expires within the reserve maintenance period (two-bank case), the equilibrium interbank market rate does not change in that reserve maintenance period, i.e. there is no interest rate smoothing in the sense that the interbank market rate will already decrease (increase) before the central bank actually cuts (raises) the repo rate.

7.3.4 Rationing

So far, we have assumed that the central bank totally satisfies the banks' demand for reserves even if aggregate demand exceeds the central bank's benchmark. This subsection analyzes within the overlapping maturities model the bank's liquidity management if the central bank never provides more liquidity than its benchmark amount, i.e. if it rations liquidity when aggregate liquidity demand exceeds its benchmark. For the sake of simplicity, we restrict our analysis to the two-bank case. As we have shown in the overlapping maturities model, aggregate demand will only exceed the benchmark if the central bank raises the repo rate within the reserve maintenance period and if $K_0^A > 0$. Consequently, we can restrict our analysis to this case. As in the previous section, we assume that $0 < K_0^A \leq 2(A + RR)$ (for details see p. 145).

The central bank's benchmark amount is equal to $2(A+RR)-K_{t-1}^A$. Consequently, $K_1^A = \min[K_1^{A,opt}, 2(A + RR) - K_0^A]$. Solving the overlapping maturities model under the rationing assumption the following will be obtained for the banks' optimal liquidity management if the repo rate is raised ($l_1 < l_2$):

$$K_1^A = 2(A + RR) - K_0^A, \tag{7.109}$$

$$K_2^A = K_0^A, \tag{7.110}$$

$$B_1^{A,opt} = B_2^{A,opt} = -(A + RR), \tag{7.111}$$

$$K_1^{B,opt} = K_2^{B,opt} = 0, \tag{7.112}$$

$$B_1^{B,opt} = B_2^{B,opt} = A + RR, \tag{7.113}$$

$$R_1^{A,opt} = R_2^{A,opt} = R_1^{B,opt} = R_2^{B,opt} = RR. \tag{7.114}$$

These results show that, as in the average rate model, in both periods the *benchmark* amount of liquidity is provided via bank A to the banking sector,[22] and that in both periods the same amount of liquidity $(A + RR)$ is transacted in the interbank market. Moreover, on aggregate reserves are provided smoothly over the reserve maintenance period despite the increase in the repo rate.

However, as in the average rate model, the extent to which the banks are affected differently by the monetary policy impulse is higher when compared to the non-rationing case. If there is no rationing, bank B actually benefits from the increase in the repo rate, while bank A faces additional costs or at least benefits less than Bank B (see section 7.3.3). If the central bank rations liquidity, it is bank A which benefits from the increase in the repo rate, while bank B unambiguously faces additional costs:

$$V_1^A(l_2 = l_1) - V_1^A(l_1 < l_2)$$
$$= -(2A + 3RR - K_0^A)(l_1 - l_2) > 0 \tag{7.115}$$

$$V_1^B(l_2 = l_1) - V_1^B(l_1 < l_2) = (l_1 - l_2)(2A + RR) < 0. \tag{7.116}$$

The reason is the same as in the average rate model: The rationing implies an additional increase in the interbank market rate. From this increase bank A as a lender benefits, while bank B as a borrower suffers. The interbank market rate is, as in the average rate model, given by

$$e_1^* = e_2^* = l_2 + q_i + 3(A + RR). \tag{7.117}$$

The comparison of equation (7.117) with equation (7.95) reveals that the interbank market rate in the rationing case is higher since it is only determined by the higher repo rate l_2, while in the non-rationing case it is determined by the average of l_2 and l_2.[23] The comparison of the equations (7.115) and (7.116) with the equations (7.107) and (7.108) shows that the extent to which the banks are affected differently is higher with rationing.[24]

---

[22] The central bank's benchmark amount is equal to $2(A + RR) - K_{t-1}^A$. Consequently, at date 1, it is equal to $2(A + RR) - K_0^A$, and at date 2, it is equal to $2(A + RR) - K_1^A = K_0^A$.

[23] For the reason see the corresponding comments for the average rate model on p. 105.

[24] When comparing the equations it shows that the extent to which the banks are affected differently by the increase in the repo rate will be higher in the rationing case if $|-4(A + RR)| > |l_1 - l_2|$. This will be the case since $|l_1 - l_2| < K_0^A \leq 2(A + RR)$.

7.4 Summary

As in the Chaps. 5 and 6 we have considered a two-period model where we have first analyzed the optimal liquidity management of a single, price-taking bank. Decisive institutional features of this model - features in which this model differs from the other models presented in this work - are:

- required reserves are remunerated at the average of the repo rates valid in the current reserve maintenance period, and
- the maturities of central bank loans do overlap.

As in the previous chapters the bank minimizes net total liquidity costs across the two periods by choosing the optimal intertemporal allocation of the required reserves and the optimal borrowing from the monetary authority. After having solved this optimization problem, we have again assumed that the banking sector is heterogenous since banks differ in their marginal costs of obtaining funds from the central bank causing an interbank market to emerge. When setting liquidity supply in the interbank market equal to liquidity demand, we have derived the equilibrium interbank market rate and could present the following results of this average rate model (for a more detailed summary of the model framework, we refer the reader to the summary of the benchmark model given on p. 68):

- If the repo rate is cut within the reserve maintenance period, the overlapping maturities of central bank credits will reinforce the problem of uneven aggregate provisions of the required reserves. This implies that the central bank borrowing deviates even more from the central bank's benchmark and that the extent to which banks are affected differently by this monetary impulse is higher than in the average rate model.
- If the repo rate is raised within the reserve maintenance period, reserves will be provided unevenly and overlapping maturities will reinforce these uneven provisions if there are central bank credits expiring within the reserve maintenance period.
- If the repo rate is raised within the reserve maintenance period, the central bank borrowing in the first period will exceed the central bank's benchmark if there are central bank credits expiring within the reserve maintenance period. If the central bank totally satisfies this demand, the overlapping maturities reinforce the frontloading of the required reserves holdings which implies that the extent to which the banks are affected differently by a monetary impulse is

also higher with overlapping maturities. If the central bank does not totally satisfy this demand, but rations liquidity by providing only its benchmark amount, reserves are provided evenly across the maintenance period but the extent to which banks are affected differently is higher when compared to the non-rationing case.

- Banks are affected differently by a monetary impulse in the form of a change in the reserve requirements.
- Holding reserves is neither neutral with regard to interest costs and yields initiated by the central bank nor with regard to overall costs and yields which implies that banks face different overall costs of holding required reserves
- In the two-bank, non-rationing case, the overlapping maturities prevent a smoothing of the interbank market rate in the sense that the interbank market rate will already decrease (increase) before the central bank actually cuts (raises) the repo rate. If a continuum of banks is considered, there will only be a smoothing of the equilibrium interbank market rate if the repo rate is cut.

8

Implications for the Eurosystem's Operational Framework

This chapter presents the implications of the theoretical analysis for the Eurosystem's operational framework. We start with a comment on the implications for the interbank market rate in the euro area. Then, we focus on the question which of the three models presented (current rate model, average rate model, overlapping maturities model) most closely fulfills the requirements that should be met by Eurosystem's operational framework. We go on to evaluate the 2004-changes to the Eurosystem's monetary policy instruments. Finally, we suggest a further measure to improve the Eurosystem's operational framework.

8.1 Interbank Market Rate

In the euro area, banks face different marginal opportunity costs of holding the necessary collateral when borrowing liquidity from the central bank (see p. 14). According to our theoretical analysis, one consequence of this heterogeneity is the occurrence of a certain kind of intermediation: Banks with relatively low marginal opportunity costs borrow more liquidity from the central bank than they need to cover their own liquidity needs in order to lend the excess liquidity via the interbank market to banks with relatively high marginal costs. Indications that this kind of intermediation occurs in the euro area are the positive spread between the interbank market rate and the MRO-rate and that only a small fraction of credit institutions actually takes part in the MROs (see section 3.1).

Furthermore, our theoretical analysis has identified, inter alia, the autonomous factors as a determinant of the interbank market rate. If there is an increase in these factors, the interbank market rate will rise, even if the central bank restores neutral liquidity conditions. The reason is that the interbank market rate reflects the banks' marginal costs of placing liquidity in the interbank market and an increase in these factors, i.e. in the banking sectors' liquidity needs, implies that these costs increase because, inter alia, more collateral is required. Consequently, the above described intermediation becomes more expensive which is reflected with an increase in the interbank market rate (for details see p. 65). On average over the months May, June, and July 2005 the spread between the EONIA and the MRO-rate (minimum bid rate) was 7 basis points. On average over the months February, March, and April 2005, this spread stood at only 6 basis points.[1] According to our analysis, one explanation for the higher spread in the summer months is the increased stock of banknotes in circulation at this time which makes up the largest part of the autonomous factors in the euro area.[2]

8.2 Current Rate Model: Fulfils Requirements Most Closely

Requirements

When drawing the conclusions from our theoretical analysis for the Eurosystem's operational framework, we have considered the following requirements that the operational framework should meet:

- On aggregate, required reserves should be provided smoothly over the reserve maintenance period to enhance the buffer function of the minimum reserve system against temporary liquidity shocks.
- Holdings of the required reserves should not impose a competitive drawback for the banks in the euro area.
- Under- and overbidding behaviour in the MROs should be avoided.
- Banks should be treated equally (principal of equal treatment), i.e., they should not be affected differently by a monetary policy impulse due to the design of the operational framework.
- Monetary policy decisions should be fed through as precisely and quickly as possible to short term money market rates (principle of operational efficiency).

---

[1] Numbers are based on time series data published by the ECB and the Deutsche Bundesbank.
[2] For a description of the liquidity conditions and monetary policy operations during these summer months (see European Central Bank, 2005a, Box 2).

In Which Model Are the Requirements Most Closely Fulfilled?

The outcome of our theoretical analysis shows that in the *current rate model* presented in Chap. 5 the above listed requirements are fulfilled most closely: Even if the central bank changes its repo rate within the reserve maintenance period, required reserves will be provided smoothly over the reserve maintenance period and aggregate central bank borrowing will correspond to the central bank's benchmark, i.e., referring to the MROs, there will be no under- and overbidding behaviour.[3] Moreover, banks will not be affected differently by this monetary policy impulse. This makes the current rate model superior to the average rate model and to the overlapping maturities model. Generally, in these models a deviation of central bank borrowing from the central bank's benchmark, uneven provisions of required reserves, and an unequal treatment of banks will only be avoided if the repo rate is not changed within the reserve maintenance period. This reduces the flexibility of monetary policy and violates the principle of operational efficiency. Consequently, the average rate model and the overlapping maturities model leave the choice open between two evils: either one has to accept a deviation of central bank borrowing from the central bank's benchmark, uneven provisions of required reserves and an unequal treatment of banks or one has to accept a reduction in the flexibility of monetary policy. On the other hand, in the current rate model neither of these problems exists.

One may argue that the ECB can react to the underbidding behaviour by only providing its benchmark amount, i.e., by rationing liquidity. Then, reserves are provided evenly over the maintenance period. However, as we have shown, this rationing implies that the extent to which banks are affected differently by the monetary policy impulse is even higher. Consequently, in the average rate model as well as in the overbidding maturities model, the bank faces a trade off. Either it has to accept that reserves are provided unevenly over the maintenance period so that the buffer function of the minimum reserve system is impaired, or it has to accept an even stronger violation of its principle

---

[3] In the models presented in this work, banks do not bid in a tender procedure for central bank funds. However, transferring our model results to the Eurosystem's MROs, underbidding (overbidding) behaviour in the MROs correspond to a situation in the models where aggregate central bank borrowing falls below (exceeds) the central bank's benchmark (see also the ECB's definition of under- and overbidding given on p. 13).

of equal treatment. In the current rate model, this trade off does not exist.

Drawbacks to Accept

However, the current rate model also has its drawbacks, but these drawbacks have to be accepted as long as the MROs have to be based on collateral. The collateralization implies that holding the required reserves is costly despite their remuneration. The credit institutions will either have to bear the opportunity costs of holding collateral if they borrow the relevant liquidity from the central bank, or they have to bear additional interest costs if they borrow the liquidity in the interbank market. Since the opportunity costs of holding collateral differ across banks, banks face different costs when fulfilling their reserve requirements which *violates the Eurosystem's principle of equal treatment* (for the relevant theoretical analysis see p. 67). Furthermore, these costs of holding required reserves will impose a *competitive drawback* on the banks if they outweigh the possible benefits from the minimum reserve system (possible benefits from the stabilization of short-term interest rates). Analyzing whether there is a net benefit for the banking sector in the euro area from the minimum reserve system is beyond the scope of this work. But it should be noted that the costs could be reduced if it were not for the collateralization of central bank credits.[4] At the end of section 8.4 we will again address the problem of the collateralization of central bank credits.

8.3 Evaluation of the Changes to the Eurosystem's Operational Framework

Right Decision

In 2003, the governing council of the ECB decided to change its operational framework with effect from March 2004 (European Central Bank, 2003a). First, the timing of the reserve maintenance periods was adjusted so that the start of a new maintenance period is now aligned with the settlement day of the MRO following the governing council's

---

[4] In the theoretical analysis of this work, this would imply that net costs of holding required reserves are equal to zero, i.e. holding the required reserves is neutral with regard to overall costs and benefits. However, in practice holding the required reserves does not only impose the opportunity costs of holding collateral on the banks, but also the costs of managing reserve holdings.

meeting, where interest rate changes are normally decided on. Second, the maturity of the MROs has been shortened from two weeks to one week so that the maturities of two subsequent operations no longer overlap.

From the point of view of our theoretical analysis the decision to change the Eurosystem's operational framework has been correct. We have argued that overlapping maturities of central bank credits may lead to under- or overbidding behaviour, and we have identified two problems associated with this unbalanced bidding behaviour: a reduction in the buffer function of the minimum reserve system and a violation of the principle of equal treatment. The crucial point is that the underbidding/overbidding behaviour is combined with postponing/frontloading of the required reserves. This reserve shifting implies that there are periods in which aggregate reserve holdings are relatively low which reduces the buffer function of the minimum reserve system. Furthermore, the cost advantage from this reserve shifting differs between banks which violates the Eurosystem's principle of equal treatment since banks are affected differently by a monetary policy impulse. Note that the crucial point is not that banks face a different increase or decrease in liquidity costs after a monetary policy impulse, but that the different increase or decrease results from the design of the monetary policy instruments.

Section 3.3 has documented that underbidding behaviour in the MROs was combined with the postponing of the required reserves. However, when overbidding occurred a frontloading of the reserves could not be observed, as we would have expected from our theoretical analysis. The reason is that the ECB did not allot the necessary liquidity. The ECB did not allot the amount of liquidity the banking sector bid for, i.e. by rationing the ECB could avoid the above described problems related to overbidding behaviour. However, it should be noted that according to Nautz and Oechssler (2003) this rationing resulted in the "vanishing allotment quota", i.e. such rationing implies an explosion of the bidding behaviour (see p. 27 for details). Consequently, from a theoretical point of view, it was correct to reduce the maturity of the MROs from two weeks to one week.

When discussing the consequences of the redesign of the Eurosystem's operational framework, two effects should be commented on. These effects are the large increase in MRO-volumes (obviously, on average they have doubled) and the higher risk of forecast errors concerning autonomous factors at the end of a reserve maintenance period.

Concerning the first effect, two problems were seen prior to the implementation of the new framework (European Central Bank, 2003e). First, increased difficulties for the credit institutions to procure necessary collateral because the increased MRO-volumes imply an on average higher turnover of collateral. According to the ECB, this problem has not occurred, on the contrary, the shorter maturity of the MROs has even facilitated the credit institutions' collateral management (European Central Bank, 2005c). Second, the increase in the MRO-volumes may increase the operational risk in the event of technical problems during the bidding or allotment process. In its subsequent publications dealing with the redesigned framework the ECB no longer addresses this issue. Obviously, the disadvantage of the increased operational risk has been estimated to be smaller than the advantages of this change to the operational framework.

The second effect, a higher risk of forecast errors concerning autonomous factors at the end of a reserve maintenance period, is due to an on average longer forecasting horizon. Under the new framework, the allotment of the last MRO in a maintenance period always takes place eight days before the maintenance period ends. Whereas before the changes in the operational framework the last allotment took place on average four days before the end of the maintenance period (see p. 16). These forecast errors have actually occurred. In response to these errors the ECB has carried out a fine tuning operation on the last day of the reserve maintenance period in the majority of the reserve maintenance periods since November 2004.

The conduct of these fine-tuning operations has implied that the maturities of two subsequent central bank credit operations overlap again (the maturities of the MRO and the fine-tuning operation). However, considering the results of our theoretical analysis, the conduct of the fine-tuning operations should not induce strategic bidding behaviour in the last MRO of a maintenance period, i.e. they should not induce under- or overbidding behaviour, as long as the two operations are conducted at the same rate. So far, the rates have not differed significantly from each other. Since the implementation of the new framework, the *liquidity-providing* fine-tuning operations have been conducted as variable rate tenders with the same minimum bid rate as the MRO which was executed prior to the fine-tuning operation. The difference between the weighted average rate of these two operations was three basis points.[5] When *absorbing liquidity* from the banking sector, the ECB

---

[5] The time series data on which this number is based on is available on the ECB's website (www.ecb.int).

invited the credit institutions to place deposits with the Eurosystem at the minimum bid rate of the MRO which was conducted prior to the concerned fine-tuning operation. The difference on average between the weighted average rate and the minimum bid rate was five basis points.[6] Although these relatively small and uncertain interest rate differentials should not induce strategic bidding behaviour it must be acknowledged, that these interest rate differentials entail costs/benfits for the credit institutions taking part in the fine-tuning operations. And although these costs/benefits should be generally small,[7] a possibility to reduce them even further (note that these costs are finally due to forecast errors of the ECB) would be to conduct these operations at the weighted average rate of the MRO which was executed prior to the fine-tuning operation.

Is the Under- and Overbidding Problem Solved Under the New Framework?

According to our theoretical analysis, the under- and overbidding problem has been solved with the implementation of the new operational framework in March 2004 - as long as the governing council keeps to its self-commitment not to change interest rates within the reserve maintenance period which is an issue we will address in the next section. We have identified two causes for under- and overbidding behaviour: overlapping maturities of central bank credits and the remuneration of reserves at the average, over the maintenance period, of the repo rates. We have argued that these two features imply that overbidding (underbidding) occurs if the central bank is going to raise (cut) interest rates. Since under the new framework the maturity of the MROs no longer overlap, the remaining reason for the bidding problems is the remuneration of reserves at the average rate. However, the remuneration of required reserves at the average rate will only cause under- or

---

[6] The time series data on which this number is based on is available on the ECB's website (www.ecb.int).

[7] In order to illustrate these costs we will look at the fine-tuning operation settled on 12 July 2005. The weighted average rate on the MRO conducted prior to the fine-tuning operation was 2.05%. The fine-tuning operation with a maturity of one day allowed the credit institutions to place liquidity with the Eurosystem at 2.00%. The average amount the credit institutions placed with the Eurosystem was EUR 873 millions, i.e. on average the credit institutions faced costs of EUR 1213. Similar calculations for the fine-tuning operations settled on the 18 January 2005 and September 2005 result in benefits of EUR 160 and costs of EUR 386. (Numbers are based on ECB statistics given in the ECB Monthly Bulletin October 2005, p. S 8.)

overbidding behaviour if the central bank changes the repo rate within the reserve maintenance period. This will not be the case in the euro area if the governing council keeps to its commitment of only deciding on interest rate changes at the first of its bi-monthly meetings only.

Even though according to our theoretical analysis the bidding problems are solved under the new framework, it should be noted that this work only explains under- and overbidding behaviour triggered by interest rate change expectations.[8] In the literature, no alternative triggers have been discussed concerning the observed *underbidding* behaviour and so far no features of the new framework have been identified which may imply that the banks have an incentive to underbid if they expect the ECB to raise interest rates, i.e. the underbidding problem should be solved.

However, a different picture may be drawn when considering the *overbidding* problem. In the literature three explanations have been discussed concerning the observed overbidding behaviour up til June 2000: interest rate change expectations (European Central Bank, 2000, 2003a; Bindseil, 2005), an asymmetric objective function of the ECB (Ayuso and Repullo, 2001, 2003), and a flawed rationing rule in the fixed rate tenders (Nautz and Oechssler, 2003).[9] Nautz and Oechssler (2006) show empirically that interest rate change expectations play an important role in the observed overbidding behaviour, but that they alone can not explain the large extent of the overbidding observed in the first half of 2000. They conclude that the overbidding problem cannot be solved by the changes in the Eurosystem's operational framework since these changes aim only at excluding interest rate change expectations as a source of overbidding. In the following, we will briefly comment on the asymmetric-objective-function explanation and on the flawed-rationing-rule explanation for overbidding behaviour in the MROs.

Ayuso and Repullo argue that an asymmetric objective function of the ECB (see p. 23 for details) led to liquidity allotment decisions, which resulted in tight liquidity conditions. These in turn implied that there was such a large positive spread between the interbank market rate and the MRO-rate that banks overbid in order to profit by arbitrage from this interest rate differential. However, even if this is an

---

[8] Note that in our theoretical analysis banks have rational expectations and there are no shocks so that the in period one expected repo rate for the second period is equal to the actual repo rate in that period ($E_1(l_2) = l_2$).

[9] If in the fixed rate tenders total bids exceed the amount of liquidity the Eurosystem is willing to allot, there will be a pro rata allotment of the individual bank bids, depending on the ratio between total bids and the amount of liquidity to be allotted.

explanation for the observed overbidding behaviour, it is rather unlikely that it can serve as an explanation for future overbidding behaviour: With the implementation of the new operational framework the ECB has started to publish its forecast of autonomous factors and its calculation of the benchmark allotment on each day it announces or allots a MRO (European Central Bank, 2005c).[10] This means that the Ayuso-Repullo explanation for the observed overbidding behaviour implies that the ECB's *published* estimation systematically underestimates the banking sector's actual liquidity needs.

The flawed-rationing-rule explanation put forward by Nautz and Oechssler (2003) for the observed overbidding behaviour also implies that the ECB provides systematically less liquidity than the banking sector actually needs - either intentionally or unintentionally (see p. 27 for details). As already pointed out above, the former is rather unlikely. The latter may trigger the explosion of the bidding behaviour as described on p. 27. The reason being that only a positive probability of being rationed can already trigger this process (Ehrhart, 2001), and if the ECB always allots the amount of liquidity, which from its point of view is the appropriate amount, there will be a positive probability of being rationed since this amount may be smaller than the total bids because uncertainty about actual liquidity needs is involved. Nautz and Oechssler (2006) argue that the rationing rule in fixed rate tenders should be changed to solve the overbidding problem completely (although they do not suggest in which way the rule should be changed). An obvious possible solution is not to ration, but always to allot the amount of liquidity the banking sector bids for and to absorb possible excess liquidity via fine-tuning operations. If this no-rationing is credible, the probability of being rationed will be zero so that the overbidding process described on p. 27 will not be triggered. If banks are not rationed but receive the amount they bid for, the theoretical analysis presented in this work will fit again, i.e. not only the underbidding problem but also the overbidding problem should have been solved with the implementation of the new framework as long as the governing council keeps to its commitment not to change interest rates within

---

[10] From January 1999 until June 2000, i.e. in the period overbidding occurred and to which Ayuso and Repullo (2001, 2003) as well as Nautz and Oechssler (2003, 2006) refer to, the ECB did not publish its estimations of the banking sector's liquidity needs. From June 2000 to March 2004 the ECB published its forecast of the autonomous factors only on the day a MRO was announced. This implied that it was not clear whether a deviation of the allotment amount was due to a non-neutral liquidity target or to updates of the autonomous factor forecast (European Central Bank, 2005c).

a reserve maintenance period. With regards to the last aspect we will comment on it in more detail in the next section.

8.4 Suggestions for Further Improvements to the Eurosystem's Operational Framework

Remuneration of Required Reserves at the Current Rate on the Main Refinancing Operations

The theoretical analysis presented in Chap. 6 captures the main features of the *current* Eurosystem's operational framework. One implication of this analysis is that the present remuneration of required reserves at the average of the rates on the MROs conducted during the concerned reserve maintenance period requires a commitment of the governing council to decide on interest rate changes only at the first of its bi-monthly meetings to avoid frontloading or postponing of required reserve holdings, over- or underbidding and the violation of the principal of equal treatment.[11]

This necessity of adhering to the commitment will be a problem if shortly after the first meeting a liquidity shock occurs. In this case, the central bank must weigh up the costs of not reacting already at the next meeting of the governing council and the costs of loosing credibility. If a small shock occurs, the governing council may wait until the "right" meeting in order not to jeopardize its credibility. However, this may involve costs which can be reduced or even be avoided if it were not for the commitment. Furthermore, the commitment implies a violation of the principle of operational efficiency, which says that the operational framework shall ensure that monetary policy decisions are fed through as precisely and quickly as possible to short term money market rates (see section 2.2). In summing up, the disadvantage of the remuneration of required reserves at the average rate is that the governing council must adhere to a commitment which reduces the flexibility of monetary policy and which violates the principle of operational efficiency.

A possible advantage of the remuneration of reserves at the average rate is a smoothing of the interbank market rate as shown by the theoretical analyses in the Chaps. 6 and 7. However, the interest rate smoothing will only take place if the repo rate is changed within the

---

[11] Note that if the governing council changes its repo rate at the beginning of the maintenance period, the same results will be obtained as in the current rate model, i.e. then the above listed problems will not occur (see p. 85).

reserve maintenance period.[12] Consequently, presently this advantage is not even used because of the governing councils' commitment. This means that if this kind of interest rate smoothing is aimed for, the remuneration of reserves at the average rate should be retained and the commitment should be given up. However, it then has to be accepted that reserves will be provided unevenly, that under- and overbidding will occur, and that the principle of equal treatment will be violated.

Considering the requirements given on p. 156 and balancing the advantage (smoothing of the interbank market rate) against the disadvantage (necessity of adhering to a commitment) of remunerating reserves at the average rate, we suggest changing the way in which required reserves are remunerated. We propose remunerating the required reserves at the current MRO-rate at the end of each week instead of at the average, over the maintenance period, of the MRO-rates. Then, as the current rate model presented in Chap. 5 has shown, the central bank could change the repo rate within the reserve maintenance period without risking uneven provisions of the required reserves, under- or overbidding behaviour, and without risking a violation of the principal of equal treatment. Consequently, the commitment to change interest rate decisions only at the first of the bi monthly governing council meetings would not be necessary anymore and could be done away with. Then, monetary policy in the euro area could be conducted more flexibly since interest rate decisions could be made when the assessment of available information suggests to do so. This would enhance operational efficiency of the Eurosystem's operational framework.

Collateralization of the Main Refinancing Operations?

Credit operations with the Eurosystem have to be based on adequate collateral to protect the Eurosystem against financial risk (European Central Bank, 2004c, p. 74). However, the question arises whether the collateralization of the MROs is sensible when balancing its costs against its benefits. A detailed analysis of this question goes beyond the scope of this work, so we are not in the position to provide a conclusive answer to this question, but we will call attention to a possible problem and leave the final solution for further research.

Concerning the risk the ECB would have to bear if the MROs were not based on collateral, i.e. concerning the *benefits of the collateralization*, it should be considered that the maturity of the MROs is only

---

[12] The smoothing is the result of the frontloading or postponing of required reserves which is triggered by an interest rate change within the reserve maintenance period. For details see p. 83.

one week and that the national central banks and/or the institution which is responsible for the supervision of the banking industry monitor the financial soundness of the credit institutions. Therefore, the Eurosystem will generally have information early if a credit institution experiences financial distress and can react accordingly. Furthermore, the question arises whether, in view of financial stability considerations, the Eurosystem could actually liquidate the collateral of a concerned institution.

Concerning the *costs of the collateralization*, it is not only necessary to consider the banks' opportunity costs of holding collateral, but it is also necessary to consider the considerable costs of managing collateral which occur for both, the Eurosystem and its counterparties. Moreover, one should bear in mind that in all of the relevant models presented in this work, i.e. also in the current rate model, banks face different costs when fulfilling their reserve requirements (for the theoretical analysis see the pages 60 and 67) which violates the Eurosystem's principle of equal treatment.

Finally, it should be mentioned that in our models the collateralization of central bank credits plays a pivotal role because it implies that banks will face different marginal costs if they borrow liquidity directly from the central bank. However, it should be noted that the abolition of the collateralization does not mean that the implications of our theoretical analysis are lapsed. The crucial point is that banks face different marginal costs when borrowing from the central bank and this heterogeneity cannot only be motivated by different opportunity costs of holding collateral, but they can also be motivated by other costs as operational costs, for example.

8.5 Summary

The implications of our theoretical analysis for the Eurosystem's operational framework can be summarized as follows:

- In the current rate model (no overlapping maturities, remuneration of required reserves at the current repo rate), the requirements the Eurosystem's operational framework should meet are very closely fulfilled. Unbalanced bidding behaviour and strategic reserve shifting, and, therefore, the related problems, will not occur even if the ECB changes the repo rate within the reserve maintenance period, and having the possibility to change interest rates within that period enhances the flexibility of monetary policy. However, the current rate model also has its drawbacks, but these have to be accepted as long as central bank credits have to be based on collateral.

- From a theoretical point of view, the reduction of the MRO-maturity from two weeks to one week in 2004 has to be evaluated positively. The reason is that a two-week maturity implies that the maturities of two subsequent MROs overlap, and, as we have shown, overlapping maturities will lead to unbalanced bidding behaviour and a strategic reserve shifting if the banks expect the ECB to change interest rates. Problems related to this liquidity management are a reduction in the minimum reserve system's buffer function and a violation of the Eurosystem's principle of equal treatment.

- Early concerns about possible negative effects of the redesigned operational framework have not proven to be true or could be dealt with. One problem is the increased forecast errors concerning autonomous factors. The ECB has solved this problem by conducting fine-tuning operations. We suggest conducting these operations at the weighted average rate of the MRO which was executed prior to the fine-tuning operation in order to reduce the banks' costs/benefits resulting from the ECB's forecast errors.

- According to our analysis, the 2004-changes in the Eurosystem's operational framework have solved the problem of the unbalanced bidding behaviour as long as the governing council keeps to its self-commitment of deciding on interest rate changes only at the first of its bi-monthly meetings. However, our theoretical analysis focusses on interest rate change expectations as being a trigger for the unbalanced bidding behaviour which, according to Nautz and Oechssler (2006), cannot explain the extensive overbidding in the first half of 2000. They conclude that the overbidding problem cannot be solved by the changes in the Eurosystem's operational framework. We argue that if the ECB does not ration and absorbs any possible excess liquidity via fine-tuning operations, the overbidding problem in the fixed rate tenders should be also be solved as long as the governing council keeps to its commitment.

- The governing council's self-commitment to decide on interest rate changes only at the first of its bi-monthly meetings reduces the flexibility of monetary policy. Therefore, we suggest remunerating the required reserves at the current MRO-rate instead of at the average of the rates on the MROs conducted over a maintenance period. Hence, the commitment is no longer necessary.

- Credit operations with the Eurosystem have to be based on collateral. Our suggestion for future research is to analyze to what extent the collateralization of MROs is sensible when balancing its costs against its benefits.

Finally, two further results of our analysis should be mentioned. First, our theoretical analysis has provided an explanation for the observed positive spread between the interbank market rate and the MRO-rate: the heterogeneity of the banking sector in the euro area. Second, we have identified, besides the MRO-rate, further determinants of the interbank market rate, such as the autonomous factors, which provides an explanation on the specific features of the behaviour of the interbank market rate.

Summary

In January 1999, the euro was launched and the Eurosystem took over the responsibility for the single monetary policy in the euro area. This creation of a new currency and a single monetary policy in a large and relatively heterogeneous economic area has been related to extraordinary challenges. Among these challenges there has been the development of an appropriate operational framework, i.e. of appropriate instruments and procedures for the conduct of monetary policy.

The aim of this work has been to evaluate the Eurosystem's operational framework against the following requirements. There should be no under- and overbidding behaviour in the MROs; in the absence of liquidity shocks, the required reserves should be provided evenly over a reserve maintenance period; the design of the Eurosystem's operational framework should not imply that banks are affected differently by a monetary policy impulse; and the operational framework should ensure that monetary policy decisions are fed through as quickly as possible to short term money market rates.

We have started our analysis by giving a brief *overview of the Eurosystem's monetary policy instruments* with a focus on the minimum reserve system and the MROs since these instruments have been the center of our theoretical analysis. Important features of these instruments are: Reserve requirements can be fulfilled on average over a reserve maintenance period and are remunerated at the average, over the maintenance period, of the rates on the MROs. MROs are credit operations which are executed weekly and which had, until March 2004, a maturity of two weeks, i.e. the maturities of two subsequent MROs overlapped. In March 2004, the maturity of the MROs was reduced to one week, i.e. since then, the maturities have no longer overlapped. A further important feature of the MROs is that they have to be based on collateral.

Then, we have documented the following *stylized facts*. There has been a positive spread between the interbank market rate and the MRO-rate. In the past, MROs were characterized by underbidding (overbidding) if the market expected the ECB to cut (raise) interest rates and holdings of required reserves were postponed if the market expected the ECB to cut interest rates.

In the *theoretical analysis*, we have modelled in a first step the liquidity management of a single bank. This bank has liquidity needs due to autonomous factors and reserve requirements imposed by the central bank. It can cover these liquidity needs either by borrowing from the central bank or in the interbank market, where it can also place excess liquidity. Both, borrowing from the central bank as well as transactions in the interbank market, are combined with increasing marginal costs. The bank minimizes its net liquidity costs by optimizing its liquidity management, i.e. by choosing its optimal central bank borrowing, its optimal transactions in the interbank market, and its optimal intertemporal allocation of required reserves. In a second step, we have first considered two banks and then a continuum of banks differing in their marginal costs of borrowing liquidity directly from the central bank. Aggregating over the banks, we have obtained aggregate demand and supply in the interbank market so that we could derive the equilibrium interbank market rate which has allowed us to determine the final results for the banks' optimal liquidity management. We have done this analysis on different maturities of central bank credits and on different designs of the remuneration of the required reserves. The first result of our theoretical analysis has been that a heterogeneous banking sector is a rationale for the existence of an interbank money market. Banks with relatively low marginal costs of borrowing liquidity directly from the central bank borrow more funds from the monetary authority than they need to cover their own liquidity needs to lend the excess liquidity via the interbank market to those banks with relatively high costs. The latter cover their liquidity needs either partially or even totally in the interbank market. This intermediation implies that there is a positive spread between the interbank market rate and the rate on central bank credits. Furthermore, our theoretical analysis has revealed that overlapping maturities of two subsequent central bank credit operations and the remuneration of required reserves at the average, over the maintenance period, of the rates on the central bank credits will lead to a deviation of the aggregate demand for central bank credits from the central bank's benchmark amount and to postponing/frontloading of required reserves if the central bank changes its interest rate within the reserve maintenance period. Moreover, our analysis has shown that this liquidity management implies that banks are affected differently by this monetary policy impulse. If, on the other hand, the maturities do not overlap and if reserves are remunerated at the current central bank rate, there will be no deviation from the benchmark amount, no reserve shifting, and banks will not be affected differently.

From the theoretical analysis, we have drawn the following *implications for the euro area*. One explanation for the observed positive spread between the interbank market rate and the MRO-rate is the heterogeneous banking sector in the euro area. The observed under- and overbidding behaviour in the MROs and the postponing of the required reserves was due to overlapping maturities and the remuneration of the required reserves at the average, over the maintenance period, of the MRO-rates. Problems resulting from this liquidity management were a reduced buffer function of the minimum reserve system and a violation of the Eurosystem's principle of equal treatment. The 2004-changes to the Eurosystem's operational framework have to be evaluated positively since the unbalanced bidding behaviour and the reserve shifting and, therefore, the related problems should not occur anymore - as long as the governing council keeps to its self-commitment not to change the MRO-rate within the reserve maintenance period. This condition has led us to a suggestion for a further measure to improve the Eurosystem's operational framework. We have proposed to remunerate holdings of required reserves at the end of each week at the current MRO-rate instead of at the above described average rate. Then, the commitment of the governing council is no longer necessary, i.e. the monetary policy in the euro area could react more flexibly to liquidity shocks.

With regards to future research, we have suggested analyzing to what extent the collateralization of the MROs is actually sensible when balancing its costs against its benefits, while bearing in mind that the collateralization is combined with non-negligible costs for both the Eurosystem and its counterparties.

Appendix

Numerical Example: Effects of a Change in the Repo Rate on the Equilibrium Interbank Market Rate

Table A.1 summarizes the effects of a change in the repo rate within the reserve maintenance period ($l_1 \neq l_2$) on the equilibrium interbank market rate. We assume that if the repo rate is not changed, the spread between the interbank market rate and the repo rate in all models will be one percentage point so that the sum of the spreads over the two periods is equal to two percentage points. In the current rate model, the change in the repo rate implies a proportional change in the interbank market rate in the second period, i.e. the spreads, and, therefore, the sum of the spreads, do not change. In the average rate model, on the other hand, there is a smoothing of the interbank market rate in the sense that the interbank market rate will already decrease (increase) before the central bank actually cuts (raises) the repo rate. However, in the two-bank case the interbank market rate changes in both periods in such a way that the sum of the spreads does not change and that the total change in e_t^* over the whole maintenance period (last column) is the same as in the current rate model. This will not be the case if a continuum of banks is considered. Then the negative transaction cost effect described on p. 98 implies that if the repo rate is cut, the total decrease in e_t^* over the whole maintenance period will be stronger and that if the repo rate is raised the total increase in e_t^* over the whole maintenance period will be weaker. This means that there is a decline in the sum of the spreads. Furthermore, the table shows that in the overlapping maturities model, the interbank market rate will only be smoothed if the repo rate is cut and if a continuum of banks is considered. In this context the table presents two examples. In the first example the decrease in e_t^* is stronger than in the average rate model, so that the overall change in e_t^* (last column) is also stronger, whereas the sum of the spreads is smaller. In the second example, there is a stronger decrease in the average rate model, so that the overall decrease in e_t^* is also stronger in that model, whereas the sum of the spreads is smaller. Moreover, the table shows that in the overlapping maturities model, the smoothing of the equilibrium interbank market rate is restricted to the case in which the repo rate is cut and a continuum of banks is considered. In all other cases the interbank market rate will not change in that reserve maintenance period if the repo rate is changed within the maintenance period.

Table A.1: Numerical example: Effects of a change in the repo rate on the equilibrium interbank market rate. Numbers in the first four columns are in percentages, in the last four columns in percentage points. CRM = Current Rate Model, ARM = Average Rate Model, OMM = Overlapping Maturities Model.

	l_1	l_2	e_1	e_2	s_1	s_2	$\sum_{t=1}^{2} s_t$	$\sum_{t=1}^{2} \frac{\partial e_t^*}{\partial l_2}$
No Change	3	3	4	4	1	1	2	0
CRM, 2 Banks								
Cut	3	2	4	3	1	1	2	1
Increase	3	4	4	5	1	1	2	1
CRM, Continuum								
Cut	3	2	4	3	1	1	2	1
Increase	3	4	4	5	1	1	2	1
ARM, 2 Banks								
Cut	3	2	3.5	3.5	0.5	1.5	2	1
Increase	3	4	4.5	4.5	1.5	0.5	2	1
ARM, Continuum								
Cut	3	2	3.25	3.25	0.25	1.25	1.5	1.5
Increase	3	4	4.25	4.25	1.25	0.25	1.5	0.5
OMM, 2 Banks								
Cut	3	2	4	4	1	2	3	0
Increase	3	4	4	4	1	0	1	0
OMM, Continuum								
Cut (1. Case)	3	2	3.1	3.1	0.1	1.1	1.2	1.8
Cut (2. Case)	3	2	3.4	3.4	0.4	1.4	1.8	1.2
Increase	3	4	4	4	1	0	1	0

References

Ayuso, J., and R. Repullo (2001): "Why Did the Banks Overbid? An Empirical Model of the Fixed Rate Tenders of the European Central Bank," *Journal of International Money and Finance*, 20, 857–870.

——— (2003): "A Model of the Open Market Operations of the European Central Bank," *Economic Journal*, 113, 883–902.

Bartolini, L., G. Bertola, and A. Prati (2001): "Banks' Reserve Management, Transaction Costs, and the Timing of Federal Reserve Intervention," *Journal of Banking and Finance*, 25, 1287–1317.

——— (2002): "Day-To-Day Monetary Policy and the Volatility of the Federal Funds Interest Rate," *Journal of Money, Credit, and Banking*, 34, 137–159.

——— (2003): "The Overnight Interbank Market: Evidence from the G-7 and the Euro Zone," *Journal of Banking and Finance*, 27, 2045–2083.

Bartolini, L., and A. Prati (2003): "The Execution of Monetary Policy: A Tale of Two Central Banks," *Economic Policy*, 18, 435–467.

——— (2006): "Cross-Country Differences in Monetary Policy Execution and Money Market Rates' Volatility," *European Economic Review*, 50, 349–376.

Bindseil, U. (2004): *Monetary Policy Implementation*. Oxford University Press, Oxford.

——— (2005): "Over- and Underbidding in Central Bank Open Market Operations Conducted as Fixed Rate Tender," *German Economic Review*, 6, 95–130.

Blum, J., and M. Hellwig (1995): "The Macroeconomic Implications of Capital Adequacy Requirements for Banks," *European Economic Review*, 39, 739–749.

BREITUNG, J., T. LINZERT, AND D. NAUTZ (2003): "Bidder Behaviour in Repo Auctions Without Minimum Bid Rate: Evidence from the Bundesbank," Discussion Paper Economic Research Centre of the Deutsche Bundesbank, No.13/03.

BREITUNG, J., AND D. NAUTZ (2001): "The Empirical Performance of the ECB's Repo Auctions: Evidence from Aggregated and Individual Bidding Data," *Journal of International Money and Finance*, 20, 839–856.

BRUNO, G., M. ORDINE, AND A. SCALIA (2005): "Banks' Participation in the Eurosystem Auctions and Money Market Integration," Discussion Paper Banca d'Italia, No. 562.

CAMPBELL, J. Y. (1987): "Money Announcements, the Demand for Bank Reserves, and the Behavior of the Federal Funds Rate Within the Statement Week," *Journal of Money, Credit, and Banking*, 19, 56–67.

CLOUSE, J. A., AND J. P. DOW (1999): "Fixed Costs and the Behaviour of the Federal Funds Rate," *Journal of Banking and Finance*, 23, 1015–1029.

———— (2002): "A Computational Model of Banks' Optimal Reserve Management Policy," *Journal of Economic Dynamics and Control*, 26, 1787–1814.

DUISENBERG, W. F. (2001): Introductory Statement, ECB Press Conference in Frankfurt on 8 November 2001, available at www.ecb.int.

EHRHART, K.-M. (2001): "European Central Bank Operations: Experimental Investigation of the Fixed Rate Tender," *Journal of International Money and Finance*, 20, 871–893.

EJERSKOV, S., C. M. MOSS, AND L. STRACCA (2003): "How Does the ECB Allot Liquidity in its Weekly Main Refinancing Operations? A Look at the Empirical Evidence," Working Paper European Central Bank, No. 244.

EUROPEAN CENTRAL BANK (1998): *The Single Monetary Policy in Stage Three. General Documentation on ESCB Monetary Policy Instruments and Procedures*. European Central Bank, Frankfurt.

———— (1999): "Economic Developments in the Euro Area," *ECB Monthly Bulletin, May 1999*, pp. 7–27.

———— (2000): "The Switch to Variable Rate Tenders in the Main Refinancing Operations," *ECB Monthly Bulletin, July 2000*, pp. 37–42.

———— (2001a): "The Collateral Framework of the Eurosystem," *ECB Monthly Bulletin, April 2001*, pp. 49–62.

————— (2001b): "Economic Developments in the Euro Area," *ECB Monthly Bulletin, June 2001*, pp. 7–64.

————— (2001c): "Economic Developments in the Euro Area," *ECB Monthly Bulletin, March 2001*, pp. 7–52.

————— (2001d): "Economic Developments in the Euro Area," *ECB Monthly Bulletin, May 2001*, pp. 7–39.

————— (2001e): "Economic Developments in the Euro Area," *ECB Monthly Bulletin, November 2001*, pp. 7–38.

————— (2001f): "Economic Developments in the Euro Area," *ECB Monthly Bulletin, December 2001*, pp. 9–71.

————— (2001g): *The Monetary Policy of the ECB*. European Central Bank, Frankfurt.

————— (2002a): "Economic Developments in the Euro Area," *ECB Monthly Bulletin, January 2002*, pp. 9 39.

————— (2002b): "The Liquidity Management of the ECB," *ECB Monthly Bulletin, May 2002*, pp. 41–53.

————— (2002c): "Measures to Improve the Efficiency of the Operational Framework for Monetary Policy," Public Consultation, available at www.ecb.int.

————— (2002d): *The Single Monetary Policy in the Euro Area - General Documentation on Eurosystem Monetary Policy Instruments and Procedures*. European Central Bank, Frankfurt.

————— (2003a): "Changes to the Eurosystem's Operational Framework," *ECB Monthly Bulletin, August 2003*, pp. 41–54.

————— (2003b): "Economic and Monetary Developments in the Euro Area," *ECB Monthly Bulletin, July 2003*, pp. 7–40.

————— (2003c): "Economic Developments in the Euro Area," *ECB Monthly Bulletin April 2003*, pp. 7–38.

————— (2003d): "Economic Developments in the Euro Area," *ECB Monthly Bulletin, January 2003*, pp. 7–38.

————— (2003e): "Measure to Improve the Efficiency of the Operational Framework for Monetary Policy," Press release, 23. January 2003, available at www.ecb.int.

————— (2003f): "Measures to Improve the Collateral Framework of the Eurosystem," Public consultation, available at www.ecb.int.

————— (2003g): "Summary of Comments Received on the Measures Proposed to Improve the Operational Framework for Monetary Policy," available at www.ecb.int.

————— (2004a): "Economic and Monetary Developments," *ECB Monthly Bulletin April 2004*, pp. 7–43.

———— (2004b): "Measures to Improve the Collateral Framework of the Eurosystem: Summary of the Answers to the Public Consultation," Public Consultation, available at www.ecb.int.

———— (2004c): *The Monetary Policy of the ECB*. European Central Bank, Frankfurt.

———— (2005a): "Economic and Monetary Developments," *ECB Monthly Bulletin, September 2005*, pp. 7–75.

———— (2005b): *The Implementation of Monetary Policy in the Euro Area. General Documentation on Eurosystem Monetary Policy Instruments and Procedures*. European Central Bank, Frankfurt.

———— (2005c): "Initial Experience with the Changes to the Eurosystems's Operational Framework," *ECB Monthly Bulletin, February 2005*, pp. 65–71.

EUROPEAN MONETARY INSTITUTION (1997): *The Single Monetary Policy in Stage Three. Specification of the Operational Framework*. European Monetary Institution, Frankfurt.

EWERHART, C. (2002): "A Model of the Eurosystem's Operational Framework for Monetary Policy Implementation," Working Paper European Central Bank, No. 197.

FURFINE, C. H. (2000): "Interbank Payments and the Daily Federal Funds Rate," *Journal of Monetary Economics*, 46, 535–553.

HÄMÄLÄINEN, S. (2000): "The Operational Framework of the Eurosystem," Welcome address at the ECB Conference on the Operational Framework of the Eurosystem and the Financial Markets in Frankfurt on 5/6 May 2000, available at www.ecb.int.

HAMILTON, J. D. (1996): "The Daily Market for Federal Funds," *Journal of Political Economy*, 104, 26–56.

HO, T. S. Y., AND A. SAUNDERS (1985): "A Micro Model of the Federal Funds Rate," *Journal of Finance*, 40, 977–986.

NAUTZ, D. (1998): "Banks' Demand for Reserves When Future Monetary Policy is Uncertain," *Journal of Monetary Economics*, 42, 161–183.

NAUTZ, D., AND J. OECHSSLER (2003): "The Repo Auctions of the European Central Bank and the Vanishing Quota Puzzle," *Scandinavian Journal of Economics*, 105, 207–220.

———— (2006): "Overbidding in Fixed Rate Tenders - an Empirical Assessment of Alternative Explanations," *European Economic Review*, 50, 631–646.

NEYER, U., AND J. WIEMERS (2004): "The Influence of a Heterogeneous Banking Sector on the Interbank Market Rate in the Euro Area," *Swiss Journal of Economics and Statistics*, 140, 395–428.

NYBORG, K. G., U. BINDSEIL, AND I. A. STREBULAEV (2002): "Bidding and Performance in Repo Auctions: Evidence from ECB Open Market Operations," Working Paper European Central Bank, No. 157.

PÉREZ-QUIRÓS, G., AND H. RODRÍGUEZ-MENDIZÁBAL (2006): "The Daily Market for Funds in Europe: What Has Changed with the EMU?," *Journal of Money, Banking, and Credit*, 38, 91–110.

RUCKRIEGEL, K., AND F. SEITZ (2002): "The Eurosystem and the Federal Reserve System Compared: Facts and Challenges," Working Paper Zentrum für Europäische Integrationsforschung (ZEI), No. B 02/2002.

VÄLIMÄKI, T. (2001): "Fixed Rate Tenders and the Overnight Money Market Equilibrium," Discussion Paper Bank of Finland, No. 8/2001.